CATCH
A Major League Life

CATCH
A Major League Life

Ernie Whitt
Greg Cable

McGraw-Hill Ryerson
Toronto Montreal

ISBN 0-07-549673-9

1 2 3 4 5 6 7 8 9 D 8 7 6 5 4 3 2 1 0 9

First Published in 1989 by
McGraw-Hill Ryerson Limited
330 Progress Avenue
Scarborough, Ontario, Canada M1P 2Z5

Canadian Cataloguing in Publication Data

Whitt, Ernie
Catch: a major league life

ISBN 0-07-549673-9

1. Whitt, Ernie. 2. Baseball players - Canada -
Biography. I. Cable, Greg, xxxx -   .
II. Title.

GV865.W55A3 1989   796.357'092'4   C89-093801-6

Jacket and Book Design: Kirk Alexander Stephens
Jacket Photographs: Jim Allen

Printed and bound in Canada

Contents

For Chrissie, the woman I adore — for all your strength and
love and support. Without you, I could never
have kept the faith and fulfilled my dream,
I could never have endured the bad times
or taken such joy in the good. Words can never say
what our life together has meant to me.

And for my wonderful children, Ashley, EJ, and Taylor
— for making home a place of happiness
and my 0-for-4 nights fade away.
With you by me, I know whenever I leave the game
I'll never feel empty inside.

–EW

Dedicated with great love to Helen and our brood
— Simon and Toby and Melissa and Jordan.
To my parents, Howard and Dawn Cable.
And to Greenly for a promise long ago.

–GC

Acknowledgements

Like any book, this one wouldn't have come together without the participation and support of many people, and we would like to both acknowledge our debt and express our gratitude to them.

From Ernie Whitt: My appreciation begins with all those people without whose support I never would have had a major league career. My thanks to first, with love, to my parents, because without them I never would have made it. I thank all my relatives and friends who encouraged my hopes and helped me along the way; all the players, coaches, and managers over many, many years who had confidence in me as a big league player; the Blue Jay organization and everyone in it for being a first-class organization all the way. I especially thank my fans in Toronto and all across Canada who've been so supportive of me throughout my career. I want to thank John Boville, my friend, advisor, and business partner, for arranging this project, and Greg Cable, not only for digging into my brain to get the story out, but for making the whole experience so surprisingly enjoyable.

From Greg Cable: My thanks go to Denise Schon of McGraw-Hill Ryerson for bringing about this happy collaboration in the first place, and to McGraw-Hill's Glen Ellis for shepherding the project through editorial. The Blue Jays' director of public relations, Howard Starkman, was helpful in arranging access both to team records and several facilities. Special thanks go to Chris Whitt for maintaining the voluminous scrapbooks, without which our job would have been much harder, and to Jennifer Hietala and Simon Cable who carried almost all the burden of transcribing many hours of tape. I'm especially grateful to Ernie and Chris for letting me wander through their lives with such ease and comfort and for making the journey so much fun. Most of all, I'm eternally grateful to my wife, Helen, and our children, Simon, Toby, Melissa, and Jordan. Without their love I would likely succeed in little in this life, and without their patience and tiptoed understanding I certainly would never have finished this book.

October 2, 1988

There'll still be a few more games for the Toronto Blue **1** Jays to play in Exhibition Stadium. But today, we wound up our last full season at the park we've played in for the last 12 years. We were hoping to have our opening home game in 1989 in the new domed stadium a mile or so away, but labour strikes screwed things up and now we won't get into our new home until June. When we get there, we'll have some new players, new uniforms and, I hope, a new attitude and a new desire to win.

We won't be too sorry to see the last of this park. Players don't like it very much. It's okay, but it's still a converted football field. The playing surface is not the greatest. There are seams in the turf that shouldn't be there. There are planks around the bases that shouldn't be there, as Tony Fernandez found out at the end of the '87 season when he broke his elbow on one.

It's not good for the fans, either, because they have to turn in their seats to see the action, whereas in a real baseball diamond all the seats are focussed on what's happening at home plate. All the seats are like bleachers, too, open to the sky. Fans don't get the intimate feeling they get at older parks like Fenway, Comisky, or Tiger Stadium where the roofs make you feel like you're inside a theatre watching a performance on stage. There's not that focussed sound coming out to us, the entertainers on the field, either.

But there are a lot of good memories for me at Exhibition Stadium, and I know I'll miss it because of them.

One of the fondest memories, personally, is hitting my first major league grand slam home run here on June 23, 1985. What made it even more memorable to me was that I didn't realize it was a grand slam until I got back to the dugout. I hadn't been paying attention to who was on base when I came up to bat. All my concentration and my anger were directed at the opposing pitcher.

We were playing the Boston Red Sox, and there was a lot of bad feeling between our two teams. Bruce Kison was pitching for Boston and in my first at-bat, he knocked me down with a pitch. Then he threw at Rance Mulliniks. And then he hit George Bell. George charged out to the mound and gave the famous karate kick that was replayed endlessly on TV sports programs. The best way of getting back at a pitcher after he throws at you is to hit a home run, and I was real happy to do just that in the sixth inning. But I was still so furious as I was going around the bases that I didn't notice how many teammates had crossed the plate ahead of me. I was just yelling at Kison, calling him every nasty name I could think of.

I'll remember September of 1987 pretty fondly, too. One night, in a game against the Yankees, I joined the handful of Blue Jays with 6 RBI in a game. Two nights later, in a game against Baltimore, I hit three home runs, the only Jay other than Otto Velez to accomplish that. What was even more gratifying was that we set a major league record that night. Lloyd Moseby also homered, Rance Mulliniks and George Bell hit two homers each, Freddie McGriff set a club rookie mark with his nineteenth of the season and Rob Ducey hit his first in the major leagues. After we won the game 18 – 3, the bats

2

Freddie, Rob, and I used to match and then extend the record were collected for shipment to Cooperstown.

I'll remember the last game of the playoff series with Kansas City in 1985. We'd been up three games to one, but Kansas City had come back to tie the series at three games apiece. Still, we were moments away from making the dream of every major league baseball player come true. Dave Stieb was pitching and the game was close. Kansas City had taken an early lead and had gone up 2 – 0 in the fourth, but we came back with one run in the fifth. The bases were loaded in the top of the sixth when Jim Sundberg came up to bat.

Sundberg hit a lazy fly ball out to right field, and I remember thinking, "Great. There's an out. All right." Then I saw Jesse Barfield turn and drift back further and further as the ball got caught up in a jet stream blowing out to right, and I thought, "What in the world is happening?" The triple broke the game wide open and ended our dreams of playing in the World Series.

I'll remember the series with the Yankees a couple of weeks earlier when New York came to town needing to win all three games to tie us for first while we only had to win one game to lock up the American League East Division Championship.

We had the Friday night game won. Then, with two outs in the ninth inning and with two strikes on him, Butch Wynegar hit a home run off Tom Henke to tie the game. There's always the thought in a player's mind that anybody in the opposing team's lineup can beat you, especially with the Yankees. But Butch Wynegar? Then in the tenth, Lloyd Moseby dropped a routine fly ball to centre and the Yankees' winning run came in.

But that was the '85 Blue Jays and things like that really didn't bother us. We were loose, confident that we had the best team, and knew that we'd get them tomorrow.

We did. With Doyle Alexander pitching for us against the Yankees' Joe Cowley, I started off the scoring with a two-run homer in the second inning. Moseby hit one that

3

day and so did Willie Upshaw. And as each inning went by, we could feel the electricity in the air, not only from the fans in the stadium but it seemed like from all around Toronto. The excitement kept growing. We could feel it. When Ron Hassey hit a fly ball to left field and George Bell caught it and dropped to his knees with his arms raised up in the air, it was bedlam. We all charged out to the mound and laughed and hugged each other and carried Doyle back to the dugout on our shoulders.

There are a lot of memories from what I guess will be considered the first Blue Jay era, when big league baseball first came to Toronto. The '77–'88 Jays went from a pretty rocky expansion club to one of the elite, a team always contending in what was, until this year anyway, thought of as the toughest division in baseball. Over the past five years, only the Detroit Tigers, in all of baseball, have a better record. As players, we can take some satisfaction out of that, especially Jim Clancy and myself, the last two players who were here in '77 and are still on the field today. We've had more than our share of disappointments, but I think we've played enough good, entertaining ball to make the people of Toronto, and all of Canada, proud of what we've done.

It's just too bad that this first era couldn't have ended on a happier note. True, we're finishing only two games back, tied for third place with Milwaukee. As our general manager, Pat Gillick, said, "Someone 25 years from now will look at the final standings and think, 'Wow, that must have been one hell of a pennant race.'" But in fact, the 1988 season will not go down in memory as one of our best. Right from spring training the year has been noted more for turmoil, controversy, and a struggle to play at least .500 ball than it has for playing to win.

And now it's come down to this last three-game series against the once-great Baltimore Orioles. If the year has been a disappointment for the Blue Jays, it's been a disaster for the Orioles. They started the year with a terrible stretch, beating the league record for consecutive losses at the start of the season by losing 21 games. Now, with our

9 – 3 win on this last day of the season, they finish 34 1/2 games back of the division champions. They also finish with the worst record in either league — 54 wins and 107 losses — the very same record the Blue Jays had at the end of the 1977 season.

We've had a good September, our best month not only of this year, but also the best month in Toronto history. And we've had the best record in the league since the All-Star break. But it's been too little too late. We've had a tremendous year against Boston. We've owned the Red Sox. We swept a four-game series in Fenway in June and a three-game series in September, finishing with an 11 – 2 advantage on games. But it's still the Red Sox who'll be meeting the Oakland A's for the pennant and the chance to play in the World Series.

This isn't the way it was supposed to be. We were supposed to win it all. Everybody seemed to think so after the year we had in 1987, even with our losing the division title to Detroit on the last day of the season. We had **5** the best team in baseball in 1987, even though the record says we were only second best.

We believed we were the best. We believed back then that we could do it "next year," and most baseball fans and writers seemed to agree. But then next year came, and the team seemed to come unstuck.

It didn't seem possible just a year ago. It didn't seem possible at all.

The Off-Season, 1987

I couldn't do as much pheasant hunting as I wanted to in the fall of 1987. My ribs hurt too much. I had to walk slowly because for the first time in my life, breathing was a problem. I couldn't get into the heavy brush, either. I had to stay on the outside and send my dog, Erica, into the thicket. A lot of times a bird would fly up, and I wouldn't be able to shoot. Erica would come out of the brush and look at me like she was thinking, "You dummy, why didn't you do something? I get in there and work my butt off and get nothing to put in my teeth."

Erica's a German short-haired dog I got as a puppy when I was playing ball in Syracuse in 1978. Some friends of mine in the Red Sox organization were raising pups down in Alabama and they shipped one up for me when the Syracuse Chiefs went into Pawtucket to play Boston's AAA club. I carried her back to Syracuse with me on the five-hour bus trip from New England to New York and presented her to my wife, Chris, when she opened the door for me at six o'clock in the morning.

I worked with Erica a lot, training her to hold her point and retrieve the prey, and now I enjoy going out in the field to watch her work. She gets so excited when she smells a bird, her stubby tail moves a mile a minute.

For the first time I took my boys out with me during pheasant season. EJ was coming up to his ninth birthday; Taylor was almost eight. They seemed to be growing up very fast. We'd played a little catch in the backyard when I got home from baseball season, and the rainbow throws I used to chase after were suddenly coming right to me, hard. It seemed time to start to teach them what to do out in the woods. By no means would I let them handle a gun, but they carried their little air rifles along with them while they beat the brush a bit. I could keep an eye on them to make sure they did things right and scold them if they didn't point their rifles straight down or straight up in the air. It was so enjoyable to spend some time together and get some exercise in the open air. I'm hoping they'll come to love being in the woods like I do.

I'm a city boy, but my parents came from the country down in the southwestern part of Virginia, near the Cumberland Gap where Tennessee, Kentucky, and Virginia meet. My dad, Ernest, came from Lee County, Virginia, near the town of Rosehill, and my mother, Dolly, came from Haysi, about a three-hour drive away, along the winding roads in that hilly country. When I was young, I thought it was a big and exciting thing to go down there and visit my grandmothers, see all the farm animals, and go back into the woods. My parents liked to hunt deer, and every year my older brother, Mike, and I would go out with them into the fields and the bush.

Now I like to go out every year as soon as baseball season's over and the hunting season starts. Chris isn't crazy about my taking off so soon after I come home from many months away. But she knows how much I enjoy it and she accepts it, as long as I don't overdo it. It's very pleasant and comforting out there, not hearing any cars or construction going on, just hearing the birds chirping. I appreciate the silence, especially after spending so many

8

days hearing thousands of people yelling and cheering and booing and having big, overgrown guys screaming balls and strikes in my ear.

In the last few years, there've gotten to be so many hunters in Michigan that it's frightening to hunt deer anywhere but on private land with people you know. So in November I head off to a patch of private property owned by Chris's grandparents up the Michigan peninsula.

I'll sit in the morning from daylight 'til nine, then start walking the fire trails with the wind in my face, just taking a few short, quick, and easy steps then stopping to scan the area, looking for movement. I like to get down on my hands and knees and stalk the deer, trying to get up close without them knowing that I'm there. They're very intelligent animals, and one flash of a hand or a crack of a twig and they'll be off. It's a challenge, crouching down and surveying the scene, just waiting for the right moment. If a big trophy buck came by, I'd probably shoot. **9** But most of the time, I just like to watch them, studying their different characteristics. It's relaxing.

I really needed some relaxation in the fall of 1987. I'd just come through the most frustrating period in a baseball career that's had its share of frustrations.

The Blue Jays had had a tremendous season, leading the American League East for most of June and never being more than three games back since just after the All-Star break. By the middle of September, we were back in first and in the heat of a tight pennant race. We went three and a half games up on Detroit with only eight days left in the season. Then we lost our last seven games. The last three games in Detroit were heartbreakers — one-run losses against the Tigers despite some of the finest pitching the Blue Jay staff had ever come up with. That was sad and frustrating to all the players and to all the fans in Toronto, but what made it even more frustrating to me was that I sat on the bench, never getting the chance to play in those last three games. I was suited up, ready to play, and would have given anything to get into a game.

But a few days earlier two of my ribs had been cracked by Paul Molitor's knee in a game against Milwaukee.

What made it worse was that I love playing in Tiger Stadium. I usually do pretty well there, and I like to think that in those close games I might have made a difference. My lifetime average isn't very high against the Tigers, but my run production — both home runs and RBI — is better than against any other team in the league. I guess there are a lot of reasons for that. But the biggest reason, I think, is just because Detroit is my home.

I don't remember much about it, but I spent the first few years of my life a few blocks from Tiger Stadium. My dad was a truck driver, and he had come to Detroit to find work in the early fifties. When I was three or four years old, we moved to a house in a suburb named Roseville. The house looks pretty small now, but when I was a kid I thought it was huge. There were only the four of us then — my parents, my brother Mike, and me. My sisters, Melinda and Bernadine, came along a few years later.

Roseville was a new suburb, and one thing that it had a lot of was open fields. There were a lot of kids then, too, and it didn't take us long to start turning any spare patch of ground into a baseball diamond or a football field. In our backyard, there were two trees that made great first and third bases, and we could always find something to throw out for second. Right next door was what is now the pretty heavily wooded grounds of St. Anthanatious Church, but was then a good-sized open area where we could play football in the fall. Right around the corner was the house where one of my best friends, Billy Burgess, lived, and along the street were the six or seven Holland kids. There was always a front or backyard to play in, and if we got too noisy or came too close to breaking windows and got shooed away, the game would just move down the street and keep on going. We'd play baseball all day, run in for dinner and run back out to play until we couldn't see the ball any more.

10

Mike and I both loved sports and my dad did, too. He wanted us to get involved in organized teams as well as playing sandlot ball. I think he had dreams of both his sons being major league players some day.

Being two years older than me, Mike was the first to get involved. Dad took the two of us to a diamond behind the Veterans of Foreign Wars post on Gratiot Avenue, Roseville's main drag. I was just going there to watch Mike get on a team, but I overheard the coaches saying they were short of players and needed a catcher. I said, "I'll catch."

They looked at me and said, "Have you ever caught before?"

We had really never had a catcher in most of our backyard games. We always tried to put the batter where there was a backstop so we wouldn't have to chase the ball. I'd played just about every position but catcher. So I said, "No, but I want to play."

The problem was that you had to be eight to play in this league, and I was only seven. But I wanted to play so bad that my parents said it was okay with them and the coach got special permission from the league. I've been a catcher ever since.

11

I was a tough kid then, and I wasn't afraid of the ball coming in fast like a lot of kids seemed to be. Besides, before the game the manager would go to home plate with the umpires and call the catchers over so they could make sure they were wearing cups. I thought that was the neatest thing in the world at the time. The first time I went up there I thought, "God, this is terrific."

The umpire said, "Let me hear it." So I banged on my cup, thinking, "Wow, seven years old. I'm not even supposed to be out here and this umpire's asking me to bang on my crotch. This is great."

I believe I was a pretty good catcher right from the start, but I don't remember that much about it. I think it helped, though, that I always played against guys who were older than me. I'm a firm believer in the idea that if you play against tough competition, it's only going to make you better.

I played in leagues all the way through elementary school, always getting better and always having more fun, and it wasn't long before I made up my mind that one day I was going to a big league player. From the earliest grades that I can remember, whenever some school form came around asking what I wanted to be when I grew up, I'd always write "professional baseball player." Of course, I didn't know what a catcher did then. I knew there were signs that you put down if a pitcher had more than one pitch. It was basic — one, fastball; two curveball. That was it. No one had ever heard of a slider or a forkball or anything like that. But one part of the position I always enjoyed was when someone tried to steal a base. To me, that was challenging. Even now I get just as excited throwing people out at second or third as I do getting hits. Right from the beginning, I've believed that the number one priority of the catcher is his defensive capability, and anything he does offensively is a bonus. I enjoy hitting home runs and driving in runs, and there's no question that all the notoriety comes from offensive abilities. Very seldom will you hear someone say, "This guy's great, and we're going to pay him for his defence." They look at you and say, "He hits such and such, but he doesn't hit that." But defence comes first with me, always.

I had a good example to follow in learning to be a catcher: all the time I was going through school I was a big fan of the Detroit Tigers. My first trip to a major league game was with one of my little league clubs. Every Saturday was kids' day at Tiger Stadium, and they'd put us all out in left field. We'd go as a team, with everyone in uniform, and we'd try to get there early to catch batting practice balls. It seemed like we would go every Saturday when the Tigers were at home.

The Tigers had a good team with a lot of outstanding players all through the late fifties and sixties. Al Kaline, probably the all-time greatest Tiger as far as class and talent went, was in his prime. He was a gentleman, with an impressive bearing. I liked Dick McAuliffe, who managed me in Bristol in 1974. He was a left-handed hitter with an open stance, and I always liked his batting style. Jim Northrup, Mickey Lolich, Mickey Stanley — I was excited about almost every Tiger player. I remember Charlie Maxwell, who was called Pow-Pow Maxwell because he was from Paw-Paw, Michigan, and would hit a home run, it seemed, every Sunday. I never did meet him, but I remember listening to him and always pulling for him to do well. He always stood out in my mind.

But the one who stood out most — the guy who really was the Tigers for me — was their catcher, Bill Freehan. Freehan was from Detroit, too, and spent his whole career with the Tigers. I always looked up to him and told everyone who would listen that I wanted to be like him when I grew up.

The Junior High I attended is torn down now, but I learned an awful lot of good lessons there. Coming out of **13** elementary school I was still kind of a tough guy. At least I thought I was. In grade school I'd been the scrappiest kid around and had learned to take a lot of punishment, especially from a wicked paddle one teacher had that I always seemed to be running into. I had a reputation, and it followed me when we transferred in grade seven to what was called Eastland Annex. There were not only kids from our elementary school but two or three other schools as well, which made for quite a learning experience because suddenly I had to battle the toughest guy from each of the other schools. There were a lot of fights, but I'd had lots of practice. My friend Billy Burgess was a tough character, and he and I had got into an awful lot of scraps.

My first big test at Eastland was a short, heavy-set guy named Larry, built really strong. He beat the crap out of me, and I figured, well, I won't have to mess with that kid anymore. The second test was a guy named Dave who was a lot bigger than I was and kept pushing me to fight with him. I kept saying no, knowing he would probably clean my clock. But he finally got to me one day, and I just grabbed him, threw him up against the lockers, and held him there. It kind of surprised me that I was able to do that, but I told him, "Look, don't mess with me. I don't want to fight with you, so just leave me alone."

After school he was waiting for me. We met at the usual battle spot — the field next to Don's Party Store, the place we'd all go to get our candy. Whenever there was a challenge, it was "Okay, I'll meet you at Don's." There was always a good audience.

Butting him up against the lockers had built my confidence up a little bit, and I thought, "Maybe I can handle this guy." After school I found out I couldn't. For the first time I actually saw stars. The kid pounded on me pretty good.

I learned a few good lessons in that field, and I learned a few in school, too. A man named Leroy Herron was the phys. ed. teacher at Eastland, and he took me aside and said, "I know you've got a lot of talent. You've got a lot of good in you, and I'm not going to let it go astray." He was the first instructor I had that took me under his wing and really set me straight.

He had a certain way of explaining things when he thought you were going wrong. First, there was "big thunder." You'd stand in front of him, and while he gave his lecture he'd emphasize his points by jabbing his finger into your chest, harder and harder and harder. Even worse was "the big squeeze." He'd sit above you up on a bleacher and start working on your shoulder and neck muscles, getting more intense all the time. It would almost bring you to your knees as he lectured you on right and wrong and told you how he was going to make you a better man. He really put an effort into it, and I have the highest respect for the man because he showed that he cared about me as an individual. I was about 12 years old, and at that point in my life there really were two roads for me — the way of the good guy or the tough bad guy — and he went out of his way to make sure that I went along the right path.

After that one year in seventh grade I could see myself changing. I wasn't going out looking for trouble anymore. I tried to back away from it and keep my nose clean. Not to say that there weren't a few instances in eighth and ninth grade. But that was because my reputation still followed me around, and there was always a new challenge. It seemed like one would come every week. I never turn down a challenge, but I found out I really wasn't as tough as I thought I was. I came to believe it was wiser to avoid fights instead of getting my brains beat out.

As I went into Carl Brablec High School, I also figured that if I wanted my brains beat out, I always had football. Sports was it for me right from the beginning, and all through school, from grade eight on, I played baseball, football, and basketball, never putting much of an effort into my studies but always doing just enough to keep me eligible for sports.

Baseball was always special, but I actually had more **15** talent for football and enjoyed playing that game more than baseball in high school. I played both quarterback and linebacker, which was a neat situation because if I was getting beat up at quarterback, I was able to take out my frustrations by going on defence and beating up the other quarterback. We didn't have that many players, so we didn't have any specialties. We always played both ways, which made it an awful lot of fun. I was probably most effective running the option play. That was a challenge, making the split-second decision of whether to hand the ball off to the tailback, pitch it back to the halfback, pass it, or keep it myself.

We played our home football games at Memorial Stadium. We'd dress at the school right next door and walk by twos from the gym to the field, feeling the momentum building. The closer you got, the more you could hear the cheering and the humming of the crowd. I loved playing high school football.

I enjoyed basketball more than baseball, too. We had some great guys on the team, and our coach was Rex

Corlis, a very low-keyed, down-to-earth man who was a defensive halfback for Michigan State the last time they went to the Rosebowl in '66. We students always thought he had the wrong job, that he should have been the head football coach. He was a super coach to play for because he knew how to get the most out of all his players.

But always there was baseball. We played our high school baseball games on the diamond in Rotary Park. I was a pretty good ball player at the time, one of the best on the team, and that kind of went to my head. Once, I got into a little disagreement with the coach, who was trying to help me out with my catching and made some comment I took exception to. I figured I didn't need any help, but I was catching the ball in a certain way and he wanted me to do it differently. I threw up my hands and said, "If you think you know how to do it any better, get someone else. I quit." To this day I remember it as one of the stupidest statements I've ever made. I took off my gear and sat on the bench while someone else finished catching the game. I apologized to him after a couple of chats with the athletic director and the football coach, who wondered how on earth I could pull a stunt like that.

It was useful getting that little dose of humility, because I knew I was getting good. I was still playing baseball in local amateur leagues, and during the summer we'd play our games in Memorial Stadium. That was the ultimate. There were always lots of open fields around, but Memorial had a fence around all four sides. It had bleachers and a concession stand, and it was almost like playing at Tiger Stadium. That's the way we felt, growing up. We played night games, too, and that was the best of all — playing in the stadium under the lights. Nothing else could make you feel so much like a real baseball player.

But it was at Huron Park, a huge facility with three fields, where I played until I was sixteen years old, that my baseball skills really developed. I played an awful lot of games — double headers, triple headers — twice during the week, then on Saturday or Sunday.

16

I was starting to feel a little special. I was one of the star athletes at Brablec, a local sports hero at the school. But it was still just Roseville, and you couldn't get to the big leagues from there.

There were some good ball players in our local leagues who I felt could have made it if they ever got out of Roseville or if scouts ever came out to the suburbs to look at them. I played with a couple of very high quality players who just never got the opportunity.

I was luckier. My dad really made my opportunity. He got friendly with a number of scouts and, when we were told that if I wanted to be scouted by professional teams I had to go to Detroit, he formed a team in Roseville, then rolled it into the city league.

Both my parents were very good about coming out to games and cheering me on. They were both very supportive and very giving of their time. I know they sacrificed an awful lot to see not only me, but my brother in sports. Mike, too, was very good in baseball. He wasn't big, but he had talent. To this day, I feel he could have pitched in the major leagues. But there came a time when he thought girls were more important. I got excited about girls, too, but I had that dream of playing in the big leagues that I'd had since I was small. And I think Dad kind of made sure that I stayed interested and active. He had seen what happened to Mike, and didn't want that to happen to me.

That kind of commitment by parents is tremendously important, but I sometimes wonder whether it has its down side when I see what happened to my sisters. They didn't turn out to be the type of people I thought they would. They seemed to get sidetracked by some bad influences. They both dropped out of school, both got involved with drugs. I often wonder whether it was because my parents, especially Dad, spent so much time with me that they felt neglected and then went off with the wrong crowd. But then maybe it was just peer pressure or the fact that my oldest sister, Melinda, is six years younger than I am and drugs were really popular when they grew to adolesence. But they got hooked on the stuff,

17

from marijuana right up to heroin, and it's only gotten worse.

They face a long road of recovery. They've had treatment, but if you don't want help to be cured, you're not going to be cured, no matter what anybody else does. You've got to want to do it, and they haven't wanted to as far as I can see. Every day, I wonder whether I'm going to pick up the phone and find out that one of my sisters is dead.

I feel fortunate that all my influences were positive, especially the teachers I had in high school and the coaches I admired and who looked out after me. Brablec's football coach, Bob Nelson, really stands out in my mind. He put quite an effort into getting me a football scholarship, and because of him over fifty universities sent me letters asking if I'd be interested in attending their schools and trying out for their teams.

18 I had a big decision to make. If I was going to go to a four-year university, I thought I could probably major in education and maybe have a pro football career. But I looked at the longevity factor. If I was going to be a professional athlete, I wanted a career longer than football could offer. And there was also my boyhood dream that I couldn't shake off. I wanted to play professional baseball, and if I went to university I wouldn't be able to sign a baseball contract until I was 21 or had graduated. Putting it all together, I chose Macomb Community College, where I could play both basketball and baseball and could sign with a baseball team at any time. I was one of the first students Macomb ever gave a scholarship to.

Once I made that decision, my football days were over. At Macomb I stuck to baseball, basketball, studies in a general education program, and all the other things young college students get up to. There were nights of cruising Gratiot Avenue, a Roseville teenage tradition that continues to this day. There were border crossings to Windsor, Ontario, where the drinking age was lower, and lots of parties with more than a few girlfriends.

Then I came across a girl I'd met once the year before, while I was still in high school. I had been planning back then to go to a house party with a good friend, Rodney Barnett, when his mother told him that he couldn't go unless he found a date for his cousin, Christine, who was in for a visit from Cedar Rapids, Iowa. He asked if I'd mind her tagging along as my date. I didn't. At the party, she went one way and I went another, which was fine because we didn't hit it off at all.

About a year later she came to Detroit again, and I told Rodney to bring her by so I could see if she'd improved any. She had definitely improved. She had matured into an interesting young woman. Of course, being nineteen, I was looking mainly at the physical side. I saw the face and figure and thought, "Oh, she's changed." I asked her out for the next night and the next. We were together the whole time she was in from Iowa, and when she went back home, the telephone calls and letters never stopped. The next summer, she moved in with her aunt in Michi- **19** gan.

Chris didn't know much about baseball, but she sure heard a lot about it soon enough. I kept telling her that I'd give anything to be drafted, and she kept wondering why I'd want to go to Vietnam. But we straightened that out, and she encouraged me and kept my spirits up when the June, 1971, baseball draft came and went without any contract being offered to me.

I had been hopeful about that draft. I knew scouts had been looking at me ever since my last year of high school. And the Tigers had open try-outs every year at Butzel Field, where the bird-dog scouts from different organizations would come to look over the local talent. I went down there every other Saturday for three years for their program of running, hitting, and throwing. I was selected for the All-Star team they put together at the camp and played games in Michigan and across the border in Canada. The Tiger scout who was pursuing me told me that the reports on me were good. Besides, that year I had done well playing for the college team. Macomb's coach, Dan Jaksen, was very helpful, and I ended the year batting .324.

But it wasn't to be. I was very disappointed, but I threw myself into basketball and not my studies and kept hoping for a better draft the following year. The basketball coach, Dennis Ambo, had an assistant named Bernie Lemieux, who became a very close friend and made playing an enjoyable experience. I wasn't the star of the team, but I was kind of a stabilizing factor. Bernie would always say that for us to win a game I had to play well. But there were many guys a lot more talented than I was. I was a forward, a dirty-work type player, always good at blocking out the rebounders, no matter what their size. At that time I was 6'2" and weighed maybe 185 pounds, and I'd be going up against guys 6'6" who weighed 220 and could jump like kangaroos. Bernie would always put me on their best rebounders.

20   It was a great way to stay in shape for baseball season, and the next year I hit .333, led the Macomb team with 32 RBI, stole 20 bases in 21 attempts and was voted the baseball team's MVP and the college's most outstanding athlete. So as the June draft came around in 1972, my hopes were high again. Just one thing tempered my optimisim. A Tiger scout my dad was friends with told him that Bill Lajoie, Detroit's director of scouting at the time, had said that he didn't think I would ever make it past AA ball. I refused to believe that. I couldn't believe that. I had an out if I wasn't drafted. The baseball coach at Eastern Michigan University had seen me play and said he'd take care of me if I wanted to go there. But I kept thinking, "I want to play professional ball. It'll work out. I will be drafted."

There's a recurring joke in baseball. Whenever we're on a team bus and we pass a wino in the street, someone almost always calls out to another player, "Hey, there's your scout." The scout who signed me was far from that. His name was Morri deLouf, an older gentleman who has now passed away. I never knew the man was around when I was playing ball in Detroit, though he had scouted me in both the Detroit and the college league. I'd never seen him, but one afternoon he called me on the phone and said,"Would you like to sign a professional contract?"

The surprise was that he wasn't a scout for the Tigers. He represented the Boston Red Sox. I didn't know anything about them. I didn't even know who their catcher was at the time. I had heard of Carl Yastrzemski, but he was the only one I knew. Detroit was the only team I had followed. I did know a little bit about Baltimore because of Jim Palmer, Brooks Robinson, and Boog Powell, and because I have some relatives there and there was always a little competition between Detroit and Baltimore among the families. And I guess everyone follows the Yankees to some extent, but Detroit and Baltimore were the only two teams where I knew many of the players.

Morri came over a couple of hours after his call, and we talked. I had never even thought about negotiations. The only thing I wanted out of it was a college education. I asked him what round I was drafted in, but he said that really it wasn't important. I was too naive and too happy to argue. I found out later that it was the twelfth round, and players drafted in later rounds were signing for substantial sums of money. But he said, "What we'll do is give you $2,500 and an allowance for college." To me, this was great. I'd never seen that kind of money before. And to get $2,500 to go out and play a game that I loved playing, this was what I wanted. It was what I had wanted since I was seven years old. It was my dream come true.

I signed that night.

The longer you're in baseball, the busier the off-season gets. There are promotional activities to do for the team, charitable organizations you get called on to work for, shows to emcee, radio commercials to record. And the number of sports banquets and benefits being held around North America seems to be growing at an amazing rate. To accept all the invitations would make the four months off almost as gruelling as the season.

One thing I don't like to do in the off-season is to think too much about baseball. There are too many rumours of moves around the time of baseball's winter meetings, too many reporters asking for comments on the latest story. In 1987, Pat Gillick was quoted as saying he was "85 per cent certain" that I'd be with the Blue Jays in 1988. It was the 15 per cent that stuck in my mind. After a while, you just try and block that stuff out.

I did get in touch with the organization about one move, though, a move I found very disappointing. The Blue Jays released Garth Iorg. Maybe I'm a little prejudiced about Garth, because we go back a long way, but I hated to see the organization give up on him. To me, he was a gamer, a guy that wanted to play every day whether he was hurt or not. He was an aggressive player who could play all the infield positions. He was a good right-handed bat coming off the bench and meant a lot to everyone in the clubhouse. He was the all-around good guy who kept us loose even if he was going through a bad spell himself.

I talked to Paul Beeston, the Blue Jays executive vice-president for business, and asked why the Jays would not want to retain him. He was still young and had a good baseball sense about him. He'd had some trouble at the end of the '87 season, but that was because he'd been a platoon player since Day One. He'd been told that he would platoon at second with Nelson Liriano. Then he found that Nelson had taken his job and he only got to play as a utility man. That's not an adjustment that can be made overnight.

Paul said, "We're just trying to be fair to Garth, too. We feel that if he can catch on with another team as an everyday player, it'd be unfair to sign him here when he'd only be a utility player. It's better to tell him now than at the end of spring training when everybody's roster is set."

I could see the point, but I still thought he was too valuable to give up on. And I was sad when the deadline for a team signing its own free agents came and went without Garth getting an offer from the Jays or any other club.

But that goes with the territory. I've seen a lot of baseball friends released, but Garth was more than that. It's funny in baseball. You spend more time with your teammates than you do with your family over most of the year. I like to feel that my teammates are my friends. But to me, friends keep track of what's going on in each other's lives, just like we keep track during the season of our friends outside of baseball. When the team melts away at the end of the season, everyone goes his own way. There's very little communication. In this off-season, I saw Lloyd Moseby and Willie Upshaw at a promotional event in Toronto and you get your Christmas cards from everyone, but the communication is just not there. The only players I spoke to on the phone were Rick Leach, who also lives in the Detroit area, and Garth out in California. But I guess that's understandable. We've all got families to catch up with and lives to get on with. We're busy.

There are business affairs to look after. Like many players, I have promotional contracts for companies that require so many days a year for travel and personal appearances at company functions.

And like most players, I think, I have my own business ventures and investments to tend to. Major league salaries may seem high, but major league careers are pretty short. If you want to maintain a certain standard of living once your playing days are over, you've got to get your money working for you. I've been very fortunate to have financial advisors who've ensured my children's education and a comfortable life for my family after I retire from the game. I have real estate investments in Toronto and California, a share in an Egyptian horse breeding operation in London, Ontario, and a major share in an investors group operating fifteen "Mothers Pizza Pasta" restaurants in cities from Toronto to Sarnia. As a group, we'll also be opening thirty "TCBY" frozen yogurt outlets in southwestern Ontario over the next few years.

It takes time to take care of business, but I try not to let that detract too much from spending time with my family. During the spring and summer when I'm travelling and working almost every day, I miss an awful lot of my kids' activities — school concerts, parent days, sports — a lot of little things that are really important to a kid.

So I enjoy the winter months. I really enjoyed the winter of '87, because I helped coach my son's third-grade basketball team. It was exciting actually doing something with my kids instead of just sitting back like during the summer when they're playing little league and soccer. Their schedules being the way they are, and off-days in baseball usually being Mondays and Thursdays, I've been able to see them play some soccer, but I've never seen them play baseball.

24   I found out one thing in my short coaching career: you have to have a lot of patience with a third-grade group of boys, and you have to have even more patience with their parents. I thought the pressures in the major leagues were bad. I had 15 kids to split up into two groups. I tried to split them as evenly as I could, yet have friends together playing on each squad. I wanted to keep the teams evenly matched because the whole purpose of the league is competition, not for winning, but for learning how to play the game. And if you have one dominant team, then the other team's only going to become frustrated and throw in the towel.

The first time I tried to divide them up, the phone rang off the hook that night. "Billy's upset because he's not playing with Joey." "Mark's upset because he's not playing with Andy."

I said, "Wait a minute, people. I'm doing the best I can. I'm trying to make it as even as possible."

The parents started saying, "We don't care. We want the best team."

I said, "But that's not the purpose of this."

I always respect a desire to win, but sports were never supposed to be this grim. A game's a game, but it seems kids now are getting pushed hard to succeed before they realize what fun it is to play a game and to play it well.

Some parents would start yelling at their kids before and during a game. Some kids would start crying after they lost a game. I'd talk with them, just saying, "Did you have a good time? Then it doesn't matter if you won or lost at this point. The biggest thing is that you had a good time. And remember that one rebound that you got? That was a big rebound. You've got to be happy about that." I was just trying to pick up on the positive things for them instead of all the negatives.

They were a terrific bunch of kids and really responded well. And when I emphasized that you can't score without shooting the ball, these guys took it to heart. As soon as they crossed the centre line, they'd throw 30 and 40 foot shots at the rim. I said, "Wait, a minute, guys. That's not what I meant. Let's run a play, let's get closer to the basket before you shoot." It was fun. I had a great time.

Our daughter, Ashley, plays basketball, too, and the winter gives me a chance to see her play and to see the shows she gets into as a singer. In 1987, the years of singing lessons that she's had led to her first paying job, singing at a dinner in St. Thomas, Ontario.

And sometime during the off-season, I play Mr. Mom while Chris takes the two weeks she takes every year to travel with a friend wherever she chooses to go. She's gone to Italy, Egypt, twice to Israel, California, even just down to Florida. After playing Mrs. Dad as well as Mom for so much of the year, she figures the kids need a break from her, and she naturally likes a break herself. She really deserves it. Baseball wives don't get nearly the credit they should for all the burdens they carry during the baseball season.

But there's only so much time. In January, spring training is just weeks away. My weight conditioning program at the health club intensifies, and I head over to Macomb College for workouts. But before all that happens, there's the hectic period leading up to Christmas. In baseball, that also often means a lot of birthdays to look after. There's a kind of family planning that goes with the game that's got less to do with the palm trees and the Florida moonlight in springtime than it has with making sure that fathers are at home when their children are born. Many players try, and we had great success with our kids — that means two birthdays in November and one in early December.

It makes for a lot of activity, but these are all special dates. Christmas, especially, is a big time for us, with friends and people from the neighbourhood coming over for our traditional open house on Christmas Eve. We run a train around one of our trees, and some of the neighbourhood kids who don't even know our names remember the train and want to come every year to see it going round and round. It's a tradition I hope will continue when our children are grown with children of their own.

26 We have two trees because one, the one with the train, is very special. It's our "memory tree," with ornaments we've collected from all over North America and from South America, too. It may be just a small bulb or a little sign, but each is a treasured souvenir picked up wherever baseball's taken us. It's taken us a long, long way.

February

I always like to get to spring training early. So as soon as
February comes around, we get organized to move the
family south for six weeks. We have to arrange with the
kids' teachers to match up their studies with the curricu-
lum in Florida and find schools with tolerable levels of
the mildew and dampness that every school in the state
seems to have. Then we pack up, spend a few days at
Disneyworld, and head for our condominium in
Dunedin.

Catchers are usually the first to arrive at camp, along
with pitchers and injured players. Catchers are usually
first on the field and the last to leave every day, too.
There's a lot of work to be done — conditioning, signs,
blocking the balls, pop-ups, pick-ups, plus catching for all
the pitchers. Being a pitcher at spring training, on the
other hand, is the easiest job in the world. We ride each
other about it. These guys pitch maybe once every three
days or so, and on the other days they get their running
in and then they get to go home. That's why pitchers are
the best golfers on any team. They have the most time.

We'll be out there slaving away and see the pitchers riding off in their convertibles with the top down and their golf clubs sticking up out of the back. They smile and wave at us as we block balls in the dirt. It's all good natured.

Some people think you have to be a little crazy to be a catcher. You certainly have to be tough and learn to take punishment of all kinds. And you can't let little things bother you. If you let them bother you, you're not going to play in the big leagues, and you're not going to play effectively anywhere.

Catchers do get beat up quite a bit. Something is always happening — a foul tip off the toe or the finger or the shoulder, a collision at the plate. During the season, any catcher's body is always black and blue. But you get used to it and you just play over it. Losing a nail or busting a toe on a foul tip is bad, but the worst is getting a tip right on the point of the shoulder, especially on your throwing arm. It stings and it's very difficult to perform when you can't get the proper movement out of your shoulder. It's a very difficult place to try to protect, because any padding would cut down the motion you need to get the ball to second quickly. The padding couldn't be any thicker than the chest protector anyway, and a ball coming off the bat at a high rate of speed doesn't get slowed down much by a pad that's maybe half-an-inch thick.

Very seldom will you see a catcher who'll go more than two or three days without something happening, which is probably why there aren't that many really good hitters among the catchers. A lot of little aches and injuries build up. You play through them, but they still affect the way you stand or swing at the plate.

Maybe you do have to be crazy. But it's a position I wouldn't change for anything. I played some first base and outfield in the minor leagues and found both positions very boring.

To me, catching is a challenge. You've got the pitcher you have to deal with. What's he capable of doing anytime and on this particular day? What's his makeup as a person? Is he the type of guy you have to baby, the type of guy you have to ride all the time, the type of guy you have to go out and pat on the butt to boost him up when the going gets tough?

You've got to know what type of hitter is coming up to the plate and what his strengths and weaknesses are. If you have a pitcher whose strength is pitching low and you have a hitter whose strength is hitting low, then you've got a problem. You think, "Can my man get him out high going out of his strength, or can he overmatch the guy low?"

Then you've got someone working over your back all the time, breathing down your neck, most of the time with bad breath, and you've also got to try and figure out what this guy's made of. Can I chew him out if he misses a pitch or do I have to pamper him?

And you're the only player who gets to see everything in front of you, so you wonder, is the runner going to go? **29** Is the infield at the right depth? How's the outfield shaded, and what does that do for the next pitch I want to call?

It's a mix of different personalities, strategy, knowledge, tight situations. It's exciting.

It's a lot of fun, too. Having fun's important in a ball game, although some players seem to forget that. You've got to go out and have fun. It's a big business sport, but it's still men playing a little boy's game. I've always said that once it becomes work, I might as well hang up the cleats and get out. I feel very fortunate to be able to do something that I enjoy doing so much.

There were some new faces, as well as some old familiar ones, when the catchers reported to Dunedin in February, 1988. Greg Myers was the top prospect, as he was the year before. Greg does everything. He's a good defensive catcher, swings the bat pretty well, and calls a good game. I feel kind of bad for him. He's been paying his dues in the minor leagues, waiting for his break. The only thing that he's got going against him is that he bats the same way I do, and the Blue Jays wouldn't want to carry two left-hand hitting catchers. He's basically an insurance policy for the club, and that's a position I was in for many years. It's frustrating thinking that your career is stopped cold. You want to be traded, but the club always says, "We don't want to trade you because if something happens to the main guy, we've got to have you as a backup."

Another familiar prospect was Matt Stark, who caught a few games for us in 1987. He had a shoulder operation in the winter, and it seemed obvious that the shoulder wouldn't be ready in time for the season. I've always wondered whether Matt could be a catcher because of his size. He's a big man, 6'4" and well over 200 pounds, and may not be able to take the wear and tear on the knees. He hits very well, though, and the organization may have to find him another position if he can't hold up physically behind the plate.

30   A new guy was Pat Borders, who only started catching in AA in 1987. Within days we could see that he threw the ball well and swung the bat really well, but he needed experience, which is a tough thing to gain if you're on a ball club that's expected to win. It's also tough to go right to the major leagues without going through an AAA team, although Butch Wynegar and Jim Sundberg both did it.

And, as always, the rumours were that the Jays were after a veteran catcher. Ever since I can remember, the Blue Jays have said, "We're looking for another catcher." It's bothered me some, because I don't feel I was ever given the opportunity to play on an everyday basis. And I've always wanted that opportunity. But I've taken on the philosophy over the last six years of, "If you can't control it, don't worry about it." I have no control over what they do in the front office. If it happens, it happens. It was just meant to be. That's easier to say than to live up to, of course. I've been irritated quite a few times with what's been said or what I've read in the papers. There have been times when I've felt that I haven't been appreciated by management.

But platooning behind the plate has been a Blue Jay tradition since I came up to the club full-time in 1980, first with Bobby Davis, then with Buck Martinez and, in 1987, with Charlie Moore. Offensively, Charlie and I weren't a bad combination, but the organization wasn't happy with his defence at all and released him soon after the season ended. Personally, I thought Charlie was a better catcher than he showed. I think he just had a bad year. Maybe he was a little rusty from knocking around in the minors for a while after getting sent down by Milwaukee. Even when he was with the Brewers, he was playing more often in right field than behind the plate. But he had played in the league for eight years and knew all the hitters. Finding a catcher with that kind of experience is a problem not only for the Blue Jays, but for every organization. There just aren't that many veterans out there.

One catcher many people had talked about over the winter as a possible Toronto acquisition was Carleton Fisk. I had heard that Pudge had approached the Blue Jays for a job, but I guess Pat Gillick and Jimy Williams didn't like what they saw in him. I know they don't like his style of catching. He's very slow, which also really bothers us when we play against him. What we try to do in the Blue Jays organization is have the pitcher know what he wants to throw before he gets the ball back from the catcher, set the hitters up by trying to think two pitches ahead, and get a rhythm going that moves the game along. I've never checked the records on him, but I'd bet the teams Pudge has played for have probably averaged the longest games in baseball. He does like to take his time.

Whoever joins the Blue Jay catching corps comes up against a hard-nosed sergeant type in our bullpen coach, John Sullivan, who's really helped me out in my career. Sully's a classic. He always comes to the park so early, at home or on the road, that they finally gave him his own

31

key to the clubhouse. He loves the game, loves to be there in the locker room. I think it's getting a bit carried away, being there before noon, but he's dedicated. Baseball's been his whole life. He's a true student of the game — he studies everything and everyone and he knows what each individual is made of, what he's capable of doing, and what he's not capable of doing. He's an ex-catcher himself, and in spring training he loves to work us out. Rigorously. But when the exhibition games start, we're in great shape and ready to play, which helps us all year.

We kind of envy the infielders who take their ten sprints then pack it in for the day, because once we've gone through our fundamentals of blocking and catching pop-ups, we do our deep-knee bend pick-up drills on both sides of the plate. We start with 25 standing pick-ups in full equipment, then 25 more three feet apart, then another 25 twelve feet apart. And those 75 quick knee **32** bends are just at the start of spring training. By the end, we're doing 50–50–50. And when we're through doing that for the day, we do our sprints, stretching out ten yards on each until we're running from the foul line to the centre field fence. We're always glad there's a fence out there because otherwise we'd be running for days. We do circle sprints, too, running the half-moon of the infield, then going further and further out until we're at the warning track, going foul-line to foul-line.

That's another thing I like about being a catcher — we're blue collar workers. Good work habits go with the position. I wish I could say the same for some of the other positions, but there seems to be a new breed of ball player coming up through the system.

What I've been seeing the past few years — and I usually only see it with kids who have been high draft choices and who have been given a lot of money to sign professional contracts — is a lot of pampering. Even in the minor leagues, they're pampered and nourished and burped along the way. Others who may have gotten $500 to sign have to bust their butts to make other people notice them. But the "bonus babies" seem to just coast along while the organization pushes them up through the system.

I can see that that makes some short-term sense from a business point of view. If I've got $100,000 invested in some guy, I'm going to keep an eye on him and push him more than I would the guy I've only got $500 sunk into. But I've seen too many kids get a lot of money to sign, then think they've got it made. They think they don't have to put an effort into improving themselves. They know they'll jump quickly from A ball right through to the big leagues because the organizations don't want to lose out on their investments. Some of the organizations are getting a bad deal.

I found that out with one of my first roommates in professional ball, a shortstop out of California. He was a real burn-out. He had some talent, but he was into the "I want my own freedom" frame of mind. He wanted to go up on a mountain and build a ranch and enjoy the open space and his drugs. When I first met him, he said "I got the first part of my bonus and as soon as I get my second part, I'm quitting."

I just kind of looked at him and said, "What do you mean you're quitting? Don't you want to play professional ball?" I had a hard time comprehending that. All my life I had wanted to play, and here was a guy who got $120,000 to sign, a lot of money back in 1972, and was just waiting for the chance to quit. In June, he got his final payment and just walked away. I never saw or heard from him again.

I know that I've played with some guys who have signed for big dollars who I've just looked at and thought, "This guy isn't worth that much. How in the world could they give that guy that kind of money? I've played with guys in Roseville who were better than him." A lot of it is just being in the right place at the right time. Opportunity is everything. But if some people find themselves in the right place it sometimes seems to go to their heads. They don't realize or don't want to admit that they'd be much

33

better ball players if they spent more time in the minor leagues learning their craft.

The minors are there to be helpful. They can be frustrating, but they can be an awful lot of fun, too. I should know. I spent a lot of time there.

When I was drafted by the Red Sox, I was maybe a little full of myself, too. I don't really remember it this way, but Chris says that at my going-away party she was worried about my getting to the airport. She was afraid my head wouldn't fit in the car. All I remember is being tremendously happy to finally be in professional ball.

I reported to Williamsport, Pennsylvania, and met up with Boston's minor league instructors. There were seven or eight other catchers in camp and I figured this wasn't an ideal situation. But they treated me very well, especially a couple of guys who took me under their wing. Sam Mele, who had managed the Minnesota Twins, was a big influence, telling me that he liked the way I swung the bat and that he thought I had a chance of being a good hitter.

That year the floods hit Pennsylvania and our season was cancelled for almost a week. When we finally played our first game, I ended up playing first base. I got two hits that night, one of them a double, and after the game, the manager and Sam called me to the lobby of the hotel and told me they were going to move me to the A team in Winter Haven. The next day I was on my way to Florida, with one game of rookie league under my belt.

I didn't do too well in Winter Haven. In 31 games, I hit a poor .183. But then, the Florida State League had its distractions. It was a great league. We got to go to Fort Lauderdale and Miami and Daytona Beach, quite an experience for a Michigan boy. I was single then, and naturally, we'd all go out after the game and do a little socializing. John Butler was managing at the time, and he once caught some of us late one night in a bar with some girls. He pulled me off to the side and said, "Son, there's two ways to this game. One of them is my way, and the

34

other one is the highway. If you play my way, you have a chance to make it to the big leagues, but you have to start obeying the rules. We don't need you around here, but if your goal is to make it to the big leagues you need us. We're here to help you achieve your goals, and if you go out and break the rules, you're not going to achieve them." I got the message real quick.

After that first year in baseball, I was invited to the Instructional League over the winter. I had heard that if they ask you to go to Instructional League, they've got some interest in you, they think you've got some talent, they think you can go on to be a big league player. At that point, I saw myself progressing nicely along the path that was laid out for me, one step at a time through the minor league system. I was happy with it. I was content.

Sam Mele was there and helped me put body into my swing by getting more hip action. I ended up hitting at a .300 clip at Sarasota and was assured of a place on the Red Sox club in Winston-Salem of the Carolina League for the 1973 season.

Then it suddenly looked like the path through the system was going to take a detour through Southeast Asia. I got a notice to report for an army physical on January 18, 1973. Chris told me not to worry. She said I was lucky and my number wouldn't come up in the draft lottery. Still, a Navy recruiter looked into a six-month deferment through a commitment to the naval air reserve program. But as it turned out, I was lucky. Before anything could be done, the war wound down, the draft was ended, and I was on my way to North Carolina instead of South Vietnam.

We had a great chemistry on that ball club. I roomed with Bill Moran, who later went on to pitch for the White Sox, and Gary Myers, a top draft prospect from California who loved to drive around in the Porsche he got with his signing bonus. When he got released in June or July, Rick Kreuger, a left-handed pitcher from Michigan, moved in. It was a fun year on and off the field. Everyone got along well together and the manager, Bill Slack, was

35

outstanding. Four of the players on the team — Steve Dillard, Bill Moran, Jack Baker, and me — went on to play in the big leagues, a high proportion as minor league teams go. I had my best year ever, hitting .290 with 50 RBI in 130 games, and at the end of the season I was invited to Instructional League again.

The Boston people could see that I could hit. I was never a power hitter — I didn't have that type of swing — but I hit to all fields, and they liked that. I think the biggest thing they saw in me, though, was that my catching was improving. I had a strong arm, and they worked hard on my release. You can always improve defensively with a lot of hard work, and the drills and individual attention in the Instructional League helped me an awful lot. Johnny Bench could just stand up and throw a guy out at second base, no problem. But if you're not blessed with an overpowering arm like Bench had, you work on other ways of getting the ball to second as

36 quickly as he could. You might have an arc in your throw, but if you have a quick release, then the ball might get there just as fast as it would with a guy with a rocket arm throwing the ball in a straight line. I think over the years that I've become a fairly good defensive catcher because of those drills and all that hard work.

Maybe it's because I worked so hard to improve my defensive skills that I enjoy the working part of the game more than the hitting that's always thought of as the fun part. With all the sweat I put into defence, it's a great feeling to throw out guys that get paid all their money to steal bases. It's a challenge, even though you're not going to do it all the time. To throw out a guy like Rickey Henderson, everything has to be perfect. The pitcher has to get rid of the ball in a hurry and the catcher has to both get rid of the ball in a hurry and make an accurate throw. Those three are very hard to put together.

If the pitcher doesn't give you the ball quickly, you're not going to throw anyone out. The pitcher should give you the ball in 1.5 seconds. The catcher should get the ball from his glove to second base in about 2.0 seconds. The average base runner can get from first to second in 3.5 – 3.6 seconds, so you will throw out your average base runner. But to get Rickey Henderson out, the pitcher has to get the ball to you in 1.3 seconds and you have to get it to second in 1.9. When all that works, you can get a Rickey Henderson out, but it's so difficult to do.

In 1974, I was moved up to the Eastern League, playing for the Red Sox club in Bristol, Connecticut. The league was split into American and National League divisions, with teams scattered around New England and Quebec, and one team, the Reading Phillies, in Pennsylvania. They were neat little towns to play in. I especially remember Pittsfield, Massachussetts, because it was the only stadium I've played in where there had to be an intermission in the game. We'd start at 7:00, but at 7:30 we'd stop for 45 minutes or so to wait for the sun to set. It set directly out in centre field and a batter couldn't see anything while at the plate.

The Bristol Red Sox was a new team then, partly owned **37** by trumpet player Harry James, who was one of the team's vice-presidents. There weren't that many fans, even though in the team's first year (1973), Jim Rice and Fred Lynn had shown their talent. The ball park was Muzzy Field, an older park surrounded by spruce trees. It was one of the prettiest little places I've ever played in, with painted signs on all the outfield fences and a beautiful grass diamond. It was a long way out to centre field and a pretty good poke to left, but right field was a short fence.

We had a good, cohesive team, especially since seven of us had played together in Winston-Salem the year before. The manager was Stan Williams, who had pitched for Los Angeles in the late fifties and early sixties, then had moved on to the Yankees, Indians, and Twins. He'd posted a 10 – 1 record with 1.99 ERA in 68 appearances in relief for Minnesota in 1970.

Stan looked at me and he looked at that right field fence and said, "With your size, you should be a power hitter, you should try and pull the ball and hit home runs." I did my best, but I became really frustrated. I saw my average dip and I didn't hit that many home runs. Then it got to the point that I didn't know what I was doing. I had my manager who was there on a daily basis saying, "I want you to pull the ball." Then I had the roving hitting instructor who would come in every once in a while and say, "What happened to your swing? You're not swinging properly." Then a third coach would come in and tell me to do something else again.

I sat down with all of them and said, "Okay, I don't care how I hit. I just want one person to tell me something and for everyone to agree on it, because right now I'm totally confused and I can't please everyone. So please come up with a way you want me to hit." They decided I should go back to hitting the ball to all fields, to 'hit it where it's pitched'.

That's the big theory in baseball. If the pitch is outside you should hit it to the opposite field, if it's down the **38** middle, you should hit it up the middle, if it's inside, you should pull the ball. I've never been much of a believer in that. Each hitter is different. There are hitters who can take that outside pitch and pull the ball, because that type of hitter likes to extend his arms. When he extends his arms, that's when he gets most of his power, so you're doing him a favour by pitching the ball away from him. And the typical inside-out hitter likes the ball inside because he throws his hands through the strike zone first and the barrel of the bat is late. He gets the bat on the ball, but on an angle where it's going to the opposite field. You're doing him a favour, too, by pitching him inside. 'Hit it where it's pitched' is not the proper way of looking at it. As a hitter, what you've got to do is focus completely on the ball and let your natural abilities take over. Just try to make good solid contact.

But I tried hard to do whatever they told me to do, and improved my skills a lot over the season. It was an enjoyable time.

I especially looked forward to the ten-day swings we'd take through Canada. Despite growing up right across the river from the country, I didn't know much about Canada and had spent very little time there. I'd crossed over to Windsor a bit and I remember as a child taking Sunday drives with my parents over to Windsor then going up around Lake St. Clair to Sarnia and back down through Michigan. But that was about the extent of it.

The team was always warned not to make any remarks while going across the border. The customs man would ask us if we were bringing anything with us and we were supposed to say "nothing." But there always seemed to be some jerk who'd answer the question with "Just a case of VD" or something. We'd all have to get off the bus and have our bags searched. Smart remarks didn't seem to be appreciated.

Quebec was quite an experience for us Americans, especially the communication problem. It was fun to try and pick up a few words in a new language and try to use them in conversation, but people seemed offended by our attempts. All the players noticed going into French-speaking communities that people looked at us a little strange because we were speaking English. We didn't know about the big strain between the English and French of Canada in the early '70s, so it kind of unnerved us. When we sat down to eat at a couple of places, people actually got up and moved to another part of the restaurant when they heard us speak. We knew it wasn't because we hadn't showered, because this would usually happen when we'd just come from the showers at the ball park.

One time in Trois Rivières, I went out to eat with Lanny Phillips, my roommate from Odessa, Texas. "Lanny A. Phillips, No. 17" was how he signed his autograph. "And the 'A' stands for Apache." He insisted he was going to order in French, but he garbled the language so badly that the waitress got all upset and the other people in the restaurant started giving us dirty looks. We eventually ordered in English and got our meals just fine. We gave Lanny a hard time about that.

39

Of all the Canadian stops on our road trips, Quebec City was the nicest place to play, although we never got to see much of the city itself. We'd usually get off the bus, play the Carnavals, go to the motel, play the next day, then get right back on the bus and head out of town. I do remember one rainout day, though, when we hung around the clubhouse until post time, then went to the racetrack nearby. Quebec City had the best facilities, but the players enjoyed meeting up with the Trois Rivières Aigles best. That didn't have much to do with the team or the facilities, but it had a lot to do with the girls in Three Rivers, who seemed to be well-endowed. Every one of them.

But in all the Eastern League, Thetford Mines was unique. Having a team there was a bit of an experiment, and the experiment didn't last long. The town wasn't really large enough to support a team. We stayed in a motel about five miles from the ball park and the only place to eat was a little hamburger joint, a dairy bar half a mile up the road that was so small we had to eat in shifts. Even though the field was brand new, there were no locker room facilities and the lighting was terrible. But it was party night for the fans, and they made playing there enjoyable. There was a wooden fence that ran along the first and third base lines, and fans would climb up on it and dance and carry on, really enjoying themselves. I don't know whether they paid too much attention to the game, but they sure knew how to have a good time. Down on the field, we spent a lot of time watching them rather than concentrating on the game. The team itself wasn't much either, but any team with Willy Randolph at second and Tony Armas in the outfield had something going for it.

I got into a terrible slump in the first half of the season. That was partly because of the early attempts at my transformation from a spray hitter to a pull hitter, but it was also because I was lonely. I shared a cabin out by a lake with Lanny Phillips, who liked fishing as much as I did, so that was pleasant enough. But I missed Chris.

Before the season started, we had gone out to dinner at Luigi's Pizza Restaurant in Mt. Clemens, right next to Roseville, and got into one of those fights we always seemed to get into, and the thought kept running through my mind, "What can I say that will shut her up?" I landed on, "Will you be my wife?" It worked. That shut her up immediately, and the tears flowed and we decided to get married after the season was over in September. My parents greeted the news by telling Chris that if she married me my baseball career would be ruined, opening up a breach in my family that still hasn't healed.

We were planning a fall wedding, but then we got to fighting over who we wanted to invite and where we wanted to have it. This wasn't turning into the joyous occasion it was supposed to be. Then in Bristol, I really started to miss her. She came out to visit at the end of May and a week after she went home, I called her and said, "I'm sick of this long distance romance. Why don't you come back and let's just get married." She came down **41** through Canada and got tied up at the border when a guard thought she might be the missing Patty Hearst, but she was in Bristol in three days. A week later, we went to a third-floor Justice of the Peace. We were married around 1:00 and at 3:00 I was at the ball park. The slump was over. I went 2-for-3 in a 3 – 1 win over Trois Rivières that night.

It was a fun summer after that, and I got my average up to .249 on the year with nine homers as Bristol won the American Division title.

We didn't win the championship, but I was invited down to Instructional League for the third year in a row. I played good ball there, so with about three weeks to go in the league, I was taken aside and told, "The winter draft is coming up and there are a lot of scouts down here. We don't want anyone to see you. We're not going to protect you on a major league roster, but we're protecting you AAA and we're inviting you to spring training next year. But we don't want you to play here anymore because we don't want to lose you in the draft. We'll pay you your money and you can either stay here on vacation or you can go home."

I was getting close to being there. Not to take Fisk's job, certainly, but as a backup. Bob Montgomery, along with Dwayne Josephson, were catching backup for Fisk at the time, but they were both older and on their way out. I could see the plan to weed out the veterans and bring up a new catcher to work with Fisk until the rookie could get his feet on solid ground. All I needed was a good spring training and some seasoning in AAA.

I went to the major league camp in 1975 confident that I would be heading to Boston's AAA team at Pawtucket, Rhode Island. There was some competition for the position — Andy Merchant, another left-hand hitting catcher who had played the previous year in Winston-Salem. But I had the best spring training of my career and figured that I had the edge. Then, just as spring training was ending, in an exhibition game on April 2, I was out in **42** front of the plate waiting for a throw from the field, when a player came charging in from third base. I didn't know who it was then and I don't know now. It was spring training and the last thing I was expecting was a collision. The runner charged in, crashed into me and ripped my left shoulder apart. I could actually tilt my head and touch my ear to the bone sticking out.

Andy Merchant went to Pawtucket. I was flown to Boston for surgery. The Harvard doctor who looked at the tendons said it looked like an explosion in a meat factory. It was the first injury I'd ever had in pro ball.

It was a trying time. Chris followed Doug Griffin's wife up on the long drive from Florida, anxious to get to Boston before I went under the knife. She arrived at the hospital and came up against another reality of baseball life. Someone had told the nursing staff that a player from the Red Sox was in the hospital, and I guess nobody specified whether he was a minor or major leaguer. Or maybe it didn't matter. Chris walked into the room to find me unconscious on the bed, my hospital gown pushed up to my neck and a nurse giving me a very careful once over.

Chris was startled, but just said, "Do you like what you see?" After that, she almost wanted to move into the room with me, but the Red Sox were already looking after her.

The Red Sox organization was fantastic to both of us, going way beyond the call of duty as far as we were concerned. It was first class all the way. I was a "prospect," not a "suspect," and Chris was given *carte blanche* for anything she wanted. And it was the same for me when I got out of the hospital. We were used to the $5–7 a day allowance that minor leaguers got while they were on the road, but we stayed at a wonderful hotel in Boston, with expensive breakfasts, piped-in stereo, telephones in the bathroom, all kinds of luxuries we'd never experienced before. It was a taste of the big league life, but we felt a little guilty about it at the time. We would have been just as happy with an Egg McMuffin in a much smaller room, so we went to see the Red Sox VP of player personnel, Haywood Sullivan, and said, "Would you like us to move to another hotel or give us some per diem money for our meals or something, because this is really expensive?"

He looked over casually and said, "Why? Don't you think you're worth it?"

I said, "Well…yeah."

"Then don't worry about it. Charge everything to the room and we'll look after it. Enjoy it."

I missed the first half of the season while I waited to get the long pin removed from my reconstructed shoulder. It was June before I got back into a game, but I had the unique experience of being suspended for three days while I was still on the disabled list. It came after a little altercation with umpire Bob Nelson in a game against the West Haven Yankees. We had a few bench jockeys in the dugout, the loudest being our shortstop, Eddy Ford, Whitey's son. Eddy was really giving the umpire a hard time because he missed a call, and all of a sudden Nelson called time out and started coming towards the bench. Without Eddy, we didn't have a shortstop, so I stepped in front of him and told the umpire it was me saying all

43

those nasty things. He said, "Okay, Whitt, you're gone."
I ran out on the field to argue and I bumped him. It was a
gentle bump, but he played it up like I hit him good, fall-
ing back dramatically. And I thought, "Oh shit, here we
go." I ended up getting a two-game suspension and a
fine, the only suspension I've ever had.

Bristol had a terrible first half under a new manager,
one of my boyhood heroes, Dick McAuliffe, who had
played for the Tigers for 14 years before being traded to
the Red Sox for Ben Oglivie. In the second half, though,
we battled back to take the division championship for the
second year in a row. It was a disappointing year for me,
since I got into only 82 games and saw my RBI total drop
to 19 from the 56 I'd had in 1974. But still, we were in the
playoffs, despite losing Dick McAuliffe to the Red Sox at
the end of August. My old manager from the Carolina
League, Bill Slack, took over and we were confident we
had a good chance of beating the heavily favoured Read-
44   ing Phillies for the Eastern League championship.

The first game of the five-game final was tough, but we
won it 10 – 8. The second game was even tougher, and we
went into extra innings tied 6 – 6. We came out the winner, 11 – 6, and went back to Bristol hoping for a three-
game sweep.

In the final game, I drove in the first run in the fourth
and we picked up one more run the same inning. But
Reading came back with two unearned runs in the fifth,
tying it up when Rick Bosetti raced all the way home from
second on a fielder's choice. And that's the way it stayed
as the night wore on. The mayor of Bristol got a special
dispensation to let the game run past midnight as we
headed into the sixteenth inning. At the top of the inning,
I came up to bat with the bases loaded and one out. Bill
Slack called for a suicide squeeze, and I laid down a bunt
on a high slider. Butch Hobson had a late start from third
but still made it across with the go-ahead run. It was all
we needed. A new pitcher, Keith Scruggs, came in to
put down Reading in the seventeenth, and Bristol had its
first championship. The champagne flowed freely, but

we all felt bad for our pitcher, Mark Bomback, who later pitched for the Blue Jays. He had pitched 16 innings without giving up an earned run, but Keith Scruggs got the win.

Came the spring of 1976 and, once again, I just knew I'd be leaving AA ball behind, especially after another good spring training. Then came the word that I would be going back to Bristol. I said, "But I've been there two years. I have nothing left to prove in AA. All I want is a chance to get on with my career."

The reply was the most common phrase in baseball: "It's a numbers game. We just have no room for you in AAA."

I said, "Well, I don't think I'm going to report." I had seen a lot of players get fed up with the game. Talented players who got blocked, then frustrated to the point where they couldn't take it any more. I always thought that they should just hang in there. I could never see myself being in that situation. It's funny how it goes. You're about to give up the game you love so much because of the hard times and disappointments in the minors, the times you don't see any light at the end of the tunnel. Then you feel that maybe this could be your year, the year you might get a shot at taking one step closer to the major leagues. Then some curtain shuts down in front of you again and you feel like you're down even deeper into the darkness. That's how I felt in '76.

45

I went home and told Chris it was time to get out and get on with our lives. Maybe I'd go back to school and finish my degree, maybe I'd go into business full-time with her uncle, installing storm doors and replacement windows. But she told me, "I've always said that I'd live in a paper bag with you. But I won't live with you if you're going to be miserable. And you are going to be miserable. You know you can play in the big leagues. I know you can play in the big leagues. But you'll always have a little doubt in your mind because you never got the opportunity. You just have to hang on. With your talent, there'll be an opportunity."

So it was back to Muzzy Field in Bristol, sharing the catching duties with Bo Diaz, who had been moved up from Winston-Salem. It was even more discouraging when Bo got sent up to Pawtucket ahead of me. But anything can happen, and what happened in late May was that Carleton Fisk pulled a muscle. Bob Montgomery caught a few games for Boston, then the Red Sox called up Andy Merchant, leaving an opening on the AAA team.

I got the call on a Wednesday afternoon to meet the Pawsox on Thursday, then went out and caught the Wednesday night game for Bristol against the Waterbury Dodgers. My mind was far away and in my first two at-bats I couldn't get a hit. In my third at-bat, I went down swinging on a terrible pitch. When I came up in the sixth with the score tied 1 – 1, the only thought in my mind was what a shame it would be to go out like this. I cracked one over the centre field fence.

46 I was almost sad to leave. I'd eloped in this town, I'd been treated well, I loved the field. I was really fond of Bristol. I hoped I'd never come back.

The Rhode Island Red Sox was kind of a crazy team, with some really strange personalities. But the oddest guy was the manager, Joe Morgan. I'd never come across anyone quite like him before. I thought he had maybe spent too much time alone in the bush or been hit in the head too often with a hockey puck. He'd do the strangest things. He was very taken with the name of one of our infielders, Dave Machemer, and he'd sit at the front of the bus and repeat to no one in particular, "Machemer. Machemer. Machemer. Machemer." It was nothing for him to argue a call with an umpire, then stroll out to centre field, stand by the wall for a few minutes, then stroll back in as everybody just stood around waiting.

In one game, we were up 2 – 1 in the sixth inning when an opposing batter lined a rocket to centre. Our centre fielder, Dick Sharon, ran hard, dived, and grabbed the ball right out of the air. It was an outstanding catch and got Dick a standing ovation. The very next batter sent another hard liner in the same direction and Dick made another outstanding, outstretched, diving catch. Joe ran out of the dugout, called time out, then raced to centre field and shook Dick's hand.

He was bizarre, but he was also very good with the players. He was easy-going, direct, and would get his point across in a friendly, understanding way. Once, when he was going over how to field a bunt, he said, "I know you guys don't want to hear about this junk, but you can win games with it."

He was also the first manager I had who I felt was completely honest with me. A lot of managers hedge or tell you what they think you want to hear, putting the best case forward as if that was the way it was really going to be. But when I came up, Joe just said, "I don't know what the organization's got planned for you. I don't know whether you'll go back to AA when Fisk gets healthy or what. I just don't know. So I'm going to play you the way I think is best for this team, and you just have to go out and do the best you can."

47

It was fun playing for him because he'd make things happen as a manager. He'd put a hit-and-run on in strange situations, do all sorts of little things you normally don't see in baseball. But it's still the honesty that stands out. Any player in the major leagues appreciates that.

I wasn't up too many days when I hit my first International League home run against the Memphis Blues and, about ten days later, against the same team, I hit the first grand slam of my professional career. In another couple of days, I hit my third homer in a 5 – 0 win over the Charleston Charlies. We were getting into some pretty good ball games. There was one really exciting one in July when the Syracuse Chiefs, a very strong club, came in and went up 6 – 1 in the early innings. The Chiefs' manager, Bobby Cox, used five pitchers, but we came back to win it 14 – 7. I came out of it with a homer and a double.

I thought I was doing well enough to get called up to Boston early, but it was Bo Diaz, along with our third baseman, Butch Hobson, who went up at the end of July because Boston "didn't want to hurt Pawtucket too much." But I got into the IL All-Star game, sharing the duties with the Memphis catcher, Steve Nicosia, and ended the season hitting .266, my best average since Winston-Salem.

On September 3rd, the word finally came. I was on my way to the Red Sox and Fenway Park.

I met up with the team a week later while they were on a road trip. The first place I had to report as a big league player was Yankee Stadium. That meant a lot to me. I never got into a game there, but I spent my time out in the bullpen near the monuments to Ruth and Gehrig and all the other Yankee greats. I'd listen to the crowd and feel the excitement and think, "I'm here. This is Yankee Stadium and I'm on the field and I'm wearing a big league uniform. I've made it."

48 By that time, Boston was out of the pennant race, almost twenty games back of the first-place Yankees. But it was still a good team, with Doug Griffin, Carl Yastrzemski, Ben Oglivie, Cecil Cooper, Juan Beniquez, Fred Lynn, Jim Rice, Dwight Evans, Pudge Fisk, and a fair number of strong pitchers, including Luis Tiant and Bill Lee. It was great to be with them.

We went back to Fenway Park for a few games, then within days, we were on the road again, with me still waiting to get into a game. I couldn't have picked a better place for our first stop if I had done the scheduling myself. We were heading for Detroit. I was so excited being in Tiger Stadium, seeing all of my baseball heroes out on the field and finding myself actually out there with them. Thousands of people were watching us perform and I was one of the people they were watching, even if I was just catching in the bullpen. It was an amazing feeling that almost brought tears to my eyes.

I had a one-inning stint in a Friday night game, and afterwards Fisk came up to me and said, "You're from this area, aren't you?"

"Yeah."

"I bet you'd like to catch here, wouldn't you?'

"Sure."

"Well, get yourself ready because you're catching to-morrow."

"Seriously?"

"Yeah, you're catching tomorrow."

I got so excited. I went home and told Chris, I called my parents, I called some friends. I didn't know what was happening. I mean, Fisk wasn't the manager. I didn't know whether he knew something or was just kidding around. I hardly slept at all that night. I went to the ball park early the next morning, and the manager, Don Zimmer, walked up and said, "Ernie, you're going to catch today. Pudge isn't feeling well."

I'll always be grateful to Carleton for that fib of his. I was on Cloud Nine being out on that field, and my heart just jumped to be behind the plate and watch these guys I'd loved for years come up to bat in front of me. Then came my turn to hit, and I walked from the on-deck circle **49** staring at a familiar figure. My idol, Bill Freehan, was standing behind the dish, looking just as he had for as long as I could remember. He said, "How you doing, kid?" I think I must have nodded at him, but I couldn't say a word. All that was running through my mind was, "God, he actually talked to me."

Playing in front of my family and friends in my first major league start, I naturally would have liked to have hit a home run or done something dramatic, but it didn't happen. I had two at-bats, walked once, I believe, and grounded out the second time. But I was thrilled to death just to get the chance to play.

I got another start a few days later back at Fenway Park, still waiting for my first big league hit. I had a couple of at-bats in the second game of a double header against Milwaukee without any success. But in the fifth inning, the Brewers' Jim Colborn threw me one right where I wanted it. I hit the ball hard and watched it sail out to right field towards the yellow foul pole all lit up in the night. I kept thinking, "Stay fair, stay fair." Then I saw the first base coach, Johnny Pesky, who had worked so hard with me in the minor leagues, jumping up and down. Then I was jumping up and down as the ball hit the foul pole and went into the stands. I don't remember running the bases. Dwight Evans was playing right field even then, and at the end of the inning he took a ball out and made a switch with the fan who had caught my homer. I still treasure that ball with the yellow paint smudge on it.

Five days after that, I doubled in a game against the Orioles, driving in Dwight and Jim Rice with the tying and winning runs. I started to feel good about my future with the Red Sox, although Don Zimmer told a reporter the next day, "I can't really say what my opinion of him is yet. He swings a pretty good bat. And he's not bad as a catcher. I haven't even seen the man throw because nobody has run on him yet. But he did come up with a big base hit yesterday."

50   I felt even better a few days later in a game against New York. We had been ahead, but Otto Velez tied the game up for the Yankees. I doubled again and eventually scored the go-ahead run.

I wasn't tearing up the league, but I had reason enough to be happy. One clipping I treasure has the Red Sox batting averages as of September 30, 1976. On top, far away from everyone else, was Fred Lynn with .314. I was in eighth place with .267. Just below me, with .266, was Carl Yastrzemski. Of course, Yaz counted 154 at-bats to my official seven, but still. I ended my eight-game stand with Boston batting .222, with one homer and three RBI.

I was looking forward to being with Boston through all of 1977, although I knew I'd never take Fisk's job away from him. He was doing far too well and was a favourite New England native son. Just one thing made the future a question mark to me — the American League was expanding, and new teams in Seattle and Toronto would be drafting unprotected players. I was willing to go anywhere to get the opportunity to play, but I didn't think too much about the possibility of going to one of the new teams. We were so confident about Boston that Chris designed birth announcements for our first child with Red Sox logos on them.

Our daughter, Ashley, was born November 3, 1976. Two days later I was taken in the third round of the expansion draft, the only catcher drafted. Ten days after that, I got a letter from Blue Jay General Manager Peter Bavasi welcoming me to "Toronto, Ontario...the fastest-growing and most livable city in North America."

In February, 1988, I was getting ready to start my twelfth season with the Blue Jay organization. Mike Flanagan had about six months on me for the title of oldest man on the club. We're veterans, and it's fun to see the old guys and the rookies come together to get ready for another season. We love this game. New breed or not, there's always some excitement in the kids getting their first taste of the major leagues. "The Show," they call it in the minors, and when you've struggled and worked and waited to get here, you never want to go back down again.

The way to stay is to have talent, work hard, get a few breaks, accept decisions, and learn — and obey — the rules. And the last is usually the first order of business in camp once everybody arrives — a meeting to go over the rules and regulations of the team to find out what's expected of you. The rules are always basically the same, covering the dress code, curfews, not being late for workouts, not being late for functions or team activities. They never change much. But they still seem to rub some people the wrong way.

Our dress code says that in spring training, we can wear sweat suits and tennis shoes. Whenever we take an airplane trip, we have to have a sport coat. On the road, we have to have slacks and a collared shirt. In the first few years we had to always wear slacks at home, but since 1984 we've been allowed to wear jeans and tennis shoes to the ball park. But we always have to have a collared shirt. No T-shirts. In some organizations, when you're on the road, you have to wear a sport coat all the time, in

51

some you can wear shorts to the ball park at home. It's whatever the manager and the front office decide. But Toronto's pretty lenient, which is good because most ball players don't really like to dress up. But players still sometimes complain.

They'll complain about curfew, too, and I'll go along with that. I think the curfew rule is overrated. I know hard-nosed managers will check curfew once or twice a week on some teams. As far as I know, it's only been checked one time in Toronto, and that was in 1980. Bobby Mattick was managing then, and he told everyone that he was going to do it. We were going through a losing spell and I think we were in Chicago when he told Roy Howell, the player rep at the time, to pass the word to all the players that he was going to check their rooms.

Bobby Mattick no longer drinks, but at that time, he enjoyed having a few cocktails. And rumour had it that he was down in the bar a little under the weather when he told Denis Menke, the third base coach, to go and make the calls. Menke told him that wasn't his job, it was Mattick's job as manager, and they got into a heated argument. Finally, Mattick went ahead and called John Mayberry's room. He wasn't in. He called Otto Velez. He wasn't in. He called all the rooms, and there were about four guys there. The next day, I went up to him and said, "Did you check the rooms last night?"

He said, "Yeah, I called the rooms, but I knew you were there because the line was busy." And I thought, "Here's a guy who's managing a big league team and it doesn't occur to him that maybe I took the phone off the hook?"

Curfew gives some protecion to the organization. If a guy wants to go out in the streets and get into trouble, the team can say, "We did have a curfew, he broke it, so now he can be disciplined." But I feel that once you get to the big league level, you don't need curfews. If a man can't take care of himself and doesn't know when to shut it down at night for the sake of his own career, then he doesn't deserve to be there. That's one of the things the minor league system is for — learning when you have to

52

shut it down, how much rest you need, how important the games are. If you want to stay in the big leagues, you won't go out carousing all the time.

As we started camp, I could see that all the rules would annoy some of the rookies, just as they still annoy some of the veterans. The younger players, though, have kind of an edge to them. They're aggresive, and that's good because you've got to be aggresive to play good ball. They're confident, too, and I love the confidence factor. You have to have confidence in your ability. But there's a cockiness to the younger guys now, a kind of over-confidence combined with an attitude that's very anti-authority.

From what I see and hear, that's true in other businesses besides baseball. But it can make life difficult when you're trying to function as a team.

53

March

I always go to spring training with optimism, thinking we can have a good year. But I had a few unanswered questions in Florida in 1988.

For one thing, a lot of people were putting weight on our pitching staff to carry us through the year. To me, our staff was a question mark. Our starters weren't. With Jimmy Key, Mike Flanagan, Jim Clancy, and Dave Stieb, I felt we had four quality pitchers. My question was with the bullpen, particularly the kids who had come up in September of '87. Duane Ward and David Wells had good months in September, but one good month doesn't prove you're a major league player. We'd also be missing Jeff Musselman for the first part of the season while he recovered from off-season surgery, and both Mark Eichhorn and John Cerutti had had trouble adjusting in '87 to not really having defined roles.

Then, when the pitchers arrived in camp, Jimy Williams called about ten of us in and told us his plans to improve the team offensively and defensively by making George Bell the designated hitter and moving Lloyd Moseby to left field. His reasoning was that Rob Ducey or

Sil Campusano could save us a few runs in centre and that George might save his knees and keep from injuring himself if he was in the DH spot. If George was injured in left, we'd be missing his bat for maybe a week or two and that would hurt the club.

I could see Jimy's point. He was just doing what he thought was best for the team. And I could understand the organization being concerned about getting some of the younger guys in. All good organizations make sure that there's a good mesh of veterans and younger players so that the team doesn't get old all at the same time. But I've also always believed that "if it ain't broke, don't fix it." With Bell, Barfield, and Moseby, the Blue Jays had what many people considered the best outfield in baseball. Some even thought it was the best outfield of all time. All three of them were just 28 years old and we'd just come off a season where we'd won 96 games, the second best record in all of baseball. Why mess with success? Especially by taking out the player who had just proved on the field that he was the most valuable player in the whole American League.

After the meeting, a few of us got together to talk about the changes. We could see a lot of problems. The word from the organization was that they had talked with George about DHing before he had signed his contract in January and that George had no problem with that. We had a hard time believing that was the case. We knew what type of player George is. He's a fierce competitor. He's the type of guy players love to have on their team and the type of guy everyone hates to play against. He's a sparkplug. He makes things happen. He's an above average left fielder with a very true throwing arm and he's the best right-handed hitter I've ever played against or with. The younger Latin players idolize him and he has the kind of personality that he gets along well with all of the players. He's been a delight to play with. In any pranks or joking around, he's always right in the middle of it. But once we get on that field, the other team is his enemy, especially the opposing pitcher. He'll do anything to win. That's what I admire about him.

But we saw a problem with moving Moseby from centre to left, too. He'd done a good job in centre for five years and we felt Lloyd wasn't going to accept the move easily. He's a fine athlete, but there was some question of whether he could make the adjustment. Left field is a tougher position to play. In centre, you can see where the location of the pitch is going to be, so you can anticipate the direction of any hit, and you can see the ball better as it comes off the bat. In left, the ball has a whole different angle on it. The lighting conditions in every park would be different, too. In Exhibition Stadium, there are no lights to worry about on a hit to centre field. In left, the ball can disappear in the banks of lights along the right field line. It would take time to adjust.

If there had to be changes, it seemed to make more sense to move Lloyd to the DH spot every once in a while, giving one of the kids a chance to develop and giving Lloyd's back a break from the pounding it takes with all the running involved in playing centre field.

But we figured that if any experimenting was going to be done, spring training was the time to do it. We all agreed, as the phrase went that would be repeated half a dozen times a day throughout spring training, that nothing was etched in stone.

Then the fireworks started. George arrived in camp on March 2, making a lot of statements I'm sure he would have liked to take back after he had a few days to think about them. But once the media gets a hold of it, there's no taking back anything. To us, he seemed like the same old George, especially when he arrived in the clubhouse and found the lawn chair Rick Leach and I had put in front of his locker, with a big "DH" sign hanging over it. He seemed in good humour.

But George is very emotional, and I think he had every right to be upset. Here he'd performed well, had carried the team a long way in 1987, had been the MVP of the

57

league and had lost his job. All he wanted to do was go out every day and play and not sit back on the bench collecting his pay cheque. How can you criticize a man for that? I couldn't then and I can't now. Salary doesn't enter into it. The man wants to play and that's the sort of player I want on my team.

But there are ways of handling situations, and George didn't handle the situation well. There came the day when he refused to DH. We play our spring training games at 1:30, and I caught wind of George's plan about ten minutes to one. I went into the locker room to talk to him.

I said, "George, I know where you're coming from. You've got every right to be upset at not getting a fair shake out in left field. They've taken your job away. But the way you're going about this is just not right. They can fine you. They can suspend you, basically for insubordination. There are ways of going about this."

58 I told him that I'd been through a lot of turmoil in my career, but that things always seemed to work out in the long run. I guaranteed that this experiment wouldn't work out and that three weeks into the season he'd be back out in left with Moseby in centre. And I said that he was painting himself into a corner by making the stand he was making that day. If the Jays did put him back into left, it would look as if they had backed down to a player. Everyone would be asking, "Who's running this team? Jimy Williams? Pat Gillick? George Bell?" He was setting up a situation where nobody could win, because all hands would be dirty in it.

But George can be very hard-headed at times. He had his mind made up. He thought the organization was screwing him, and he seemed to blame Jimy more than anyone else. I don't know what happened in the inner meetings in January when they were negotiating George's contract. There were conflicting stories. From my understanding, George had said that if he was paid $2.5 million he would DH. The Jays said they wouldn't pay him that but then used his original statement that he was willing to DH to move him out of left field. I don't know whether that's true or not, that's just what I heard. But refusing to DH was George's way of protesting. There was nothing anyone could do to change his mind. He insisted on sitting out the game.

Jimy Williams had Willie Upshaw ready to DH because George had already told our batting coach, Cito Gaston, that he wasn't going to play. But Jimy put George in the lineup anyway and when his time came to come up to bat, the PA announcer called George's name. Jimy waited for what was probably seconds but seemed like five minutes, then sent Willie up to the plate. Immediately, Jimy left the dugout and walked down toward the left field bullpen where George was sitting and called him into the office. Pat Gillick, Paul Beeston, and a stream of reporters followed in behind.

They met for about an hour and the result was a fine and a one-day suspension for George. That was the extent of it. Needless to say, there was quite a wedge brought on by that confrontation, and it coloured the whole spring training. Reporters kept asking all the players for comments over and over and over again until everyone was sick to death of it. It was hard to figure out where to stand on the question, anyway. We felt that George had a case, but that he should have gone along with a change that shouldn't have been made in the first place. It was confusing. It was an ugly scene that was bound to affect us to some extent. The players weren't happy, and when the players aren't happy, even though they say they're ready to go out and give one hundred per cent on the field, they're not really ready mentally to go out and play. The fun goes out of the game.

It was hard to stay loose with George not being his usual self. A lot of fans don't see the side of him that we do and don't realize how much fun he can be. With Garth gone, we needed everyone we could get to lighten things up around the clubhouse. There can be a lot of tension in spring training. Everyone's exhausted from working hard in the hot sun every day, the blowing sand and grit gets into your eyes, some players get moved around and are unsure of their roles, others wonder whether they'll even make the team.

There are dreams and futures on the line, and any controversy doesn't help. Maybe on the Yankees they're used to upheaval, but the Blue Jays aren't used to it at all. This turned into a very different spring training camp from the first one I attended.

When I think back on it, my main impression of the first spring training day at Grant Field in Dunedin is of a lot of cameras, microphones, and newspaper reporters all jammed into the clubhouse. The TV lights were bright and the flashbulbs never stopped popping. There was a lot of media hype, because this was the beginning of the Toronto Blue Jays.

Roy Hartsfield started off the meeting by introducing himself and saying, "This is a unique situation we have here this year. This is probably the only time until another expansion team comes along that every position is open for the taking." He introduced his coaches and told us that they were there to work, to help us progress in our careers. Then he introduced Pat Gillick, Elliott Wahle, who was in charge of player personnel, the director of public relations, Howie Starkman, the trainers.

And then he introduced the general manager, Peter Bavasi, who must have had his speech ready for weeks. What sticks in my mind, and what the few of us left still joke about, is that he said, "Gentlemen, you are the sizzle of the steak to come." We realized we were just going to be there to warm up the fans of Toronto. Instead of promoting the Blue Jay players, he was going to promote the stars on opposing teams coming in. There'd be changes until there was a real good ball club in the city and then he'd promote the Blue Jays. But until then it was going to be, "C'mon, see Reggie Jackson and the Yankees. C'mon, see Carl Yastrzemski."

You've got to give the organization credit. They laid out their game plan and, in effect, told the fans, "Give us

60

seven years until we build our farm system. It'll take time. And if we ever need a player to put us over the top, we'll go out and get him." They were very honest with the fans and the fans were very patient. They did an outstanding job.

There was a lot of good feeling coming out of that first meeting, even some optimism. But mainly I guess it was just a spirit of adventure, of being part of a brand new team that would someday mean something in the world of baseball. Everyone seemed to feel it.

Looking back, though, I have to laugh about Hartsfield saying that every position was open. Every organization has its mind made up on who is going to be at most positions. There might be two or three positions on the twenty-four man roster they're maybe in limbo about or they might change their minds about. But in most cases, the roster is set before spring training even starts. Every year the manager will always say — Bobby Cox and Jimy Williams both said it — that there are a couple of positions or a couple of spots on the pitching staff that are open. They're saying, "All the other positions are basically set, but show us what you can do. We're here to get a look at you in case there are some injuries." And that's the way it should be. Why lie about things? Why make a farce out of it? For a guy to make a statement like Hartsfield did seems asinine to me, though I didn't think so at the time. I listened and thought, "Maybe I really do have a chance."

61

I had been really hopeful of making the club right from the expansion draft. The only competition, for a few hours anyway, was Phil Roof, an older journeyman catcher the Blue Jays had purchased from the White Sox in October, 1976, as the team's first acquisition. But the draft was barely over when the Jays traded a right-handed pitcher, Al Fitzmorris, to Cleveland for first baseman Doug Howard and catcher Alan Ashby. A month later, they sent Rico Carty to Cleveland for outfielder John Lowenstein and another catcher, Rick Cerone. Phil Roof was going to be used mainly as a bullpen catcher, but both Alan and Rick had more major league experience than I had.

With four of us at that first camp in Dunedin, I felt a little like the forgotten man. Experience was a factor, but somehow I had acquired a reputation of having a slow release and a poor throwing arm. I didn't think I deserved that reputation, but in baseball reputations are almost impossible to shake. All it takes is for one person in authority to say something about a player or a manager, and that word will travel around the league for years. I knew my arm wasn't as strong as Ashby's or Cerone's, but I felt that I made up for that in accuracy and what I believed was a quick release. I had worked hard on my release and had thrown out the fastest runners in the minor leagues.

I worked my butt off in that spring training, always making sure I led in the wind sprints, always trying to show my enthusiasm for the team. Nothing seemed to get **62** through to Roy Hartsfield, although he did admit in March that I was a "surprise" when I threw out runners. I thought if he was surprised, it was only because he rarely got to see me play. Every other catcher got more work than I did. I didn't even start in a game until March 20, and in that game against Kansas City I hit a two-run homer and threw out three of five guys trying to steal a base.

I accepted the fact that Roy would take Phil Roof for maturity behind the plate. Phil would be able to keep the pitching staff in line. And I figured he would probably go with Alan Ashby because he was young but had still caught over 200 games in the big leagues. But Roy had said positions were wide open, and I still believed the third catching spot could be mine. I thought my chances were good since Rick had only one hit all spring training and I was the only one of the young catchers to hit a home run.

As the last week of spring training wound down, the roster was slowly cut back. Catchers are usually the last to go since the team needs them to work with the pitchers, so I wasn't surprised when no decision was announced on my future. Then two fielders and three pitchers — Jim Clancy, Jeff Byrd and Butch Edge — were sent down. There was one more player to go.

On the last day of camp, I was told to have my stuff at Grant Field at three o'clock for the truck going north. I got there at two and found that the truck had left at ten that morning. I also found out that Hartsfield wanted to see me. It was "a numbers game," he said.

Back at the hotel, Chris and I were packing up the last few personal things when Rick Cerone came up in the hallway and said with a smirk, "Where are they sending you, Ernie?" Chris felt like kicking him.

Where they were sending me was to the Charleston Charlies. Toronto didn't have a farm system in 1977, so players who were sent down scattered to a number of clubs. The Charlies were part of the Houston Astros' organization, and that year were introducing probably the ugliest uniforms in all of baseball.

63

As soon as the season started, I was off on a two-week road trip, leaving Chris and Ashley in Charleston to try and arrange accommodation. My roommate was the other Blue Jay on the Charlies, Garth Iorg, who I'd played against in the Eastern League when he was with the West Haven Yankees. We discovered that our wives had even played against each other in a softball game between West Haven and Bristol. We became good friends on that trip and for the first time, but not the last, I let him talk me into doing something I didn't really want to do.

The big rage in hair styles then was the "natural" look, and Garth and I talked a lot about whether that kind of hairdo would suit us. I had my doubts, but Garth was persuasive and when we got to Syracuse we both decided to go for it. He insisted that I go first. Then when he saw the terrible job the guy did on me, all tight and really frizzy, he refused to get his done. My teammates were all over me with ridicule that day. God, it looked awful. And Chris just about dropped when I got back to Charleston.

Catch

There's a saying in the big leagues that if you buy a house in the city you play in, you'll be traded. In the minors, the saying is if you buy a ton of groceries, you'll be moved. We were unloading bags and bags of groceries outside the house in Charleston towards the end of May when a kid came over from the ball park to say the GM wanted to see me. Rick Cerone had been the opening day catcher in Toronto but had broken his thumb five days after the home opener. Ashby had taken over the regular catching duties while Rick was on the disabled list, and now Rick and I were going to trade places. I was going to be the Blue Jays back-up catcher.

We made the journey from West Virginia to Detroit the first night, then headed to Toronto the next day, hauling a blue, home-made trailer full of stuff behind the two-tone Monte Carlo I'd bought with my signing money back in 1972. We made it almost to London, Ontario, okay, but then the car started overheating. It seemed like every ten or fifteen minutes we'd have to pull off the road and find water for the radiator.

At every stop I'd call Elliott Wahle to tell him where I was and ask how much longer it was going to take me to get to Toronto. I'd never been to the city before. He was a little tentative in his answers, and when I told him I was near the city of Woodstock, he said, "What are you doing there? Listening to music?" And it suddenly sunk in that almost the whole organization was in Toronto for the first time and had no idea about the towns in the surrounding area.

We finally limped into the city and pulled up to the classy Hotel Toronto right downtown. Out of the '72 Monte Carlo with the makeshift trailer stepped a guy with a hacked-up natural and a woman with a five-month-old baby under her arm. Here come the Whitts! People were looking at us like we'd stepped out of "The Real McCoys."

We checked in and I raced downstairs, got in a cab and took off for the ball park. I didn't get there until after seven and the team had already done with infield and batting practice. There was no way I was going to play that night, but I had made it. I walked into the clubhouse to report and went up to Roy Hartsfield. He didn't even look me in the face. He stared right at my tight, frizzy curls and said, "Nice to see you," with a frown on his face as if he was thinking, "Where'd we get this bozo at?" I kind of read between the lines and got all the curls cut off real close the next day.

It didn't help. I was called up May 23 but didn't start a game until June 25. I wasn't too impressive in my Blue Jay starting debut, going 0-for-3 at the plate against Baltimore and being charged with a passed ball. I did better in my next start a few days later, hitting two doubles and throwing out Mickey Rivers to beat the Yankees. But I stayed pretty much on the bench, getting used mainly in double headers or being called on to pinch hit against guys like Nolan Ryan and Dennis Eckersley, which didn't do much for my average.

65

Alan Ashby was the main man. But then, in the middle of August, Alan pulled a hamstring. He could still catch, but he couldn't run. Finally, this was my chance to show what I could do.

On August 16, after an hour's rain delay, we took the field against the Angels. In the top of the fifth, the Angels catcher, Andy Etchebarren, was on second when Jerry Remy singled. Etchebarren rounded third, driving for home where I waited for a perfect throw from Bob Bailor in centre field. I caught the ball, Etchebarren's cleat caught some dirt still wet from the rain and we collided with tremendous force. Andy was down on his back when Ron Luciano called him out. He had a mild concussion and had to leave the game. I stayed in for the rest of the inning, but I was down and out, too. The tendons around my left ankle had been torn from the bone. I spent the rest of the season with my leg in a cast.

I had played in all of 23 games and in 41 at-bats had managed to drive in six runs. My average was .171, the lowest it had ever been in my career.

I didn't go to spring training in 1978 with too much optimism. Alan and Rick had a lock on the position and Roy Hartsfield again didn't seem to pay too much attention to what I could do. I tried not to let that get to me. I had confidence in my ability. I did start to wonder about Hartsfield's ability, though, and I wasn't alone in that.

When he came to the Blue Jays, Roy had a reputation as a players' manager — a man who would stick up for his players and never run them down as long as they gave a hundred per cent on the field. He would stand behind you and beside you. I didn't find that to be the case. Just the opposite. I found him to be a very nervous individual, very unsure of his situation. Mind you, he was put into a tough situation, being an expansion manager who wanted to win the race but didn't have the horses to do it. He was battling in a losing cause. But he would rip his players in the papers, saying things like, **66** "These players don't belong here" or "We can't compete in this league with the players that we have." A manager's not going to get too much support from his team if he says things like that.

The only thing that made that spring training memorable was that we found it impossible to live in a hotel with a small baby, and one rainy day we went out to look for an apartment. We found a nice looking building near the Gulf and went in, but the agent said there weren't any apartments for rent, just condominiums to buy. He gave us a price, but we weren't too interested. Then he said he'd paint it for us, then he said he'd furnish it, he'd throw in a TV if we brought other players around to look. He came up with a deal that we couldn't refuse. We bought it and brought Alan Ashby around a few days later. He liked it, too, and bought the condominium a few doors away.

We were set for a place to live in Florida, but the summer was going to be spent in Syracuse with the Blue Jays new AAA club, the Chiefs. At least I had a job there, or so I thought. I'd been told the position was wide open, but that was a lie. The organization was bringing up Pat Kelly from AA and was committed to seeing him develop as a catcher. I ended up playing first base and right field. I was disappointed, but playing there was fun, even though we didn't have a good year. The manager, Vern Benson, was a wonderful man to play for. There was a nice mesh of players, too, some on their way down and some on their way up. The hero of the Jays' first opening day, Doug Ault, had been sent down. Alvis Woods and Hector Torres spent part of the year with the Chiefs, along with Garth Iorg, new guys like Willie Upshaw and Danny Ainge, and Jack Baker, an old friend and teammate from my days in Bristol.

The Jays had got off to a worse start in 1978 than they had in 1977, but in the summer they picked up. In the beginning of August, they really went on a tear and ended up with 16 wins against 14 losses for the month, the first month in the team's short history that they played over .500. By the end of August, though, they were sinking fast. When I was called up on September 3, Rick Bosetti had gone 0-for-19, John Mayberry 1-for-11, Bob Bailor 0-for-14, and Willie Horton 1-for-25.

The call-ups from the Chiefs didn't help, and the team headed into their worst September ever. All I can say about my contribution is that my Hartsfield fan club was still in high gear. I got into two games and in four at-bats, I walked once, struck out once, and grounded out twice, leaving me with a big .000 batting average.

I was starting to think that I would never play with the Blue Jays. But, once again, my optimism came back in the off-season. For one thing, we had our second child, EJ (Ernest Jordan), which made me think of the future in a positive way. But also, in November of 1978, Alan Ashby was traded to Houston for Mark Lemongello, Joe Cannon, and Pedro Hernandez. When Alan was traded, Pat Gillick bought his condominium in Dunedin, and the standing joke ever after was that if he had liked our condo better, it would have been me who was traded. We've been neighbours ever since.

With Alan gone, I figured I was ready to maybe take the top spot or at least battle Cerone for it. I was dreaming. In the 1978 winter draft, the Blue Jays acquired Bob Davis, a catcher who had played for Roy Hartsfield in the Pacific Coast League's team in Hawaii. In spring training for the 1979 season it was the same old story. I didn't even play the first ten days of camp and when I did get into games I never stayed in long. Cerone and Davis would play nine innings, but I'd be lucky to stay in for six. I was even replaced in one game by Tim Johnson, a utility infielder. It was humiliating.

Still, I felt I was having just as good a spring training as the other catchers offensively and a better one defensively. Hartsfield suggested that the Blue Jays might go with three catchers and said, "Whitt is the best hitter of the bunch. We would be free to use him as a pinch hitter and still have a third catcher available." I was skeptical, but against all reason, I kept my optimism.

68 I really got hopeful and excited after one game right near the end of camp. We'd been playing the Cardinals who were known even then for having a bunch of rabbits on the base paths. I'd had a couple of hits and threw out three of the four runners who tried to steal a base. I was feeling good about things. Then, after the game, the equipment man came over to my locker. In baseball, that's kind of like the arrival of the Angel of Death. They always send the equipment man who'll say over his shoulder, "The skip wants to see you." That's when you know you're on your way out.

I headed down to Hartsfield's office, really upset. Roy was sitting behind his desk, with Pat Gillick and Elliott Wahle on the other side of the room. Roy said, "We've taken a good look at you this spring and it's the consensus of myself, the coaches, and Pat that you'd be better off playing in the minor leagues another year. I personally don't think you're able to catch at the big league level. You have a difficult time throwing people out. And that's the decision I voted for."

I said, "How can you judge me like that? I've had just as good a spring as any catcher down here. I've thrown out more base runners than any catcher down here. And you make a statement that I can't throw runners out? Did you or did you not watch that game today?"

"I watched that game, young man."

"Did you or did you not see me throw out three of the four base runners?"

"I saw that, but they were slow runners. And the guy that made it you should have thrown out."

"Excuse me? The guys I threw out were slow base runners? Lou Brock? That was their speed team out there. They were not slow base runners."

"Well, that's my opinion and that's what I'm sticking with. I just don't think you can catch at the big league level and you'll definitely never catch in the big leagues for me."

"Well, Roy, I don't think you can manage at the big league level. You don't know talent."

I turned to Pat Gillick, who hadn't said a word through all of this, and said, "Pat, obviously the man does not like me. There's something there, I don't know what it is, but it's not going to work out. I'd like to be traded and if I can't be traded just give me my release."

He said, "We're not going to release you. We'll do everything we can to accommodate you, but we're not going to give you away. We'll see what we can do to trade you, but you'll just have to go back to Syracuse."

"Well, I don't think I'll do that. I mean, I'll talk with Chris and we'll make a decision, but I really don't think I'm going to go. I think I'll probably just hang it up."

I meant it. I was heartbroken. I called Chris to come and pick me up at the field. It was the first time she'd ever seen baseball make me cry. I said, "We might as well call it quits. There's no point in going back. Let's just go home and start something different in our lives."

But, just as she had in 1976, she kept my spirits up. She said, "You're in Triple A. You're one step away. One step.

You'll never know if you quit now. You'll go to bed every night and your head will hit the pillow and you'll lay there and think 'I wonder if I could have made it if I'd just stayed in.' The only way you're going to find out is if you hang in there."

We went to Syracuse. But it kept running through my mind that I'd spent five years in the Red Sox organization trying to get to the major leagues, only to be blocked by the fact that as long as Carleton Fisk was there I wouldn't get the opportunity to play. I'd been happy to come to the Blue Jays because I thought I'd finally get that opportunity. Now in my third year with Toronto, my opportunities had vanished as long as Hartsfield remained as manager.

It was depressing, and my mood wasn't helped by arriving in Syracuse to find that Pat Kelly had been told he would be the Number One catcher. The thing was, Luis Rosado, who had been picked up on option from the Mets, had been told the same thing. On the roster, I was listed as the designated hitter.

But I was determined to enjoy the season. I knew it was either going to be my last year in the minors or it was going to be my last year in baseball. It could have been my last year with the Blue Jays, too, even if I did stay in baseball. The organization had run out of options, which is also part of the numbers game. Up until 1979, the Jays could bounce me back and forth between the minors and the big leagues and not risk losing me. In 1979, they'd either have to call me up or put me on waivers.

That season, I had the most fun I'd ever had. Vern Benson created a winning atmosphere and we had a terrific group of guys. I was still hoping for some movement, though, and when Pat Gillick came into town in May I asked how good my chances were to be traded.

He said, "We're still looking for you. Just try and keep your chin up and things will work out."

I don't think he ever actually tried to trade me. Or maybe he asked for Dave Winfield in return just so he could say he made the effort. But the options and numbers games aren't unusual with a franchise building for the future. Teams that are expected to have a shot at the pennant don't usually play those kinds of games. They just take the best players available.

In the summer, Pat came back to Syracuse with Bobby Mattick, the Blue Jays' director of player development, and I asked again if there was anything happening. He said, "Well, I can't tell you what's going on, but there are going to be some changes made." I kind of read between the lines and figured that they had already decided that Hartsfield was going to be fired.

It wouldn't have been surprising. The Jays were having a terrible year. They were over 30 games out of first place by the beginning of July and almost 40 games out by the beginning of August. By August 19, they were mathematically eliminated from the race, which still stands as the earliest elimination date in team history. The same day, Tom Buskey, the team's best reliever and the second best reliever in the league at the time, publicly called for Hartsfield's replacement. Other players started complaining, too, saying that Roy just didn't have the respect of the players.

71

Maybe the thought I picked up from Pat Gillick inspired me a little bit, because I had a very good year. It was especially satisfying throwing out the quickest base runners. When I threw out one of the Blue Jays in their annual exhibition game with the Chiefs, one of the local broadcasters came up and said, "I guess you showed them something last night, throwing that guy out at second."

I said, "Who, me? Everyone knows I can't throw guys out at second. It must have been someone else wearing my uniform."

I wasn't too disappointed when I wasn't among those called up in September. The Jays had a clubhouse in turmoil and ended up with a dreadful record of 53 – 109 on the season. Maybe I couldn't catch well enough for Roy

Catch

Hartsfield, but I had the Silver Glove Award as the best defensive catcher in the minor leagues.

Nine years later, the clubhouse was experiencing some turmoil again. The George and Jimy situation just wouldn't go away. There were still unanswered questions, still some uneasiness among the players about authority. The organization tried to put any questions to rest around the third week in March when Peter Hardy came into the clubhouse for a meeting, something he had never done before.

Mr. Hardy has never had much of a profile in the press or among the fans in Toronto. Many people don't realize what he means to the organization both as the Chief Executive Officer and as a person. I learned long ago in Boston that the tone of an organization is set at the top, and that's been very true in Toronto. As long as I've been with the Blue Jays, I've found Mr. Hardy to be a sincere, caring gentleman who is very concerned with the well-being of the players and who has always maintained an open-door policy if any player had problems or special needs.

He's the backbone of the organization, and it was quite a sight to see this seventy-one year old man come into the clubhouse to offer what he called his "grandfatherly advice." He made it clear that the administration and the Board of Directors had hired Jimy Williams and the coaching staff because they had confidence in their abilities and that the players should make no mistake about that. He also said, without mentioning any names, that no player should paint himself into a corner, because it could be very difficult to get out.

But the confrontation between George and Jimy wasn't the only thing troubling the team. Lloyd Moseby was unhappy, Juan Beniquez felt he wasn't getting a fair shake, Tony Fernandez seemed to be having some trouble regaining his form after the pins were removed from his elbow at the beginning of camp, and the rookies competing for positions were on edge. Then on March 25, the roster was cut back from 36 to 35. Willie Upshaw was going to the Cleveland Indians.

It was hard seeing a player who had meant so much to this ball club leave the team. Willie was a quiet leader, a great man to have in the clubhouse. He was the type of player who played through an awful lot of injuries that no one knew about. The fans saw his numbers going down, but didn't know that he was playing hurt quite often. He'd given Toronto some outstanding years.

His leaving seemed to affect Lloyd more than anyone else, but that was only because their tearful goodbyes were caught by the media and made public. He meant a lot to all of us. To me, Willie was a good friend, a person I could confide in. We were neighbours in Toronto for five years and we travelled back and forth from the ball park together many times. Our families were fairly close and our kids played together all the time during the summer. The kids just hated to see the trade happen. He was one class individual, and I can't say enough good things about him. He was a gentleman, he was a good father, and a good teammate.

73

But the trade was good for him because the organization had already made the decision that Freddie McGriff and Cecil Fielder were going to get the opportunity to play first base rather than platoon in the DH spot as they had in '87. George Bell was going to be the DH. It got to the point of us wondering what Willie's job was going to be. Was he just going to be a left-handed bat coming off the bench? He wouldn't have been happy with that. All the players would much rather see him playing every day for another team than see him suffer sitting on the bench with us. So while I was sad that he was leaving the organization, I was happy that he was going to a place where he could play. It wasn't like those times when a person is released outright and left with no job.

He would take some leadership to Cleveland and with some of his problems corrected over the winter — some surgery that would help him pivot better at the plate — he'd have some good seasons yet. He's a fine defensive player, with tremendous range as a first baseman. A lot of people didn't realize that he got an awful lot of balls that most first basemen wouldn't get to, and that's something Cleveland has needed because their defence has been shaky for years. Willie doesn't make that many mistakes.

When you've been in the game a long time, you know your teammates are only going to be around for a while, what with the constant trades, the constant movement from the minor leagues to the big leagues, from the big leagues to the minors, from in baseball to out of the game. It's always seemed like a transit line running in a circle with people getting off and on all the time. You get used to it, but it still hurts to see good men go.

When I think back over the times we had in the middle of the eighties, it seems to me that Garth and Willie provided a lot of the glue that held this team together. Now they were both gone.

74 But the game goes on, and it wasn't the loss of players or the clubhouse feuds that made me worry about the upcoming season. At one of our meetings part way through camp, I had to speak up on one thing that was really bothering me.

I said, "We have the talent here, but just because we have the talent we can't just throw our gloves out there and say we're going to win. We've got to work. We've been here for three weeks now and I still see only two people working hard on their positions. We've got all sorts of outfielders and all sorts of infielders, and the two people working hard from what I can see are both Gold Glove winners, and that's Tony and Jesse. It doesn't take anything to get a coach out there to hit you ground balls and fly balls, maybe twenty-five a day just to work on it. But we've got outfielders in the infield taking ground balls, just goofing around passing the time instead of going out and catching a few fungos."

It was bad enough that the veterans weren't doing it. But the kids we had wouldn't do it. During training and even later during the season, Jimy Williams would take them out to the outfield and hit them fly balls, but he would have to call them over first and say, "Let me hit you some." Jesse was always working, every day, and he'd make sure to call a coach over and say, "Hit me some balls." "Hit me some" instead of "let me hit you some" — that's a little difference that makes a big difference.

There were some bright spots, though. I don't think anyone could help but be impressed with Pat Borders. He did work hard and worked himself right onto the team. He proved in practice and on the field that he deserved to be there and I was really happy to see him make the club.

It's always tough for the staff to make the last cuts, and it seemed it was going to be especially tough to make the last decision which revolved around the pitching staff. John Cerruti had been taken out of the starting rotation and the last spot could be filled by either Bob Shirley or Todd Stottlemyre. Shirley was a veteran who was almost unbeatable in the early going at spring training.

When it became apparent that Todd might be the one to be sent to the minor leagues, I went first to Al Widmar and then to Jimy Williams and said, "I know my vote doesn't mean anything, but I really feel that Stottlemyre should make this club the way he's been throwing. I think he can pitch in the big leagues. I'm very confident about that."

75

I felt funny about doing it, yet I felt that I needed to say something. I've been around baseball long enough to know talent when I see it and I know Al and Jimy well enough that I can express my feelings towards them or about them or about some other player and they'll accept it with no repercussions coming back on me. Neither one would say, "I'm running this fucking team and that's the way it's going to be," though there are plenty of managers and coaches around the league who would say just that.

But I had never done anything like that before in all my years on the team. Maybe it's my getting older and knowing that I'm not going to be in the game much longer and wanting to win and go out as a World Champion, but I think you've got to take your best people and not play the options and numbers games that organizations some-times play. To me, if you're trying to win it all you've got to take the best personnel and Todd was throwing the ball better than any of our other pitchers in spring train-ing.

He pitched himself onto the ball club. He's got a good arm and he's got the makeup to be a good pitcher. He's confident, but he's not overly cocky. He'll challenge the hitters and he'll take the blame if he screws up. Most young pitchers who make a bad pitch blame the umpire, a fielder, the catcher, anyone but themselves. A batter might drive a hard-hit ball that goes though the shortstop's legs, and the young pitcher will say the short-stop should've caught it. And you just want to grab the pitcher and say, "Hell, you're the one who threw a hang-ing breaking ball up in the guy's eye. He almost tore the glove off the shortstop's hand."

76   You wouldn't have to do that with Todd. He's got good baseball sense about him. Maybe that's been bred into him because of his dad's background as a big league pitcher. But he's got the arm, and all he needs is to de-velop consistency in throwing strikes and utilizing all of his pitches. That's a learning process and it's awfully tough, especially with the pressure of being on a team that's supposed to win.

Whether my opinion made any difference, I don't know. But I was pleased that Todd made the team.

As we broke spring training, it would have been nice to put all the confrontation and confusion and bad feeling behind us. We were all hoping that we would. But on the last day, the whole season started off on the wrong foot.

It's odd how one little incident can make so much dif-ference to the way a team feels. There was an incident in Boston in 1986 that made quite a difference at the time and still has an effect. Then, Jimy started Duane Ward in a game against the Red Sox, pushing Joe Johnson out of his normal spot in the rotation. The thing was that Joe had been very effective against Boston only a week earlier and

Duane was making his first big league start. Why that all had an effect on the team was that we hadn't been eliminated from the pennant race and we were still eager to give the Red Sox a run for their money. By making the pitching change, the organization seemed to be sending us the message that they'd given up on us. Boston clinched the division title as we got blown out that day, and the team got so deflated we lost almost all the rest of our games. By all accounts, it had been Jimy's decision to start Ward, but at the time we wondered whether he was in full control of the team or if he was being pressured by management to make certain moves. Jimy has carried the burden of that uncertainty ever since.

This year, the little incident came about because of a dinner. Every year on the last day of camp, Mr. Hardy holds a dinner where the players mix with the Blue Jay diplomats. It's always very pleasant, but it also always comes at a time when we're getting our families prepared to go back north, when we're packing up and trying to spend some time together because we won't be seeing each other for weeks or even months. There is some sacrifice involved, but the dinner is considered mandatory.

Of all the Latin players on the team, only Tony Fernandez showed up. The others stayed away as some kind of protest, although they said they had transportation problems. George and Juan had cars and the hotel was maybe a five-dollar cab ride away from the dinner, but they just couldn't seem to make it. There was no disciplinary action taken. There were no fines. Nothing was even said, as far as anyone knows. And a lot of players started to wonder, "How come I have to do this and these other guys don't? How come the rules aren't the same for everybody? Why is it okay for him and not for me?"

It was a little incident. But it left behind some bad feeling between the players and it lost Jimy Williams a little respect. He lost some control of the team that day. We weren't happy campers as we left for Kansas City and opening day.

April

It was a terrific way to start the season and a great way for
George Bell to silence his critics, at least for a while. We
opened the season in Kansas City on April 4th and
George let his bat do the talking for him, hitting three
home runs off Bret Saberhagen for our first win of the
season. Two days later, with Mike Flanagan up against
Charlie Leibrandt, George went 5-for-5, the first Blue Jay
ever to hit that mark. George was back in left field for that
game, filling in for Lloyd, who was having problems with
his hip.

George wasn't the only impressive player in the game.
Pat Borders made one hell of a major league debut. He
had led the team in average in spring training with .373,
so we were expecting big things. But for a guy only
months out of AA to hit a triple and two singles for five
RBI wasn't too shabby at all.

Kansas City had never dropped their first two games of
the season, and we started feeling pretty good about the
year ahead as we travelled to Minnesota. Things fell apart
a bit when we got there. Dave Stieb didn't have any
control early in the first game of our series, and Jimy

Williams got ejected for arguing, rightly, with umpire Joe Brinkman. We lost 6 – 3, but we came back the next day to blow them out 10 – 0. George, Jesse, Nelson Liriano, and Freddie McGriff all hit home runs, and Jimmy Key gave up only three hits over six innings. By the time we headed home to Toronto, we were 3 – 3 and ready to take on New York.

We've had crazy home opening days before, but nothing to match what happened against the Yankees. New York had jumped to a fast start and were 5 – 0 coming into Exhibition Stadium. They seem to like playing there. No one's been able to figure out a reason for it, but they have a habit of beating up on us at home, while we tend to do the same to them in Yankee Stadium.

It looked like that tradition would continue in the first inning of the opening game. The match-up was Mike Flanagan against Rick Rhoden. Rickey Henderson led off for the Yankees and beat out an infield hit, then stole **80** second, then stole third. As he went in, he took Rance Mulliniks out of the play and out of the lineup for a couple of weeks with a twisted knee. By the time Meacham, Mattingly, Ward, and Winfield were through, three runs were scored. In our half, Lloyd singled with one out, then Tony hit what should have been a double play ball, but Rafael Santana bobbled it. George walked to load up the bases, then I drove in two with a single. Kelly Gruber hit a fly to right that Dave Winfield lost in the sun, Jesse drove me in on a ground out, Freddie McGriff walked, and Rick Leach cleaned the bases with a double. After one inning, it was 6 – 3.

It was just one of those games. It went on for four hours and fifteen minutes, just three minutes short of the longest nine-inning game in major league history. By the time it was all over, Kelly had gone 4-for-6 with two home runs and five RBI. I had three RBI on two hits. Everybody in the lineup except Freddie had driven in at least one run. The final score was 17 – 9.

The next three games were just as crazy, but not in our favour. By the time the Yankees went home, they'd outhit us 52 – 37 and outscored us 33 – 24. Only ten games into the season, and we had already given up 11 unearned runs and made 12 errors. Flanagan, Clancy, Stieb, and Stottlemyre had a combined ERA of 7.50. Only Jimmy Key put in a strong performance, but his elbow was giving him problems.

When the Twins came in and beat us 3 – 2, it was obvious that some changes had to be made. Cleveland was leading the division with New York half a game behind them. We were already in fifth place, five-and-a-half back. The spring training experiment in the outfield was over. George and Lloyd were back in their usual spots and Juan Beniquez and Rick Leach were a platoon DH. Sil Campusano and Nelson Liriano were on the bench.

We managed to split the series with Minnesota and blew out the Royals 12 – 3 behind Jim Clancy, who has always been effective against Kansas City. Jesse helped things along with a grand slam, and maybe that hit also helped the speculation as we went into New York the next weekend that Jesse and Dave Winfield were going to be switching teams.

Trade rumours and all the intensity of the media coverage in New York were the last things we needed. All we wanted to do was put a big dent in the Yankees' winning record. Cleveland was still leading the league, but practically everyone expected them to fade. No one expected that the Yankees would.

The series was really a surprise. We faced two right-handed pitchers, Rick Rhoden and Rich Dotson. When Lou Pinella was managing, he'd never throw a right-hander against us. He'd push a guy ahead or drop someone from the starting rotation to get his left-handers in. Other teams would try and give us left-handers, too, but New York seemed fanatic about it. We used to try and do the same to them, of course, because we felt they were weaker from the right side. But that changed in 1988, with Winfield, Henderson, and Clark. With Mattingly, it doesn't seem to matter who you put out against him. You could have an octopus on the mound with balls

81

coming at him from all over the place and he'd still hit over .300.

But I guess Billy Martin had confidence in his right-handers. Dotson has always pitched us tough, even when he was with Chicago. We took two out of three from them.

It was nice that we kept up the tradition of winning in the Bronx. But there was another tradition followed in the series that we weren't happy to see — questionable calls against us by a particular umpiring crew.

I guess a lot of fans for every team think umpires are all bums and blind pigs. But they're human and they're going to make mistakes. Most of them are really good people, good guys who I have to work closely with. I approach them by kind of saying, "I know you're human, I know you're going to miss a pitch now and then and that's fine. I can accept that. As long as you're consistent in the strike zone, we're going to get along great." Besides, I don't want to get on the bad side of any of them, because if you get on their bad side they start taking pitches away from your pitchers.

The ones who really upset me are the ones who are so hard-nosed they won't listen to anything. The kind that if the pitch is obviously a strike right down the middle of the plate, belt high, and they call it a ball and I ask why, they say, "Because the fucking ball was high." I have a hard time dealing with the few of them out there who think they never make a mistake. But most of them are easy to get along with.

Players have their favourites and they have the guys they hate seeing around. Durwood Merrill is probably one of the most entertaining of them all. He's a showboat, a good guy from Oklahoma. He's not the best umpire in the league, but he's not bad. He loves to put on a show and the players just laugh at him and along with him. He always comes up with little sayings that are just a treat. In spring training this year, Steve Carlton was pitching for the Twins and Rob Ducey was up at the plate. Carlton threw a slider down and away, an obvious ball, but

Durwood rang up a strike and Ducey backed out and started complaining. Durwood said, "Son, that man's made himself into a Hall of Fame pitcher with that pitch and when you get some dirt in your cleat, then you can come back and talk to me. That's protocol right there."

Another good umpire is Larry Barnett, a guy who gives a hundred per cent behind the plate. He really busts his balls to do a good job and that's what players like to see. Sometimes umpires look like they're bored, like they don't even want to be there, and that upsets the players. There's no reason for them not to be into the ball game for the three hours they're there. Larry is good about that and the players respect him for it. He's become one of the better umpires in the league because of his good work habits.

I've been kicked out of only one ballgame in the major leagues and it was Larry who kicked me out. The Jays were playing in Baltimore and there was a play at home plate that I had to argue. I was holding my mask in one hand and the ball in the other and while we were arguing I tossed my mask down. I wasn't cursing him, but he said I was out of the game for throwing my equipment. Bobby Mattick argued the ejection, but umpires never reverse those decisions. What was frustrating was that the next batter hit a home run and we ended up losing the game.

83

Kenny Kaiser and Steve Polarmo are probably my two favourite umpires, and that goes back to my coming up through the minor league system with them. We know each other, we've worked together for a long time, and we have a good time behind the plate.

Kaiser is just a big dorky-looking guy who used to be a professional wrestler. A lot of times I'll walk up to him and hit him right in the cup, just to set the tone for the day, and he'll say, "Oh, you cocksucker, I'll get you." And, sure enough, I've walked away from games with bruises on my ribs where he's rabbit-punched me or closed his knees up hard into my sides. Quite often, I'll get down in my position and he'll have his foot sticking up so that I'll sit right down on his toe. We have a great time.

In 1977, Kenny was behind the plate on a Sunday afternoon when I came up to pinch hit in the ninth inning. Nolan Ryan was pitching for the Angels at the time, and I'd never faced him before. Some of the players tried to prepare me for it, saying, "Just think of the fastest guy you've ever faced and add two feet onto the fastball." And I was thinking, "Come on, this guy can't throw that hard." I went up to the plate, said hi to Kenny, watched Ryan go into his motion, then heard the ball hit the mitt.

Kaiser whipped out, "Strike one."

I stepped out of the box and looked back at him with a big grin on my face. I said, "Kenny, I didn't even see that ball and I know damn well you didn't see that ball."

"That's right."

"So how could you call it a strike?"

"It sounded like a strike."

84   Steve Polarmo is the same way. He's easy to work with plus he's a very good umpire. He's very consistent. We goof around all the time. We've often pulled a little routine on rookies where the kid comes up to the plate and the first pitch might be a ball outside and I'll start screaming at him through my mask so that no one can see, saying, "How in hell can you miss that pitch? My God, the pitch is right on the corner. This is a rookie kid up here and you're not going to give us a strike on that?"

And he'll start yelling back at me, "Just catch the fucking ball and throw it back."

"I'll just catch the ball when you call a fucking strike a strike." And the kid just steps out of the box thinking, "Geez, these guys are really going at it. What's going on?" Then we just wink at each other.

You've got to joke around just to ease the pressure a little bit. We work in pretty close quarters and there's often a lot of tension. Sometimes, it's very close quarters. I've had to tell a few of these guys to back off, that I'm already happily married, although Davey Phillips is the only one who actually pushes instead of just resting on my back. It makes life difficult, especially in a possible base-stealing situation, when you're up on your toes and some hulk is pushing you forward. Timing gets all out of whack.

But a catcher has to learn which umpires he can get on, because it doesn't bother them, and which he can't. As soon as you yell at Joe Brinkman one time, he's messed up for the whole night.

With most of the umpires, I'm constantly carrying on conversations. I get along with most of them and I think that's helped our team. We've now got to where our pitching staff won't say anything or show any kind of emotion, which is good. The umpires hate it when a pitcher shows emotion out on the mound over a questionable call. We've got to where I will do the talking.

All we really want is consistency behind the plate. If he calls a high pitch a strike in the first inning, he should call it a strike in the ninth. If he calls a low pitch a strike, he should consistently do that. The same with pitches on the corners.

85

There are hitter's umpires, guys like John Shulock or Steve Polarmo. For them, the ball has to be on the plate for it to be a strike and they're fairly consistent about it. But there are more pitcher's umpires than hitter's umpires. Pitcher's umpires will extend the strike zone an inch or so on each side, so instead of 17" that a pitcher has to shoot for, he can shoot for 19". Most of the time, if the pitcher is throwing the ball an inch or two off the plate, but he's consistently there, you can talk an umpire into gradually giving you that pitch. It's a matter of setting up and catching the ball properly. If the catcher is receiving the ball properly and makes it look good, framing it there for the umpire, he'll often get a strike on it.

Sometimes framing and gentle suggestion don't work and you have to get upset and say, "The frigging ball's a strike, let's go. Bear down a little bit back there. I've got a pitcher working his butt off making some quality pitches and you're not calling them."

Whether you can do that depends on the umpire's personality. Certain umpires I know will never hold any outspokenness against me. There's an honest directness in our relationship that goes both ways. Most umpires know when they're having a good game or a bad game and they'll talk quite openly about it. They'll say, "God, I've got to wait a little bit longer before I make that call." Once the batter's out of earshot, some of them will ask me, "Was that pitch a strike?" I'm very honest with them and they all know it. If they call a strike and I think it's a ball, I'll tell them that too. I think they appreciate that honesty. And I think that helps the team's relationships with most of the crews.

I think we get a pretty good shake from the umpires, and that, I think, goes back to our staff dealing with them as individuals, knowing how to handle them, knowing what you're capable of doing with them, what you can argue and what you can't, how much you can argue without them starting to grind an axe for you.

86

But there are certain umpiring crews that have it in for a team, and any close call will go against that team. It's unfortunate, but that's the way it is. That's part of being human too. Umpires hold grudges and there are a few crews that just don't like the Toronto Blue Jays.

Joe Brinkman's is one of them. It's gotten bad over the last two years, but Joe's attitude actually goes back to when Bobby Mattick was managing. All the umpires hated Bobby, but Joe had his run-ins with Bobby Cox, too. Now he hates Jimy Williams. He always calls him "little cocksucker" and he's thrown Jimy out a few times over situations that were absolutely nothing. Every close call with Brinkman and his crew goes against the Blue Jays. It infuriates the manager and it infuriates the players.

It's not all grudges against managers, though. On the Blue Jays, we have some players who complain a lot. Umpires don't want to be shown up, and when a guy starts showing his disapproval of a call at the plate, it gets the fans going. When the fans get going, they get on the umpire and umpires don't want that. There are ways you can argue, ways you can get your point across without showing up the umpire, although sometimes that is necessary if he's consistently terrible.

A lot of umpires don't like George Bell because of the antics he pulls at the plate. Lloyd Moseby and Manny Lee are the same way, and it doesn't do any of them any good. Working with umpires, I know they have their favourite players and they have players who are on their shitlist, and if you get on their shitlist, any questionable pitch is going to go against you. I've had many umpires tell me, "Hey, just get the ball close to the plate and it's going to be a strike." Sometimes they just don't like the hitter, sometimes the hitter has pulled something to show him up, and the umpire will do anything he can to get back at him.

But Joe Brinkman hates our ball club. I used to talk to Joe all the time until 1987. Now we don't speak at all. He's one of the few I purposely won't speak to because I think he's gone downhill as an umpire. He's incompetent. And **87** the scary part is he runs an umpiring school. I thought he was pretty fair until the last couple of years, then I think he took on an attitude of, "I'm going to get you guys."

In New York in 1987, a Yankee batter, Phil Lombardi, had a swinging foul on a third strike. It was close to the dirt, but I caught the ball. Naturally, with a right-handed hitter on a checked swing or a ball close to the dirt, the home plate umpire is sometimes blocked and you immediately appeal to the umpire on the opposite side of the hitter. So I appealed to the first base umpire, Joe Brinkman, the crew chief. I knew I caught the ball, and it shows on replay I caught the ball. There was no doubt in my mind, but being in the game, you instinctively ask just to make sure.

Brinkman said, yes, it's a catch, batter's out. I started throwing the ball around and Lombardi started walking toward the dugout. Suddenly, Lou Pinella told him to run. He was almost to the on-deck circle, but then he sprinted to first base. Who cares? I didn't care. The umpire said he's out and that should be the end of it.

Lou ran out and started arguing that the ball hit the ground and that I should have tagged him or thrown to first. Brinkman came in, then Tim Welke came in from third and said no, the ball hit the ground, the guy is not out. And Brinkman let him do it. He let a rookie umpire from the opposite side overrule him, and that should never have happened. We ended up losing the ballgame because of that.

In our fourth game of the '88 season in Minnesota, a similar thing happened when it might have been to our advantage. The Twins' catcher, Tom Nieto, dropped the ball on a third strike to Rance Mulliniks, but Durwood Merrill couldn't see it from behind the plate and he appealed to Welke, who said, yes, Nieto did drop the ball on the pitch. When Tom Kelly argued, Brinkman said Nieto dropped it in the act of throwing. He was working first base and shouldn't have made that decision with a left-handed batter up, but he said, "I'm not going to let someone overrule the crew chief." I exploded. Jimy argued and Joe ran him out of the game.

Then, in our series in New York, we had another ground rule single called on us. That's right, a ground rule single, for anyone who's heard of that. Brinkman's crew called one on me in New York in 1987. I hit the ball down the first base line, a double all the way. In Yankee Stadium, the seats are close to the line and a fan reached over and interferred with the ball, so it was up to the discretion of the umpire whether it was a double or a single. Last year, it cost me a double and cost the team a chance to score a run. This year, Tony Fernandez hit one down the line and went into second base, but a fan had reached out again and they called Tony back, saying, "No, it's a ground rule single."

It's unfortunate that that has to happen. Players and teams should be able to get a better shake than that, although I guess every team goes through a similar experience. In the early years, we always felt the umpires weren't giving us a fair shake. It seemed like the more experienced teams coming in would get all the calls.

Detroit News

Ted Archer

(top)
Macomb's catcher tries for the tag in the Roseville summer league.

(lower)
The call goes against the Bristol Red Sox. (Photos: Courtesy of Ernie Whitt)

(top)
July, 1976. A three-run homer in the fifth wins the game for the
Pawtucket-Rhode Island Red Sox. *(Photo: Courtesy of Ernie Whitt)*

(lower)
April, 1978. The first home run of the season takes off at
MacArthur Stadium in Syracuse. *(Photo: Courtesy of Ernie Whitt)*

The Globe and Mail

(top)
Roy Hartsfield goes finger-to-finger with umpire Jim McKean.

(lower)
Saying goodbye to Chris and Ashley before hitting the road with the Charleston Charlies in 1977. *(Photo: Courtesy of Ernie Whitt)*

John McNeill

John McNeill

Work and play in Dunedin, Florida, in 1978. *(Photos: Courtesy of Ernie Whitt)*

Canapress Photo Service

Thomas Szlukovenyi

(top)
Bobby Mattick in conversation with Derryl Cousins.

(lower)
Watching Billy Martin express his feelings to Terry Cooney, 1981.
(Photo: Courtesy of Ernie Whitt)

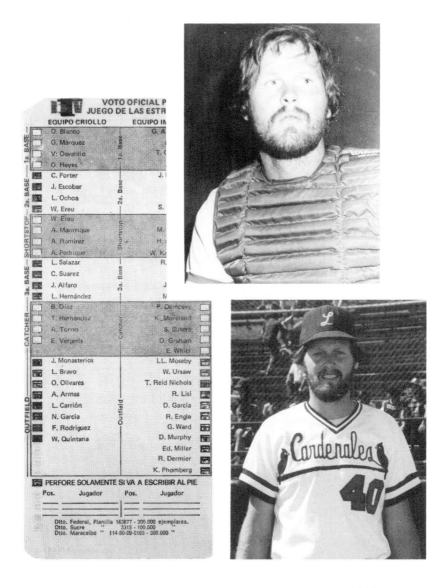

With Los Cardinales de Lara, Barquisimeto, Venezuela, 1980.
(Photo: Courtesy of Ernie Whitt.)

With Chris, Ashley, EJ, and Taylor, Dunedin, 1983. *(Photo: Courtesy of Ernie Whitt)*

Anything close would always go their way. We thought that was because we weren't expected to win and because they didn't really know us as players. But the main reason, we felt, was that they were squeezing the team to get back at Bobby Mattick.

When Bobby Mattick took over as manager of the Blue Jays after Roy Hartsfield was fired in 1980, he had never managed before. There were some things he didn't seem to know much about, like handling baseball situations on the field. The umpires hated him because he didn't know how to argue. He'd come out and say something foolish and the umpires would just look at him and say, "What the hell are you doing out here?"

He'd argue balls and strikes, which a manager can't do and shouldn't do. He'd argue balks. He'd argue every close play and umpires get sick and tired of that. They kept telling me they'd never come across a guy who argued like that before. They also hated him because he was constantly carrying on in the dugout. An umpire would miss a pitch and Bobby would yell or throw his hands up in the air. They'd just look over at the dugout with contempt.

They did get a kick out of some of the foolish things he did, though. In one game he went out to the mound to make a pitching change and almost absent-mindedly made some motion with his left hand. I think it was Paul Mirabella who had been warming up in the bullpen at the time and who came running in. Bobby wasn't paying any attention at all. He actually wanted a right-hander. Mirabella ran right up to the mound and Bobby looked up, saw him there and said, "What the fuck are you doing here? I don't want you here. I don't want you. You've got to go back. You've got to go back."

The umpire said, "Oh no, you wanted a left-hander. He's got to stay in." Paul proceeded to give up a home run and we lost the game. The umpire just laughed.

The players got a kick out of some of his antics, too. He always had this act of taking his hat off and tossing it up

89

in the air to show his displeasure with something on the field. In Baltimore, he was on the top step, something happened, he took his hat off, threw it up in the air and it didn't come down. It had sailed off up into the stands and he kept looking around all over the place, saying, "Did anyone see my hat?" We were just rolling.

As far as managing on the field went, Bobby had a lot to learn. But he was good as far as knowing baseball talent. At least, he saw something in me. I respect the man because he gave me the opportunity to play in the big leagues. If it wasn't for him, I don't know where I would be right now.

He had seen me play in Syracuse while Roy Hartsfield was still managing in Toronto. He had come into town with Pat Gillick when Pat told me there would be some changes made. I was never quite sure why he was appointed manager, although I think the organization had already decided that they wanted Bobby Cox and just put **90** in the first available man until Cox could be freed from Atlanta.

But I think he was instrumental in the trade in November, 1979, that sent Rick Cerone, Ted Wilborn and Tom Underwood to New York for Chris Chambliss, Paul Mirabella, and Damaso Garcia. That trade opened up a spot behind the plate.

The first critical move Bobby made was to bring in a new coaching staff. I can't remember one coach who was happy during Hartsfield's years. They didn't seem to enjoy coaching under Roy and didn't really seem to do much. Bobby Doerr did well as the hitting coach, but he couldn't be there that often. And Jackie Moore tried to do a good job at third base. He was always willing to come out early to help the players and it hurt him every time we lost. But other than those two, the coaching staff seemed to be basically filling a spot and to have an attitude of, "We're supposed to lose, so why put an effort into it?"

When Bobby Mattick became manager, only Bobby Doerr stayed on the staff. John Felske, who had managed the Eastern League team in Pittsfield, Massachusetts, when I was with Bristol, worked with us in the bullpen, Al Widmar was appointed the pitching coach and Denis Menke and Jimy Williams looked after first and third base.

The day he was appointed, Mattick called and said I would be his starting catcher and that he was confident I could do the job. After three years of Roy Hartsfield, those were good words to hear, but I don't know that I actually believed them. In spring training that year, I'd keep hearing and reading that I would be the regular catcher "unless a deal is made." I figured I'd believe it when I heard the national anthems being played in the Kingdome in Seattle on opening day.

As it turned out, I did start. But I didn't do well at all, making a few errors early in the season and getting into a terrible hitting slump. A big part of the problem was that I was putting pressure on myself, trying to do well, wanting to do well, wanting to stay in the big leagues. A lot of it was not being selective as a hitter.

91

It was a learning process for me. There aren't too many players who become instant successes in the big leagues. The exceptions are mainly superstars like Canseco or Boggs. It usually takes time to work yourself up.

The differences between the minors and the majors aren't many, but they're critical. The biggest difference is in the pitching staff. In AAA, there are usually only two real good pitchers going for the team, while in the big leagues, there are three or four sometimes outstanding talents and a fifth starter of average ability. The pitchers in AAA have good velocity on their fastball, and that's what they specialize in. They can throw it in at 92 or 93 miles an hour, which is extremely fast and difficult to see with the lighting conditions being what they are in the minors. But a pitcher can't make it in the major leagues with just that one pitch. The hitters will catch up to him and bang him around. Hits that you get in the minor leagues are caught in the major leagues. The range of the fielders is better and the playing conditions, especially the lighting, are so much better that a pitcher has to diversify. If a pitcher has a 94 – 96 mile an hour fastball with movement on it, he can make it in the big leagues, but only in relief. No one can keep up that velocity over nine innings.

After seeing minor league pitching for so many years, it was difficult for me to make the transition. It took me so much time that Bob Davis got most of the work in the first half of the season. I never really knew Bob that well, but he was a good guy. He was a quiet gentleman who never said anything bad about anyone. He was a hard worker.

I was just fortunate that the only other candidate for starting or back-up catcher was Pat Kelly, who I'd played with down in Syracuse. Pat had an awful lot of talent, with probably the best arm I've ever seen as far as throwing went. But he was a "phenom" who got the "heebee-jeebees." He couldn't throw the ball to the pitcher. He had this mental block where he couldn't get the ball back without overthrowing or short-hopping it, and if there was a runner on first, he'd be really paranoid.

I've seen it happen to other players at different positions. Steve Sax had the "heebee-jeebees" with the Dodgers in 1987. He'd field a ball well, then couldn't get it over to first without throwing it away. But it's usually a short-term thing. A coach will usually work with the player, telling him to maybe hit his glove a couple of times before he gives a good, firm throw. A lot of position players go through it and have to double-clutch, or tap twice, before they make the throw, to keep their concentration. It helps them get a good feel on the ball and get the proper rhythm.

But it's an occupational disease for catchers that I've fortunately never suffered from. The "heebee-jeebees'"was the reason Atlanta turned Dale Murphy into an outfielder. He had a tremendous arm, but he'd overthrow getting the ball back to the mound or hit the pitcher in the back or the back of the head when he threw to second base. He just couldn't control his arm. Rick Cerone

92

went through it, too, and he'd also have to stand up and tap the glove a couple of times before he threw the ball back. When he was with the Yankees, he got into the habit of flipping a rainbow toss to the mound whenever he ran into trouble. We knew about his problem, and Alfredo Griffin once timed it perfectly and stole a base while the ball was in the air.

But Pat Kelly never got over the problem and he appeared in only three games with Toronto in 1980.

Bobby Mattick followed a basic platoon system, but he had a habit of playing hunches that really confused not only the catchers, but all the players. You could never be quite sure whether you would be playing on any given day until you got to the ball park.

I remember one game in 1981 when I got really angry because we were up against a right-handed pitcher in Cleveland, yet I wasn't in the lineup. I was sitting down in the bullpen, there were two outs in the ninth and I think it was Danny Whitmer, another Jays' catcher at the time, who was due up. The bullpen phone rang and I knew it was Mattick calling for me. I yelled at the bullpen coach, John Felske, "Don't answer it. I don't want to hit." I was some kind of hot anyway over not being in the lineup, but it was also a cold, wet night and I really wasn't prepared. Usually if you're going to pinch hit you're given the word at the beginning of the inning so you can get yourself ready. The thought of going straight from the bullpen to the batter's box didn't really appeal to me. Of course, Felske had to answer the phone and up I went. I guess I should be grateful because that one at-bat got me to Cooperstown — as the last out on the scorecard of Len Barker's perfect game.

There just seemed to be no rhyme nor reason to some of the things Bobby did. I remember starting a game in Minnesota at the old Met against left-hander Geoff Zahn, which surprised me. It was another one of Bobby's hunches. Zahn was very effective that day and we were shut out. He gave up only four or five hits, and I had three of them. The following week, Zahn pitched against us in

Toronto and I wasn't in the lineup. I thought, "I had three off him last week. Why wouldn't he play me against him this week? Has he simply forgotten what happened?" But that was just Bobby's way.

He got another hunch when he found out that Sparky Anderson and Roger Craig were calling pitches for Lance Parrish. Roger was the Tigers' pitching coach then, and he and Sparky weren't happy with Lance's pitch selection, so they started to call the pitches themselves. Bobby heard about it and decided that our pitching coach, Al Widmar, would call the pitches, too. I totally disagreed with that. I felt they were taking away part of my job. Setting up the opposing hitters is the main part of the catcher's job. That's the fun part of the job. I talked to Lance about it, so I know he felt the same way in Detroit, but we both knew that we only signed contracts to play ball, not to make decisions.

94 I protested, but Bobby was playing his hunches. He said, "We're struggling right now and we're just going to try to change things. I don't know how long it'll last, but if we're successful with it, we'll go that way."

We were playing the Tigers when the new system was put into effect, and Jim Clancy was pitching. The Tigers caught on very quickly to Al calling the pitches on the side and started getting hits in the second inning. Finally, Mattick sent Denis Menke out to the mound to say, "Okay, guys. You're on your own. It's not working. You can start calling the pitches now." Clancy and I looked at each other, looked around the bases to see each one occupied by a Tiger with nobody out, and just cracked up. Even Menke was laughing. That's how long the experiment lasted. Two innings.

But for all his bizarre behaviour on the field, Bobby was putting together a team that was miles ahead of any Blue Jay team Roy Hartsfield managed. The defence was getting better, but there were still a lot of problems on the mound.

One thing the Blue Jays never had either when Hartsfield was there or in Bobby Mattick's two years was any depth in the pitching staff. A lot of times, the pitchers would be in the ozone. They really wouldn't know what was going on. They'd get lost whenever they got out to the mound, becoming so excited they wouldn't know what to do. Catchers had to go out a lot to try and calm them down.

Butch Edge, for example, was a very talented young man who was the sixth player taken in the expansion draft. He had a great arm, but he lost all his senses on the mound. He was only up with the club in 1979, the one year I stayed in the minors, but I remember catching him in a spring training game when I put down a fastball sign and he threw me a curve. I went out and said, "Butch, I put down a fastball and you threw me a curve."

He said, "Oh, oh, oh, yeah, yeah, I know. I just got to the top and I remembered I wanted to throw a curve."

"Well, shake it off and I'll call a curve. Just let me know what's coming."

"Okay, Ernie, I'll do that."

I went back, called a curve, Butch shook his head "yes," then he wound up and threw me a fastball. I went to the backstop to pick up the ball, went back out to the mound and said, "Butch, I called for a curve and you shook 'okay' but you threw me a fastball. Do you not know the signs? Is this what's happening?"

"Yeah, yeah, I know the signs. But, Ernie, I got to the top of my windup again and I wanted to throw a fastball."

This went on for three or four innings. It was ridiculous. As a catcher, it's like being on roller skates back there if you don't know what's coming. There has to be communication between the pitcher and the catcher, and that was something we didn't have in the early years with the Blue Jays.

An incredible number of pitchers came and went over the first few years, especially young prospects who never panned out. The first year was really crazy. One who I thought was going to be really good in 1977 was Jeff Byrd, a right-hander out of the Texas organization. He threw the ball hard, with good movement, and had a fine curveball, but he just got a cup of coffee in the big leagues. Same with Mike Darr, a tall right-handed prospect who didn't know where he was throwing the ball at times, but threw it extremely hard. He ended up pitching only one inning for the club.

Bill Singer had pitched for a number of years and was taken from the Twins in the expansion draft. I guess he was supposed to be the dependable veteran, but he had a terrible year in 1977, ending up with a 2 – 8 record and a 6.75 ERA. It was his last year in the game. He was one of the few pitchers I've caught who threw a spitball. He had a pretty good one and he'd give me a special sign when he had it loaded up.

Bill was pitching when I got my first start with the Blue Jays in a game against Chicago, and before the game he said, "Ernie, you don't even have to give me a sign. The first pitch is going to be a fastball right at Ralph Gar's head." I thought, "Okay, this guy's been around. I guess he knows what he's doing." Bill had a reputation for throwing at hitters and he had some message he wanted to send to the White Sox. He did exactly as he said he would. I still don't know how Gar got out of the way of that pitch.

Jerry Johnson was another one-season man. He was called in to pitch in relief in 43 games in 1977, but only made five saves. He was a total animal, and I say that in a good way. He had pitched for the Dodgers and when we played L.A. in a spring training game, Jerry went right over to one of the Dodger pitchers and the two of them started beating the hell out of each other. They were pounding as hard as they could. I thought they were going to kill each other. It turned out that they were good friends and this was just their way of goofing around. He was such a physical type that when he got out of the game he went into the stunt business.

There were some who survived past the first year. Dave Lemanczyk was a starter who lasted from 1977 right through to 1980. I'd come across him when he was pitching for the Memphis Blues and had hit a home run off him. He was another pitcher who was a great guy most of the time, but turned into a fruitcake whenever he got near the mound. The other mainstay of Hartsfield's starting rotation was Jerry Garvin, who went 10 – 18 the first year, 4 – 12 the second, then pitched pretty well as a reliever in 1979 and 1980 before fading off into the sunset. Between them, Dave and Jerry still hold a lot of Blue Jay records — for most losses, most hits allowed, most runs allowed, most wild pitches, and on and on.

Tom Underwood was another pitcher I'd come across in the minors, a small left-hander with a great arm, a good fastball, and a good breaking ball, but who didn't have what it took inside. He'd pitch well for five or six innings, then if the game was close he'd start reaching down and touching his ankles to signal that he was tired and wanted out of the game. I always felt that he could have been a big winner if he had a better makeup about him. He just didn't have the guts to stay out and finish the job. **97**

But the best arm in those years, and I think one of the best arms the organization has ever seen, belonged to Jesse Jefferson. He had a great curveball and a fastball that was consistently 90-plus miles an hour. He could be totally awesome at times, but at other times he wouldn't have it at all. You could never tell beforehand whether he was going to be on or off, and what any organization looks for in a pitcher is consistency and dependability.

The Blue Jays certainly found dependability in the lone survivor in the pitching staff from the team's first year. Jim Clancy was just a very talented prospect, a kid, when he first came up. He needed a lot of tutoring along the way, but he worked his ERA from 5.03 in 1977 to 4.09 in 1978 down to 3.30 in 1980. It's rarely risen above 4.00 ever since.

And consistency came in 1979 with a young guy who had been converted from an outfielder to a pitcher only the year before and who jumped right from A ball in Dunedin to AAA in Syracuse to the big leagues in just a few months. Dave Stieb pitched 18 games for Toronto in

1979 and ended the season with an 8 – 8 record. He was the first Blue Jay starter ever to finish without a losing record. The next year, he made it to the All-Star game.

By the end of Bobby Mattick's first year as manager, David and Jim were the main guys on the mound. Luis Leal had joined the staff, along with Paul Mirabella and Joey McLaughlin. On the field, Rick Bosetti, Alvis Woods, Bob Bailor, John Mayberry, and Otto Velez were still the foundation of the team, but Lloyd Moseby, Damaso Garcia, Alfredo Griffin, Garth Iorg, and I were all getting more and more work.

We were coming together and by the end of the 1980 season, we were playing for pride, something we didn't seem to have a lot of in earlier years. It was the first year that we had an effect on the way things turned out in the AL East. In the first three years, any team that was scheduled to face us in the last couple of weeks looked at it as an easy way to extend a lead or make up some critical

98 ground. But in 1980, the Orioles were trying to catch the Yankees when they came into Toronto. We beat them two games out of four.

We finished up with a 67 – 95 record, the first time we'd made it through a season without a hundred losses. We were 27 games back of New York, but we hadn't been eliminated until September 7. We would never be eliminated in August again.

Personally, I had turned things around offensively. On June 18, I had hit a home run, the first since the one off the foul pole in Fenway Park in September of 1976. On July 7, I hit a three-run shot off Jack Morris into the upper deck at Tiger Stadium, my first in Detroit and the first big league homer that Chris was there to see. For the whole second half I improved. After my really poor start, I hit .275 after the All-Star break to raise my average to .237 for the year, but I had only six home runs and 34 RBI.

It was pretty clear that for the sake of my career I'd have to play winter ball, so soon after the season was over I headed off to the Liga Venezolana de Beisbol Profesional. I was assigned to Los Cardinales de Lara in Barquisimeto, Venezuela, about three hours inland from Caracas.

That was sure different. A lot of people talk badly about playing winter ball in Venezuela, but it was a learning experience. We certainly learned to appreciate North America a lot more by going down there, appreciate so many little things like even being able to run down to the store to buy milk or some diapers. In Venezuela, it's a lot more difficult to do things that we take for granted.

We had heard some terrible stories about the place before we left. We had heard that if you had blond-haired kids, especially babies, to hold on to them with your life. Barquisimeto is about 20 miles from the jungle, and an American man from Chicago had been kidnapped and taken there recently. We heard that blond-haired, blue-eyed kids were kidnapped and taken into the jungle, too, then sold for high prices back in the cities. We wanted to brush the idea off as just a scare story. But our three kids were all blond and were all going to celebrate their birthdays there. Ashley was going to turn four, EJ two, and our second son, Taylor, was going to turn one. The stories didn't make us feel very good. As a precaution, before we left Michigan, Chris bought shoes for the kids that squeaked so loud when they walked it would drive anyone insane. She had the kids wear them in the airport so she'd always know where they were.

99

We had heard nightmare stories about the ball parks, too, but Chris thought she had to see for herself and came to the opening game. There was broken glass angled all around so that nobody could climb up and get in free without ripping their hands apart. In the stands, everybody was constantly drinking beer then peeing in their cups so they wouldn't miss any of the game. And everybody wanted to touch the blond-haired kids. After the opening game, she figured she'd seen me play enough and just stayed home.

Home was an apartment complex where all the American players lived, eight couples altogether. It was a pretty decent place, decently furnished. And we all tried to look out for each other. We knew we were in for some interesting times.

One night, a group of people who had been promised apartments in the complex arrived to find that there were no rooms for them and decided that they were going to take over the building. We called it the "national uprising." Chris slept through the whole commotion going on down in the parking lot, but I thought we were going to have to fight our way out of there. It was getting hostile, with people throwing things at the lone security guard who was always at the door holding a gun. But he held them off until the police and the National Guard arrived.

We were kind of amazed that the guard was able to do it, because to that point he hadn't done anything to make us feel secure. Just the opposite. One afternoon after our usual Sunday morning game, a bunch of us were throwing a football around in the parking lot, then stopped to catch our breath before heading upstairs for a beer. We leaned up against a car and tried out a bit of Spanish with the guard, who tried out his English on us. As soon as we got upstairs, we heard a gunshot. We raced to the window and looked down in the parking lot. The guard had been playing with his gun and had blown out the side of the car we'd just been leaning against.

The Venezuelans love their baseball, especially in the winter months when they get to see major league players. And they love their local heros. Luis Leal was from Barqisimeto and pitched for the Cardinales when he got home from Toronto. He was almost like the honourary mayor of the town.

But the playing conditions weren't exactly ideal. The clubhouse facilities were terrible — cement floors, cold water most of the time for the showers, dirty uniforms that looked like they were all done in one wash with about half a cup of soap. The stench was terrible, the mosquitos were bad, and you'd see rats running around everywhere.

There were six teams in the league. Besides Barquisimeto, there were two teams in Caracas, the local one and another team called La Guaira. La Guaira was actually on the other side of the mountain from Caracas, but Caracas was their home field. I believe there were two teams in Maracaibo and another in Valencia. Maracaibo was the worst place to play, especially the Sunday day games, because the heat was almost unbearable. Scattered around the league were some pretty good young players — Lloyd Moseby, Tony Armas, Bo Diaz, Sal Butera, Garth Iorg. On the Cardinales, we had a lot of players from the Giants' organization, like Chris Bourjos and Eddie Murray's brother, Rich.

Road trips, either by plane or by bus, were frightening. We were flying on some airlines that had the worst record of crashes in the world and we felt that the pilots were all kamikazes. When they took off they went straight up, and when they landed they came straight down. There was no gentle way of flying there.

The bus trips were no better. Winding roads through the mountains, a bus driver who didn't know anything but fast, and animals walking out onto the road all the time — dogs, mules, cows. You'd see a lot of accidents with cars hitting pedestrians, hitting animals, flipping over. The travel wasn't great. We'd stop at little road-side places and see skinny dogs scrounging around for food and kids coming up and begging for money. One thing we had been told was, don't give them money. If we wanted to give them something, we were supposed to buy a sandwich and watch them eat it, because parents would send their kids out to beg and the kids would never see any of the money.

I struggled the whole time down there. I don't think I hit over .200 and I'd pick out a few Spanish words in the paper, things like, "Great defence, no hit." And I caught some kind of virus that terrified both me and Chris. We never did find out what actually happened, but I became so weak that some of the other players had to carry me down the four flights of stairs to get me to the hospital. Randy Benson, a left-handed pitcher, spent the first night with me in the hospital. Chris wanted to, but with three

101

babies to look after she had to spend the night at home worrying and praying.

I had never been that sick before in my life. I couldn't keep any food in me and I almost went into shock from being so dehydrated. I honestly thought I was going to die. I couldn't understand the doctors or nurses until the second day when they brought in a doctor who spoke a little English and could ease my mind and relieve some of Chris's tensions.

I wanted to go home, but I was told that a contract is a contract. Luckily, I started to feel better after a few days in the hospital. When I went back to the team and put my uniform on, a polyester double-knit that had been really tight, I felt like I was back in the old days when ball players wore baggy outfits. I had lost that much weight.

But you can make what you want to make out of any experience. Despite the illness, we had a good time in Venezuela and we look back on our months there as an adventure. And we remember it mainly for spending time together as a family and having one of our most enjoyable Christmases ever.

102

We went out and bought a Scotch pine and cut the trunk down so that it could fit into a big five-gallon container we drank our fresh water from. We strung popcorn and little paper loops and rings for decorations. Chris had brought gifts for the kids in trunks, and we wrapped them in newspaper and red and green ribbons and handed them out Christmas morning.

It was a warm, country, family-type Christmas. But being from Michigan, eighty degrees and a tropical breeze blowing in on Christmas Day just didn't seem right. So Chris went into the little freezer compartment of the old ice box, scraped off some crystals and started throwing them at us around the tree. The kids laughed and loved it. It was snowing in Venezuela.

The Blue Jays have never had as bad a start as we had in 1981. We were dreadful. I was never quite sure why, but maybe the labour problems looming up ahead had something to do with it, since we were a young team and unsure of what might happen. We went 16 – 42 in the first third of the season, then we all went home. The players were on strike.

At first, I thought it was great. I hadn't had any time off in the summer since I was a kid, and all of a sudden I could do summer-type things. We went boating, we visited Chris's mom in Iowa, and went horseback riding. It was really nice to be able to spend so much time with my family.

There were some problems, though. Chris and I find that when we have tensions in our marriage, it's when we have to readjust to being a family together. I think a lot of ball players experience the same thing. You get home after the season and there's the parent who's been the disciplinarian, who's been handling being both mother and father, who's been making all the decisions and maybe feels that it should stay that way, and you want to assert some authority yourself and get back into being the man of the house. It makes for some difficult **103** days or weeks every year. And here we were in the middle of the season, in summertime, with a lot of adjusting to do.

But the strike came at a good time for us. Maybe it's my background in the Baptist Church or Chris's moral upbringing, but we always believe that there's a purpose to everything. Everything happens for a reason. And just when the strike got underway, our son, Taylor, was going through a terrible time. The same sort of thing had happened with the other kids. I remember Ashley, especially, would always seem funny whenever I came home. In the first few minutes, it would be hugs and kisses and "Daddy, Daddy." Then she'd turn away like she was afraid that I would leave home, and leave her, again.

But neither Ashley nor EJ ever had the problems that Taylor had. Everything with him was "No. No. No." Over all those 59 days of the strike that we spent together as a family, there was almost a total personality change. He came out of that shell and became a happy kid.

As pleasant as it was, after a few weeks I found the strike unsettling. Partly, it was that I hadn't been in the big leagues long enough to have much money to fall back on. Partly, it was that I still didn't feel secure. These were days when I could have been out playing the game, could have been getting better at my job, could have been enjoying myself on the field, could have been learning and developing and showing people what I could do. As it stretched on, I started to get worried.

But the break must have been useful for all of us. When we re-assembled for the second part of the season, we played close to .500 ball the rest of the year. We had finished the first part 19 games back of New York. We finished the second part seven and a half games behind Milwaukee. We were still in last place in the league, but we had some optimism for the next season.

A few days after the season ended, Bobby Mattick resigned as manager. A week after that, it was announced that the Atlanta Braves' manager, Bobby Cox, would take over the Blue Jays in 1982.

104

One thing Toronto fans rarely did in the early days was boo our performance on the field, even though we often deserved to be booed. That sure changed in 1988.

As we ended the first month of the season, we were on a six-game losing streak that had started on the last day in New York and had included a sweep by Oakland at Exhibition Stadium. When we lost the first game of a series with the Angels, the fans really got on us. George took it personally after he had to chase a few balls in the corner, but I felt they were booing the whole team. I couldn't blame them.

Everything seemed to be going wrong. Our defence had been shaky all month. We still didn't have the right combination in the middle infield and Tony had to sit out a few games after his knee swelled up. There was a possibility Jimmy Key would be lost to the team for months with his elbow problem. The rest of the starting rotation had trouble making it past the first few innings. Todd

Stottlemyre had pitched pretty well in spots, but whenever he pitched we never seemed to score any runs. By the end of April, Todd's ERA was 7.50, and Jim Clancy's wasn't much better.

Before spring training I had been worried about Duane Ward and David Wells. They were both young and had strong arms, but didn't know where they were throwing the ball. A few weeks into the season, they still didn't know. I'd put down a sign to throw down and away and the pitch might be up and in.

I'm the type of catcher who likes to move and shift so that the pitcher has the whole body to throw at. It's easy to catch guys like Key or Clancy or Stieb or Henke or Flanagan. Call for a pitch outside, and it's going to be outside. They're pitchers and know what to do with the ball. A catcher has to look for the ball in a certain area. The plate's only 17" wide, but if you're set up on the outside part and the ball comes in 4" on the inside part, it might not seem like much but that's a long way to go to catch a 90-mile-an-hour fastball. You're doing well just to knock it down.

105

After the first month of the season, I told John Sullivan, "I can't move on these guys anymore. I set up outside, it's inside. I set up inside, it's outside. The ball's getting by me, so I'm just going to set up down the middle of the plate and let them throw the ball where they want to."

The few bright spots were in the batting order. George, Pat Borders, and Fred McGriff were all hitting over .300. I was in the middle of the pack with .260, so we weren't doing all that badly. But pitching and defence, not hitting, wins ball games.

The rumours about a Jesse Barfield trade kept making the rounds, too, and that had an unsettling effect. The worst part was that Jesse never got a straight answer as to how close a deal was. The biggest complaint baseball players have is that they're so rarely told the truth about things that have tremendous consequences for them and their families. There are executives, managers, and coaches all around the league who will sit across a desk and lie to a player's face. Players have a right to know at least whether a decision on their future is in the works. Maybe they don't need to know the details, but someone in authority should tell it like it is. A grown man can accept the truth, no matter what it is. If he can't, he shouldn't be in the sport.

Jesse tried to not let the uncertainty get to him. And he tried to get things on the right course for the team by calling a "players only" meeting as we went into the second month. Jesse, Lloyd, and I all spoke. We talked again about work habits and how they had to improve if we were going to do the little things we had to do to win. We weren't executing the hit and run, the squeeze bunt, driving in a guy from third with a fly ball — all situations to move runners over that we practice every day. But if players didn't put their all into the practices, we'd never execute properly.

We talked about picking up our teammates. When a runner's left on third, no one feels worse than the guy who doesn't bring him in, especially with less than two outs. But a player can't take that all on his own shoulders. His teammates have to say, "It's okay, the next guy will get him." A pitcher has to forget it if a fielder boots the ball and bear down harder on the next batter. Everyone is going to struggle at some time and needs his teammates to help him through it. We all have to pull for each other.

When I spoke, I said that what I was seeing in the club was what it used to be like in the '70s and early '80s. We'd play pretty good ball for five innings or so and then some attitude would come over us, like we were thinking, "When are we going to lose? When are we going to botch up a play?" I said it took us years to get a positive attitude, and it could be lost a lot quicker than it could be gained. For three or four years now, we would win a lot of games in the seventh, eighth, or ninth inning. We would be close and we'd bear down and pull those games out because we would say to ourselves, "We've got the best team, let's get out on the field and prove it." Now, all of a sudden, we were back to losing our concentration after the sixth inning, just laying back with an "oh, well" frame of mind.

There were a lot of things to work on, a lot of things to change if we were going to turn the season around. We'd dug ourselves a big hole, down all the way to just above Baltimore. We had a long climb ahead and without the proper attitude, we'd never make it.

May

Sometimes it's amazing what a meeting can do. After the players get-together, we went up against the Angels and snapped our losing streak by beating them 6 – 4. Dave Stieb was really effective for the first five innings, and we staked him to a 6 – 0 lead with some good hitting and heads-up running. Lloyd hit a two-run homer, and Jesse showed his leadership on the field by hustling and turning a double into a triple.

We were 10 – 13 as we flew out to the west coast for a week-long road trip. We left with some bad news — Jimmy Key was going to have to have surgery to get the bone chips out of his elbow and would be gone probably until July.

We also left Nelson Liriano behind. He was on his way to Syracuse and Rance was coming off the disabled list where he'd been since the opening game in Toronto. The thing was, Manny Lee had hurt his shoulder sliding into second in the game against the Angels, but he hadn't mentioned the tenderness he felt to Jimy; and Rance felt able to hit but didn't have the flexibility in his knee to be able to shift properly at third. So when we got to Seattle,

Manny couldn't play and, without Nellie around, we had the ridiculous situation of Cecil Fielder playing second base for the first time in his life and alternating at third with Kelly Gruber depending on whether the hitter was batting from the right or left. The next night Pat Borders played second. It didn't make for a very strong middle-infield, especially since Tony had just come back from missing three games with his sore knee. Juan Beniquez had played some third before, but he told Jimy he couldn't handle the assignment because of a sore arm.

In the second game against Seattle, the weakness didn't hurt us. Todd Stottlemyre had a perfect game going before he hit a Mariner with a pitch in the seventh inning then lost both the no-hitter and the shutout two batters later. He got his first win of the season. He had pitched effectively before, but we had never given him much of a cushion to work with. In this game we did. I got my first home run of the season, a three-run shot. Rance got his first, too, and Freddie McGriff just crushed two.

110

When we were in Oakland later in the week, Mike Flanagan and I rode out to the ball park with a couple of Jimy Williams' old friends, guys he used to play college ball with. We started talking about Jimy, and while I didn't ask his friends to talk to him, I was hoping they would because I wanted to get the message across that Jimy had to loosen up a bit and relax. All the losing and all the tension was eating him up inside, turning him into a walking time bomb. A manager has to stay relaxed to make sure the players don't get on edge. He should be able to have a calming effect, be able to say, "Hey, it's okay. You're all right."

There's been quite a change in Jimy since he was the third base coach. I guess that goes with the territory, being at a higher level, always being in the spotlight, maybe having to answer to management for certain moves that he makes. I don't know how much pressure he was getting from the organization, but the media were sure asking questions after the first month of the season.

With the personnel we had and the record we've had for the past few years, why weren't we winning?

We weren't winning because we weren't playing very good baseball. Our pitching wasn't consistent, and we were terrible defensively. Was that Jimy's fault? He wasn't out on the field. But when a team's struggling the first thing people look at is the manager, and the first thing they come up with is the oldest saying in baseball — that it's easier to change one person than it is to change twenty-four — even though that's not always the case.

He was getting criticism for not being able to motivate some of the players. But you look at it another way and ask, why should a guy have to motivate a player who's making over half a million dollars a year? That doesn't make a lot of sense. The player should take some personal pride and go on from there. You have to take responsibility for your own performance and look to the manager for encouragement, not motivation.

111

I don't know whether Jimy's friends talked to him or not, but after our west coast trip he did kind of ease up and start handling things better. Winning two out of three in Anaheim might have helped, too.

Our first day back in Toronto, Jimy called me into his office and said, "I've known you for nine years. You're a leader on this ball club and a lot of guys look up to you. I know you're having a rough time and I know it's getting to you, but I want you to start relaxing."

We talked a bit. It was a few words, a quiet conversation, but it made me feel good that he pointed out a lot of positives instead of negatives and that he made a point of recognizing my frustration and telling me not to worry, that he was behind me. It was a plus that put me in a better frame of mind, even if we did lose to Seattle that day.

He was right about the frustration. A few weeks into the season, and I felt I really stunk. I came out of spring training with my arm feeling good, swinging the bat well, and yet my numbers were really low, offensively and defensively.

It was the defensive numbers that bothered me most because defence is my top priority. It seemed that if I made a good throw the runner was stealing off the pitcher, and with the guys that I should have thrown out, I was making bad throws. Putting those two together made for very low numbers.

But I could take some consolation in the fact that defence also means getting the hitter out, and I wasn't giving in to the hitters. There's always a choice, and if there's a runner on and I know he'll be going but the hitter is better with a fastball than a breaking ball, I can't give in to the hitter and call for a fastball just to help me throw the runner out at second. A breaking ball will give the runner an extra half step, and it might be in the dirt so I'll have to dig it out. It's not a good pitch to throw a runner out on, and that had happened a number of times. But still, it was frustrating.

112

My batting was frustrating, too. I've never been known for strong first halfs. I don't know why, but it seems to take me a while to find my groove. I'm usually much stronger after the All-Star break and often very strong in September. This year was no exception. Coming into May, I seemed to be in a slump, although my numbers weren't really far off what they were in the early going of 1987, the best year of my career. It was just that then the team was winning, and winning hides a lot of things.

Hitting is very hard to do at the best of times, the most difficult thing in baseball. Somebody gives you a round object, somebody else throws a round object at you, and you're supposed to hit it square. I remember reading someplace a few years ago that scientists of some sort figured that, theoretically, no one should be able to hit a big league fastball at all. It's all hand-eye coordination, picking up little clues like where the ball is coming out of the pitcher's hand, the rotation on the seams, the colour the ball gets on certain pitches. I know a lot of fans find it hard to believe that anyone can distinguish different rotations on an object travelling 90-plus miles an hour from only 60 feet away, but when you've seen it and worked at doing it day after day over many, many years, you get to notice the little clues.

When a hitter looks for the seams on the ball and sees a dot, for example, he knows it's a slider, the pitch of the seventies, a hard, sharp, breaking ball. The pitcher uses a sinking fastball grip and it's thrown as a fastball, but he puts more pressure on the ball with the middle finger. The extra pressure has the effect of cutting the ball in on the hitter. It comes to the plate and breaks or slides maybe 4 inches across and 2 to 3 inches down just when it gets to the hitting zone. Some guys grip the ball differently and a dot might not be visible, but with the common slider the dot on the rotation is pretty clear as it comes to home plate.

The ball looks different on every pitch, and it looks different depending on how you're doing. When you're on a hot streak, it looks like a softball, sometimes even like a beachball, coming in. When you're in a slump, it looks more like a golfball. If you do know what's coming, though, the advantage shifts in your favour. Knowing how a fastball or a curve or a slider behaves, you adjust and keep trying. It's still hard. If it was easy, there'd be a lot more players hitting .300. There aren't many who do. With hitting, you're doing very well if you fail only seventy per cent of the time.

Since I was still trying to get to the point of hitting my weight, I talked things over with Cito Gaston. Was I open too much? Was I blocking myself out when I went into the ball and so keeping my hips from coming through? What it came down to was that my mechanics were all right — my feet were positioned okay, my hands were in the right place — but my timing was off. When I'm at the plate, I have to be rocking and I have to rock back at the right time to get the bat through the hitting zone. Being a little off, I was hitting a few to left field and centre. I always have hit balls there, but not as many as in the first few months of 1988. Ever since Stan Williams changed

my style in Bristol in 1975, I've been basically a pull hitter. I've hit a lot of balls hard to centre field, but I haven't
got enough pop in my bat to hit the ball out in centre. I
think I've hit two home runs to centre in my life. I've got
to pull the ball to hit home runs.

I worked hard on the problem with Cito, who's done a
terrific job with the Blue Jays since Bobby Cox brought
him in as the hitting instructor in 1982. Apart from his
talent, what really made a difference was that he was the
first full-time hitting instructor the team had.

In the first five years, Bobby Doerr had the title, but he
wasn't around much. I loved the guy dearly, and he did a
tremendous job when he was there. He knew hitting. His
record speaks for itself on that. He was the star second
baseman for the Red Sox from the thirties right through
to the fifties. In Boston history only Ted Williams and
Carl Yastrzemski are even in the same league as Bobby in
every offensive category — hits, extra-base hits, homers,
RBI, total bases, you name it. But with his health the way
it was, and the health of his wife the way it was, Bobby
would be around for two weeks, then he'd be gone for a
month. Another coach would fill in — Dennis Menke,
later Jimy Williams — sometimes Bobby Mattick. You'd
have four different opinions coming at you. It was hitting
instruction by committee, which isn't good at all

You need a guy around who sees you all the time and
can work with you all the time. Cito's been great, helping
me change my style a few years ago. I used to have a
closed stance, but we experimented in spring training one
year and I opened up a bit and found I could see the ball
better and get my hips through the ball a lot better. That
year I put up some of the best offensive numbers I've ever
had. I've batted the same way ever since.

But hitting is also learning what the opposing pitcher
likes to throw in certain situations and being more selective at the plate. When I first came up, I was swinging at
everything. What Cito's always emphasized is having an
idea of what you want to do when you get up there and
waiting for the pitch you want. Naturally, if you're up

114

against a guy who throws breaking balls seventy per cent of the time, you'd be foolish to go up and sit on the fastball, because you might only see one fastball all night.

That's why it's so important to know what the pitcher is going to do, and in that area Cito has been exceptionally good. He'll look for little tip-offs, like maybe a finger flying up followed by a fastball. Then he'll watch again and see that the finger stays down and it's a breaking ball. With some pitchers, positioning in the glove gives you something to look for. If it's high in the glove, it's a changeup, low in the glove, it's a breaking ball. With others, it might be how far they open up the glove when they go into their motion. Anything that let's you know what's coming helps.

Hitting is timing, too, and if the stance is right and you even know what's coming but the timing's off, you're not going to hit the ball. When I'm rocking, I want to be rocking on the back foot as the pitcher is getting ready to release the ball, and I want to get cocked in that position so that the next natural motion is forward, creating the bat speed. If I'm caught between rocks, my hands aren't moving and I'm swinging from a set position. That makes the bat drag through the hitting area, and when the bat drags you can't get the pop out of it that you need.

There are certain pitchers who are very easy for me to time and others who are difficult, and with the tough guys I had to come up with a new system to time my pushback so that the head of the bat would get through the hitting area at the right moment.

We considered whether enforcing the balk rule was having an effect. I was having more problems with a pitcher out of the stretch than out of the windup. Out of the windup, pitchers were still consistent. In other years, a lot of pitchers would come, boom, right to the plate. When there was someone on base, the pitcher would change his motion, a lot of times speeding up rather than coming set and holding the ball. If he held the ball for a couple of seconds, either the hitter would back out or the pitcher would move off the rubber. This year, pitchers

115

were suddenly very conscious of having to come set, and it became more difficult to know when they were going to go into the stretch. Hitters had to learn their moves all over again.

But there's only so much you can do when you're in a slump. Coaches can sometimes emphasize mechanics too much and the player can think too much about rocking or where his hands are or where his feet are. When that happens, you lose concentration and the ball gets to you before you know it. At some point, you just have to go back to believing that if you concentrate on seeing the ball your natural abilities will take over and everything else will take care of itself.

It's funny how it goes. Once I worked through everything, I started hitting the ball as hard as I ever did, maybe harder. But they'd always seem to go right to somebody. Other batters would launch these soft bloopers, no power at all, and I'd look up and see their average was over .300 while mine was around .215. That can drive you crazy. You've just got to stay on an even keel knowing that sooner or later the hits will start dropping in. I'm an optimist, and tomorrow's always another day.

That kind of steady attitude, the feeling that the season is long and the sun's still going to come up in the east no matter what happens, is a hard thing for young players to learn, but it's one of the most important things to learn. There's no way an individual or a team can make it through 162 games without keeping a positive attitude. That's why encouragement, not finger-pointing and criticism, is so necessary for a team to play well.

And that's why I wasn't happy at the beginning of our home stand in Toronto to see some comments from Pat Gillick in the newspaper. He said that we were lucky to be only six and a half games out of first place, considering the way we'd been playing. He said he thought the younger guys had been been doing well and that "It's the experienced guys — Barfield, Moseby, and Whitt — who haven't been doing the job."

116

Before the game the next day, Fergie Olver, one of the TV colour commentators, interviewed me for the broadcast that night. His first question was, "What do you think about being criticized by the general manager?"

I said I was upset about Pat's comments and that I didn't think it was fair to single out three guys. I said I was the first to admit that I was struggling. I struggled last year, too, but this year it had been magnified because the team wasn't winning. Yet I hadn't criticized Pat for not having enough healthy players around to avoid playing a catcher and a DH at second base. End of interview.

As I was walking back, Jimy was standing by the batting cage with Pat and called me over.

Pat said, "I'm sick and tired of all this bullshit."

"I'm sick and tired of it too."

He said, "There're two guys on this team who criticized me to Ron Hassey when we were in Oakland. It got back to me."

"Which two guys?"

"Moseby and Bell."

"Did you talk to them?"

"No."

"Well, why don't you talk to them?"

The discussion was kind of animated. Pat was pointing a finger, I was gesturing with my hands, reporters seemed to be trying to get closer to hear what we were talking about.

I said, "I don't think you should have criticized me in the paper. I mean, this is a team concept here and you picked out three guys and nailed us to the wall."

"I'm sorry, but I was pissed off at the time."

"Well, if you're pissed off at two other guys, don't crucify me."

Anyway, we both apologized and said we wanted to put an end to all this stuff. When I saw Fergie, I asked him not to run the tape that night and he said, no problem, he'd cut the interview, and that was the end of that.

The next day, the papers were full of how Pat and I had had a heated, nose-to-nose argument, how he had

117

chewed me out over my performance and how I'd given it to him about all the things that seemed to be going wrong with the team. The whole incident was blown out of proportion. But the reporters seemed to think it was a good thing to get attitudes out in the open, and as evidence they talked about the game after Pat and I were through. I went 2-for-4, with an RBI single in the first inning, Kelly and Rance both homered, and Dave Stieb took a no-hitter into the eighth. We won 9 – 3.

I really don't think the talk behind the batting cage had anything to do with that result. The score probably had more to do with Dave's slider coming back and a hitters' meeting with Cito before the game. Not much good can come out of a negative experience. If there's one thing we've proved on the Blue Jays over the past few years, it's that only positive attitudes get results.

118 Every year for the first five years in spring training, the Blue Jays would have the meeting where the manager goes over the goals for the season. And every year, the sense we got as players was that the organization was just trying to field a product that wouldn't be an embarrassment to the owners, the management, or the city. It was always, "We don't want to lose a hundred games this year" or "We don't want to lose ninety games this year." There was always something we didn't want to do. There was an assumption that we were bound to lose and as long as we didn't become a laughing stock we'd be doing well.

So it was quite a surprise in the spring of 1982 when our new manager, Bobby Cox, spoke to us in the clubhouse in Dunedin. He said, "Okay, guys. Our goal this year is to win 85 games."

My mouth just dropped. I thought, "What? We're talking in a positive sense here? This man actually believes that we can win 85 games?" I was impressed.

Before that spring, I didn't really know much about him. I knew he had managed in Syracuse and I had seen him when the Chiefs played the Pawsox, but that was about it. Other players had told me that he was a players' manager, that he'd go to war for you if you didn't dog it in the field. And that's what I saw first-hand. He was someone you could respect as a boss and as an authority figure, but he was a good human being.

He had a good sense of humour, which helped in a lot of situations on and off the field. Coxy always stood up for his players with the umpires, for example, but unlike Bobby Mattick, he was a pretty good arguer. He could go out and really give an umpire a piece of his mind and get away with an awful lot because he did it the right way. He got his point across.

His humour could get him into trouble, though. One time we were all chirping a little bit from the bench, and Coxy was doing some bench jockeying himself, yelling at the umpire over a called strike. Drew Coble was behind the plate and he was in his first or maybe second year in the big leagues. He whipped off his mask and started coming over towards our bench. As soon as he got close, Coxy pointed to the line by the dugout and said, "Don't you come past that line." Coble just froze like he was wondering if maybe he wasn't allowed to step over. Coxy was just goofing around with him, but it caught him off guard. Then he looked at Coxy and started screaming at him, "Don't you tell me what I can and can't do!" Coxy was laughing at him, saying, "Hey, just relax."

When Coxy came on board, I really started to progress as a player. I started to become comfortable as a catcher because he made me feel comfortable with the position. He didn't put a lot of pressure on me. Compared to the two managers we'd had previously, he hadn't been out of the game that long and knew that a player would have good days and bad days. He understood. I always had the feeling with Mattick that if a player went 0-for-4, he could never be sure whether he was going to be in the lineup the next day. With Cox, I might go 0-for-4, but if there was a right-hander pitching the next day, I knew I wouldn't have to check the lineup when I got to the ball

119

park. I knew I'd be in the game. That helped me relax more than I could in the past.

It wasn't just me that felt that way, either. He made all the players feel more relaxed. With the positive outlook he brought to the team, a lot of things started to go in the right direction, though we still had a long way to go. He had to work with a lot of young players who were still learning. Moseby was only in his second full season. Barfield was up for his first full-time season and was platooning with Hosken Powell in right. Jimmy Clancy was really just coming into his own as a pitcher and had his first winning season.

There were a lot of players who were still "potential" big leaguers, and that first year it was almost like Coxy was just sitting back and watching the players, getting to know their abilities, getting to know their personalities. He had run-ins with Lloyd and a few of the others, mainly about not making an effort on the field, yet the

120 players respected him because they knew deep down that he was the main man, that there was no one else making decisions for him. And that carried a lot of weight. That carried an awful lot of weight with the players.

What was noticable was the farm system beginning to pay off. The process of younger players gradually working in with the veterans, making the transition from minor leaguers to bona fide big league players, was moving along. The other part of that process, of course, is that some veteran players were weeded out.

One veteran I was very sorry to see go in 1982 was John Mayberry. He was a funny guy. He was from Detroit, too, and I'll always remember when we would go into Tiger Stadium he'd say to me, "Well, got to hit some into the upper deck. The family's here." And it seemed like every time we'd go to Detroit, we'd both hit one up there. He had a lot of power. He had a delight in the game, too, despite all his years in it. With some players that seems to get ground out of them after a while, but not with John. I remember when he got his thirtieth home run in 1980, the first Blue Jay to hit that many. He was like an eight-year-old kid on Christmas morning, with a big smile I could see from the dugout as he went around the bases.

Big John didn't have the range at first base to make him an exceptional fielder, but he had real good hands, soft hands that would pick balls out of the dirt at first better than almost any other first baseman. He worked very hard with Willie Upshaw, knowing Willie was going to take his job from him. He was willing to share all the insights he'd acquired when he was with the Royals, where he'd had all his best years. He was a class act, and I think Willie would agree that he owes John an awful lot for the success that he's had.

With Willie taking over at first and Garth Iorg and Rance Mulliniks platooning at third, the corners were solid. And with Alfredo Griffin at short and Damaso Garcia at second, the middle infield was one of the best in the league. Alfredo was the iron man, out there every day making plays most shortstops only dream about. And Damo, when he wanted to play, was one of the best second basemen in the game. Fortunately, he wanted to play most of the time in 1982 and '83. In '82, he had his best year offensively, hitting .310, driving in 42 runs and stealing 54 bases. The next year, he almost matched those numbers, except for the steals. His knee was bothering him a lot, but he still manged to steal 31.

Our defence was getting better and we put some pretty good numbers up at the plate. 1982 was Cito Gaston's first year with the club, and our team average went from the .226 of 1981 to .262. I had my best year up to that point, hitting .261 with 42 RBI and 11 home runs. In '83, my average dropped a bit to .256, but I had 17 homers and 56 RBI, fourth highest on the team. And the team average of .277 that year was the best in the league.

The pitching staff was still a problem, though. The starting rotation was getting better. Dave Stieb had become one of the dominant pitchers in the league. He won 17 games for us in both '82 and '83. Jim Clancy put two very strong years together. And Luis Leal, after two not very good years under Bobby Mattick, started to become

121

the dependable third or fourth starter he would be for several years.

Luis had a good arm and a good slider, but he had to have everything working for him to be effective. He had a Luis Tiant-style of pitching, sneaky quick, but he was always afraid to pitch inside, which is something you have to do to win in the major leagues. You have to keep the hitters honest. With Luis, it seemed whenever I'd call for an inside pitch, he would leave it out over the plate, and that's a cardinal sin. If you're going to miss with an inside pitch, you have to miss with it off the plate towards the hitter. The ball that misses down the middle is the ball that's hit hard.

Luis was such a nice guy, a quiet, polite gentleman who was tremendously popular with the fans in Venezuela when he played with his home-town Cardinales de Lara. He was always one of my favourite people, an enjoyable man to be around. I rarely saw him get upset about anything, although once, after he had a terrible day and had been pulled out in the first inning, a local columnist wrote that because it was Submarine Sandwich Day at the park Luis probably wanted to get back to the clubhouse to get his hands on the food. He really took offence to that and was all over the reporter the next day. It was an insult he didn't like or deserve.

Luis was a good pitcher, but I thought he could have been a much better one. He always worked hard in a game and worked extremely hard between starts. He'd throw harder than any of our other starters and work on different things more than anyone else. Sometimes I thought he would throw too much on the side, up to half an hour at a time, which is an awful lot for a guy who pitches every four days. But he had success doing it. He pitched well for many years until he lost his slider, which was one of his best pitches. I don't know what happened to it. He just suddenly couldn't throw it for strikes anymore. It stopped being a good, hard, tight, spin slider like he'd had previously. Once he lost that, he wasn't able to adjust to anything else and eventually worked himself right out of the big leagues.

Other than Dave, Jim, and Luis, Coxy had trouble finding a consistent starter. Jim Gott was a starter for a while, then he was moved to middle relief, then short relief as the organization tried to find a position for him. He had a strong arm, but his control wasn't that good. He had a hard time throwing strikes.

But the team's biggest problem was with the bullpen. It seems almost funny to think of it now, after Tom Henke alone got 34 saves in 1987, but in 1982 the entire Blue Jay relief staff managed 25 saves. The next year, the figure got up to 32, with Randy Moffitt accounting for ten of them.

Back when Mattick was managing, Joey McLaughlin was the main man in the bullpen. Joey was a fastball, knuckle-curve, changeup pitcher who came over from the Atlanta Braves with Barry Bonnell before the 1980 season. With the offence we had then, he didn't get all that many save opportunities in his first year with the club, and when he did get the opportunity, he didn't do much with it. His best year was the split 1981 season. He had a losing record (1 – 5), but he got his ERA down to 2.85 and managed 10 of the 18 saves the bullpen got that year.

When Bobby Cox took over, Joey was still one of the mainstays in relief, along with Roy Lee Jackson and Dale Murray. Coxy went to him a lot over the next couple of years, although with less and less confidence. It got to the point in later years that whenever Joey came in, you could almost hear a gasp or a groan from the fans in Toronto. We kind of felt the same way in the dugout.

To me, Joey was a pessimist. He never had a lot of confidence in himself, and if there's one thing a pitcher can't do on the mound it's doubt his own ability. I hate to hear my kids, my teammates, or anyone else use the word "can't," and I certainly never want to hear it from any pitcher I'm handling. I believe that if you set your mind to something and work hard enough you can do anything

123

you want to do. Whatever anyone else says, if you keep a positive attitude and keep trying you'll achieve your goal. Joey never had that attitude. He was always a negative pitcher, and it showed in his performances.

Roy Lee Jackson had a different kind of attitude problem. Overall, Roy Lee did a good job for us. One game he pitched really sticks out in my mind, and that was against Detroit. We were leading when Roy Lee faced Dave Bergman, and the two of them got quite a duel going. Bergman fouled off twelve or thirteen pitches, all really nasty pitches right where we wanted to pitch to him. The fourteenth pitch Bergman took into the upper deck to beat us, but the confrontation itself was a classic, one of Roy Lee's gutsiest performances.

A lot of the time, though, Roy Lee seemed to be too laid back, without the drive and desire and competitiveness a pitcher needs on the mound. He was very deeply into his religion, and his beliefs started affecting his work **124** habits in a negative way. He felt that the Lord would take care of him, so there was no need to worry. Whether he worked hard or not, God's plan for him would unfold.

I had some trouble coming to terms with some of the attitudes and practices Roy Lee was spreading around the team. It wasn't that I felt he was wrong in bringing religion into the clubhouse. We've always had a lot of Christian players on the Blue Jays and still have from ten to twelve guys out after batting practice every Sunday morning for Baseball Chapel. I know there are managers around the league who think worship belongs someplace else, but with all the travelling that we do, players need their own non-denominational place to congregate and get their minds off the game for a while and onto something bigger than themselves. Baseball Chapel serves that purpose. Whether we're at home or on the road, we have speakers who come, usually into the weight room, to talk and pray with us for a few minutes, then speak to the visiting team as well. There's a Chapel co-ordinator in every city so that services are always available.

I was instrumental in setting up the Chapel in Syracuse when I was with the Chiefs and have served as Chapel leader in Toronto as well. So I certainly had no objection to Roy Lee organizing Bible study groups or preaching the gospel. But I disagreed with some of the things he was telling the players.

I remember seeing a quote from the Dodger's Orel Hershiser, who said, "Just because I'm a Christian doesn't mean I'm a wimp." What I think he meant was that he would do anything on the mound to get the job done. He was getting paid to get hitters out, and if that meant always being tough or even knocking a batter down, he would do it. He would always be out there battling.

Roy Lee didn't always battle. He seemed to give too much up to the Lord, and that had a negative effect on his numbers and on the team. He seemed to promote a kind of "don't worry about it" attitude about a lot of things. A poor performance on the field? It's all part of the plan. Spend money on expensive clothes or jewellery? God wants you to have it. You won't be in baseball forever.

He was always trying to convert people to his beliefs and get them to pray together and speak in tongues. I know he and his wife put quite an effort into converting Joey and Robin McLaughlin. Then he and Jesse Barfield became inseparable. Gradually, I could see Jesse changing. I had known him since Instructional League as a very hard worker, but I saw him slack off a little bit.

I asked him about it, and he said, "The Lord's going to take care of me."

I said, "That's fine. The Lord's going to take care of me too, but He put us on this earth to work hard. He gave us arms and legs so we could achieve things. We're not going to get things handed to us on a silver platter. God gave us this talent and it's up to us to bust our butts every day to push on with it."

I could never decide whether Roy Lee's influence was good or bad in the long-run. Jesse's still a very religious man, but thankfully he got his good work habits back.

125

Tony Fernandez is the same way, a man who gives all praises to God, but who works hard all the time at improving himself. With Tony, Roy Lee seemed to have a positive effect, really helping him cope with injuries and personal losses in his family when Tony was just coming up. But on the field, Roy Lee did a pretty good job. His ERA slipped from 3.06 to 4.50 over 1982–83, although he got it back to 3.56 in '84.

When Joey and Roy Lee declined in '83, Randy Moffitt and Dave Geisel got almost half the bullpen's saves. Randy was very effective, but Dave I remember more for his investment schemes than for his work on the mound. He'd always be hanging up maps in the clubhouse to show us where oil fields were located off the coast of Texas. All that I and a few other players had to do once we sunk our money into these wells was wait for them to come on-stream, then sit back and watch the royalties pour in. I was just starting to make good money then, and I hadn't invested any of it. Chris and I talked it over and decided to give Dave the cash to drill those wells. Four or five other players chipped in too. Every month, we'd get a royalty check, but it always seemed to be for $10 or $12. I said, "Dave, when's the money going to be rolling in?" He kept saying that I should wait and they'd start producing. We lost about $7,500.

I don't know whether it was just a coincidence, but in 1983, Mr. Hardy asked me if I would be his guinea-pig in a financial program he was developing. He said he was concerned about players making so much money, not doing anything but spending it or giving it over to others to invest, then finding themselves out of the game with nothing to fall back on. Around that time, there were a lot of stories about some agents putting players' money into shaky investments. Guys who had played ten years in the big leagues for good dollars were filing for bankruptcy. So Mr. Hardy explained that the club was going to work with a financial services firm, the Etherington Group, to help players with their financial planning, and the club would pick up half the cost. He asked me to go through the procedure and report back to the club on how helpful it was.

The idea sounded good to me. I'd always been conservative about money. I always worked when I was in school, and when I was in the minor leagues I'd work in the off-season with my uncle's towing company or a replacement door and window outfit owned by Chris's uncle. In the minors, I never made over $1,500 a month for five months of the year, so off-season income was essential.

We would sometimes supplement my pay by bowling. Back when Chris and I were dating, we'd go up to Frontier Lanes in Mt. Clemens where they'd have the "moonlight doubles" on Saturday nights. All the lights in the bowling alley, except the pin lights, were turned off and couples would bowl for prizes. Chris was a decent bowler and I could bowl a 200 game with no problem so long as I popped my thumb out of the hole, as Chris was forever telling me. We won first place three or four times. There'd sometimes be jackpots, too, and I'd win a couple of them every Saturday. We'd come away with $200 or so, more than some people made in a week in those days. We'd also time our drives to spring training to stop off in Cincinnatti for the Hoinke Tournament, one of the biggest on the circuit. I could make a couple of thousand dollars every year in bowling tournaments.

And for a couple of years I was paid as the assistant coach of the Macomb College basketball team, but I don't even remember how much I made. I wasn't doing that for the money. I was helping out my friend, Bernie Lemieux, the head coach. I was staying in shape, and I was having a wonderful time. A couple of times, Bernie left me to coach the game on my own, once up in Alpena, Michigan, where the refs come out of the backwoods and are known for doing anything to make sure the home team wins. In that game, we were up by 20 points with three minutes to go and lost. If the ball ever got near one of my players, some violation was called. One of my guys took a pass, and as soon as he touched the ball, he was called for double-dribbling. The other game I coached was in a tournament in Ohio where we lost by one point in the last minute against the number two ranked college team in the country. It was thrilling. Not well-paid, but fun.

Despite the low pay back then, I was still able to buy a home for my family, a cute, three-bedroom brick house in Roseville. We ate a lot of Hamburger Helper, and Chris wore the same dress to church every Sunday, more as a joke after a while than out of necessity, but we never wanted for anything. Chris always said we were both magicians. I could turn a dollar into a hundred dollars while she could make a dollar disappear. It's funny how attitudes change. In the "moonlight doubles" all she wanted was the trophy, and I wanted the money. Now she keeps track of the dollars while all I want is a couple of new rings, one for winning the AL pennant, one for the World Series.

That I'm secure enough to concentrate on getting those rings I owe to the program Mr. Hardy started. A financial planner from the Etherington Group, John Boville, met with Chris and me to go over our budgets, what we needed in the future for the kids, where we wanted to be when I got out of the game. I was impressed, especially by the fact that the group was basically in the insurance business and never once asked me to buy insurance.

I reported back to Mr. Hardy and every year after, the group would come and present the program to the players. I think over the years that only about half a dozen Blue Jays have used the program, which is frightening in a way. Some of them are making very good money, but are collecting all of it now. I'm afraid to think of what might happen to them when they leave baseball. It's got to be tough going from $900,000 a year to maybe $60,000 if you're lucky

I know that my future is set. John Boville split off from the Etherington Group and set up PlanVest, which works with a number of players. With John's help, we've worked out a plan where we live on a fixed income of twenty per cent of my salary, with the rest deferred to later years. I look on that as my retirement money, so that we can live on at least the same income as we live on now for twelve years or more after I get out of the game. Along with an accountant, Norm Allen, and an operating manager, Jim Dimitroff, John is also one of my partners in Aldwych Management Inc., which owns and operates fifteen "Mother's Pizza" franchises. We felt that we could capitalize on my name in southwest Ontario, do some promotional events like special dinners and give-aways of autographed balls or gloves and turn the restaurants into more profitable enterprises. We offered investment units to other guys on the team and several showed some interest. Lloyd Moseby and Rick Leach, for example, both came in on the venture. It was through our "Mother's" group that we acquired the southwest Ontario franchising rights for "The Country's Best Yogurt" chain, which is operated out of Little Rock, Arkansas.

With the investments in food and my other ventures with a number of different partners, I know I can leave the game with a lot to show for my career and never have to worry about the bill collector coming to the door. I sometimes wonder where I would be if that program hadn't opened my eyes to looking to the future. It really turned things around for me and my family, and it was typical of the way the Blue Jays organization operates. I've had my disagreements with front office over negotiations, but that's just business. The organization has always treated me well.

My finances turned around that year, and so did the team. We suddenly became a contender for the division title. At the beginning of June, we were in first place by half a game. That same month we acquired a new pitcher, Doyle Alexander, who went on to win seven games for us that year. On July 1, we were leading by two games. By the end of August, we had slipped out of the lead, but were only one and a half back. We were getting excited, the fans were smelling "pennant" and the papers were full of us being the Cinderella team.

129

Then it all fell apart, and I remember the night it happened. We were in Baltimore and tied the game in the ninth. In extras innings, the Orioles made a change because they had sent in a pinch runner for the catcher, and Len Sakata was behind the plate. Tippy Martinez came in to pitch. Our first hitter got on first and Martinez picked him off. The next hitter got on and he picked him off, too. The next hitter, same thing. Even with being a left-hander, there was no way Martinez could have picked them off legally. The last runner, Barry Bonnell, had only taken a one-step lead-off. Every one of those pick-offs was an obvious balk, but the umpire wouldn't call it. In the Orioles half, Len Sakata hit a home run off Randy Moffitt to win the game.

It seemed like that was the end of the year for us. We went into Detroit and lost one-run ball games in our final at-bats. It was in that series that Roy Lee had his confrontation with Dave Bergman, giving up a three-run homer in the bottom of the ninth. The next day, Joey McLaughlin gave up a homer in the ninth. We just seemed to go downhill after that. We finished in fourth, nine games behind Baltimore, but for the first time we had won more than we had lost. We had played .549 ball, and would never see a sub-.500 season again.

On May 18, 1988, we lost 4 – 0 to the Rangers in Texas. The loss put us at 16 – 23, seven games under .500, the first time we had sunk so low since 1982.

That game was tough on Todd Stottlemyre. He had struck out eight over six innings, but gave up two home runs in the seventh to get his fifth loss on the year. In those five losses, we'd managed to score a total of six runs. The game was tough on all the players, and it must have been tough for Jimy Williams. Every newspaper in Toronto was calling for him to be fired and one of the papers was running a readers' poll on the question.

By May 30, after series against Milwaukee, Texas, and Chicago, we had added five games to the win column to

130

go with six more losses. Something had to happen, and something did. Juan Beniquez was released.

Juan thought that he was being made a scapegoat and left with some pretty harsh statements about the organization. He felt the coaches were against him for trying to help out some of the younger players with their hitting and he seemed to think that both Jimy and Pat Gillick were against him.

I thought Juan's fate was sealed in the game in Seattle when he said he couldn't play third base or the outfield and forced Jimy to use Pat and Cecil at second. Quite a few players expected that he wouldn't be around long when that happened. He was a very good and experienced pinch hitter coming off the bench, but with a 24-man roster it's hard to carry a guy who can only pinch hit and that's all Juan said he could do. As for the coaches being against him, I guess he meant Cito, and if that was the case Juan had brought that on himself by going behind Cito's back. George Bell has always worked with some of the younger Latin players, kicking them in the butt if he thought they'd done something wrong, not letting them slack up, but he has always been up-front about it. He'd be out at the batting cage, giving a few pointers, then saying to Cito, "Do you think that might help?" Juan didn't do that. He'd tell them things that might or might not have been in conflict with what Cito was telling them. Cito's very open-minded and if Juan had been up-front Cito would have listened.

I liked Juan and respected him as a hitter. I'd played with him on the Red Sox in 1976. But when a guy moves around from team to team, you have to wonder that maybe something's wrong somewhere. Why does no team want him for any length of time? To me, he was pretty much of a loner and he never bothered me at all. But I think he had a negative influence on some of the young Latin players. He was often huddled with them in a corner, saying I don't know what. I'm sure they looked up to a veteran like him with so many years in the big

131

leagues, and sometimes they'd get rebellious and not work as hard as they should or complain more than they should. I can't put all that on Juan's shoulders, but maybe he made them feel they could get away with certain things. It's just speculation, but maybe in spring training, Juan's first with the Blue Jays, he thought about Mr. Hardy's dinner and said, "I'm not going to that thing, you guys are crazy if you go." I don't know that he said anything like that, but the incident happened and it drove a wedge into the team.

No one is happy to see a player leave, especially if his path goes right out of the game. But not too many were upset the day Juan left. Juan seemed pretty cheerful himself. He got the news, as always, after the game, and when he finished talking with Jimy he came back into the clubhouse, went up to every player, shook hands and wished us all well. I probably would have handled it differently, but I guess you get used to it after it happens eight times.

132   We were happy to see Cecil get the chance to be the right-handed DH, though. Some fans seemed to think that the move meant that management had given up on us for the year. Releasing a guy hitting .290 and keeping another hitting .167 didn't calculate properly. But we felt Cecil had been working hard in batting practice, had been swinging the bat well, and just needed some playing time.

Our bats were starting to come alive anyway but, again, hitting doesn't win ball games. We were near the top of the league in runs scored, but we were just as high in the standings in runs allowed. Jim Clancy was really struggling and we were still missing Jimmy Key and Jeff Musselman. What we needed to get us going was a strong performance from one of our starters.

We got one. If there was a perfect way to end the month, it was to see the dominant Dave Stieb of a few years ago come back. On May 31, Dave pitched a super game against the Brewers that we won 9 – 0. He had all his pitches and threw all of them well, except for one slider that didn't go where it was supposed to. B. J.

Surhoff singled, ending Dave's try for a no-hitter. It would have been his first, the Blue Jays' first, and the first that I would have caught in the major leagues. But we had to be happy with the win and very happy with the first one-hitter of Dave's career.

June

The date kind of sneaked up on me. I wasn't really aware of it ahead of time, but the game we played against Milwaukee on the first day of June was my 1,000th game in a Blue Jays uniform. Only Lloyd Moseby and Willie Upshaw have been in more games. It's a very special feeling to be with one organization for such a long time, especially one like the Blue Jays. I've been very fortunate in my career that both organizations I've played for have been class acts all the way. And it's a special feeling when I think back to the years of differences with Roy Hartsfield and realize that I've outlasted the 18 other catchers who've worked behind the plate for the Jays before this season. I'm proud of that.

After going back over all the years of my career with reporters in Toronto, it seemed somehow appropriate that when we left for a road trip on June 2, the first stop was Fenway Park. The series was going to be a real test of our new attitudes and desire. We had never done extremely well in Boston — 25 – 42 over our 11 seasons — and we were going up against Hurst, Boyd, and Clemens, their three best pitchers.

Catch

We're a good fastball hitting club, so we weren't too worried about Roger. We've usually done pretty well against him. Hurst could have been more of a problem, but the Red Sox were going into Yankee Stadium after our series and McNamara wanted Bruce to pitch there, so we faced him in the Thursday night game, rather than in either the Saturday or Sunday day games. He's always been tough on us anyway, but his record in day games at Fenway is unbelievable. It's always hard to hit there in the day because the ball comes out of the white shirts in the centre field bleachers and it's very difficult to pick up. With Hurst, it's even more difficult. I think he's won every day game he's pitched against us there. But we beat him that night.

In my first at-bat against Oil Can in the Friday night game, I hit one hard and it headed toward the right-field foul pole I'd lit up with my first big league hit twelve years ago. It fell short and was caught, but a run scored from third. We added a few more and drove Boyd from the game. The Red Sox brought in Dennis Lamp in relief.

It was getting to be like old home week. Lampy was on the mound and behind the plate was Rick Cerone, a guy who seems to have more lives than a cat. After he left Toronto, he really had only one good year with the Yankees then struggled the rest of the way. I think Boston just took a chance on signing him when Rich Gedman got hurt, then when he played good ball in AAA, the Red Sox called him up. And here he was in early June going with every pitch and hitting .350. He was just having that type of year.

Having seen so many of Dennis Lamp's pitches should have made it easier for me to get a hit off him, but he struck me out. I knew him as a sinkerball pitcher, very successful when he got the ball down at the knees, but he always had trouble throwing a fastball in on a left-handed batter. He wasn't able to keep us honest off the plate. This night, he went and threw a fastball up and in on me for a strike. I had to swing at it. As I ran past him on the way to the dugout, I yelled, "When did you start being able to control that pitch?" He just laughed. I think he knew that we knew that he couldn't get the ball in there, so he got a couple of us out with that pitch.

We beat Oil Can, Roger, and Bruce and started thinking "sweep," something we had never accomplished in Boston, although we had swept the Red Sox three times at Exhibition Stadium. I hated to think about it, but the way things had been going for us I wondered whether in the last game Jeff Sellers, who was 0 – 5 at the time, would beat Dave Stieb, who was becoming the ace of our staff. It's a crazy game. But I didn't have to worry. Sellers couldn't find the strike zone and walked in a couple of runs, then Mike Smithson came in. I singled one off his leg to drive in a run and he gave up four more over the next couple of innings. Dave didn't last past the fifth, and Eichhorn, Wells, and Ward all took a turn. We won 12 – 4.

Taking all four games got more confidence flowing, but there was still an uneasiness on the club. Wells and Ward were still having a hard time with location. They couldn't get the ball in the zones where we wanted to pitch certain hitters. There was some uncertainty about both John Cerutti and Jose Nunez, as well as Mark Eichhorn.

137

Mark was between roles. He had been set-up man for Tom Henke for a couple of years but really had no set job in 1988. His problem started when the batters caught up to his sidearm delivery. In 1986, when he worked his way onto the team in spring training, he was incredible, winning 14 games and getting 10 saves. His ERA that year — 1.72 — set a team record. But in 1987, he had to start doing things a little differently because he had to work on his pick-off move. He hadn't been holding anyone on first and whenever he came into a game, the runner would go with the first pitch. I think I threw out only one runner when Mark was pitching in the whole 1987 season. It was a real problem for the coaches, because speeding up his motion could take away from his pitching ability. But you can't let guys run wild on the bases. When a pitcher can't hold the runner, it puts a lot of pressure on the defence. And in a close game, the manager is almost forced to make a pitching change if there are no outs and a runner with only average speed gets on first. You can't give the guy second base free.

I was sorry to see Mark lose the role of set-up man for Tom Henke, which he had played very effectively. There was good contrast there, with Mark getting slower, slower, slower, while Tom came in with nothing but power. That gave the hitters something to think about and adjust to. This year, with Wells, Ward, and Henke all throwing the ball hard, there was no contrast at all.

If there was some uneasiness about our offence, it was mainly because Jesse Barfield still wasn't swinging well. But at least two guys were picking up the slack. If Fred McGriff and Kelly Gruber had played in 1987 like they were playing in 1988, we would have had a cake-walk through the division. It always takes players time to put everything together, though, and this year they started playing super.

138   Kelly's inexperience in the field at the beginning of the '87 season cost us some games, and he hadn't learned to hit big league pitching at the time, but he always had the tools to be a great ball player. He cut his swing down tremendously this season, staying behind the ball instead of trying to jerk or pull it all the time, and he started to go up to the plate with an idea of the pitch he wanted. Freddie had a good rookie season in '87, with 20 home runs, but he wasn't hitting for average as he was this year. He's probably got the best eye of anyone on the club. He knows the strike zone extremely well and very seldom swings at a bad pitch. He hangs in tough against left-handed pitchers, and he's so damned strong that he can get jammed and still hit one off the wall.

My own average was inching up in June. It was still low, but when the weather gets warmer I do, too. Averages can get turned around in a week, and what I look at more is the RBI totals. I usually come through in the crunch and so usually have pretty good numbers, whatever my average is. Since 1982, I've always been sixth or seventh on the team in terms of RBI, as high as fourth a couple of times, which is good for someone on a team with a lot of fine hitters and who doesn't get a chance to play every day. When we were in Boston, a reporter mentioned to me that catcher was the most potent position on the team offensively, as it had been the month before. I had 19 RBI at the time and Pat Borders had 15 or 16, so our totals were up there.

Pat's the best right-handed hitting catcher this organization's ever had. Only a couple of months into the season and he was hitting about .270 and had already surpassed the total RBI of right-handers in the 1987 catching platoon. That's why it almost floored me when he came up to me in early June and said, "What do I have to do to stay in the big leagues?"

I like what I see in him. He's young, he's enthusiastic, and he's a gamer. He's really a tough kid. He goes up to the plate very aggressively, and he doesn't get cheated on any of the swings. He swings hard. But I told him, "If you drive in a lot of runs, that's great. But that's extra. Your number one priority is your catching duties."

There was some room for improvement defensively. Being in the platoon situation where the communication just has to be there, I felt kind of like a teacher for him. In all his little league and minor league experience, he'd only caught about a hundred games, so if I saw him doing something not quite right, I'd mention it to him. We talked constantly. He's very coachable. Say something to him and he puts it into effect immediately and continues to work hard on it. He's always trying to improve, and managers and coaches like that in a player as much as I do.

He already blocked balls well, although sometimes, maybe from lack of concentration, a ball would get past him. He just had to learn to set up in such a way that he could get his whole body in front of the pitch. One thing we talked about was not trying to set up too soon, especially with a runner on second base. Every team tries to cheat a little bit, to take advantage of the other team by stealing a sign or the location of a pitch and transmitting

139

it to the batter. With a runner on second, the catcher has to set up down the middle of the plate and stay there as long as he possibly can before moving inside or outside. That way the runner doesn't have a chance to pass on any information.

What he mainly had to work on was receiving the ball properly. His throwing was fine. He's got a good arm, although his accuracy was sometimes a problem. When a catcher rushes a throw, he gets into trouble. It's all timing. You have to have quick feet and quick hands and get them working together. If you rush, your feet are out in front of your hands and all of a sudden your shoulder's going to fly open and the ball's going to sail on you or sink. To keep everything coordinated, you have to establish a rhythm and maintain it consistently. Receive the ball, throw it. Receive the ball, throw it. That's hard to maintain when you see a guy get a big jump at first or if you're working with a pitcher who doesn't get the ball to **140** you quickly. With experience, you learn to keep that rhythm and you learn, as the saying goes in baseball, to stay within yourself — you do what you're capable of doing and try not to do more than that. If you try to do more than what you're capable of doing, you're going to get into trouble.

Right from the start of the season, Pat was calling a pretty good game, and that's because we always study the opposing hitters and try to pitch to their weaknesses. You can get carried away with that, though. If a batter is a good low ball, fastball hitter and you have a fastball pitcher on the mound whose strength is keeping the ball down, you have to go with what's strongest for your pitcher. It's power against power and the best man's going to win. Usually it's the pitcher.

It's very tough to tell a low ball pitcher to throw the ball high in the strike zone and get away with it. Sometimes you do have to try to get the pitcher to go out of his strength when certain situations arise, like when a hitter makes an adjustment in the box. Frank White with the Royals, for example, will move in the box and you have to watch him all the time. He's a first ball, high ball, fast-ball hitter who likes the ball down the middle of the plate. At times, he'll move his feet a little differently and a catcher has to pick up on that and think, "Wait a minute. He's not trying to pull the ball. He's trying to hit it the opposite way." So you have to change your thinking and come up with a new game plan on the spot.

You also have to adjust your thinking when a hitter is sitting on a pitch. Throw somebody two fastballs down the middle of the plate and he takes them both for strikes, you'd be doing him a favour to throw him the breaking ball. Same with a runner at second with nobody out. In that situation, the hitter should be hitting to the right side to advance the runner to third and, with a right-handed hitter, you have to put down the sign to make the hitter pull the ball to keep the runner where he is.

At times, the pitcher will shake you off and you have to go out to the mound and explain your thinking. At that point, you've done your job as a catcher. If the pitcher still feels he wants to go a different way, then fine. To me, a catcher suggests the game, but the pitcher has the final say. The game can't start until he releases the ball.

141

I've heard managers and coaches say, "You've got to make him throw a certain pitch." To me, that's totally wrong. I would much rather have a pitcher give me one hundred per cent on a pitch he's confident about throwing than to make him throw a pitch he's not too sure of and so may only give me seventy per cent effort on. I've seen that happen too many times. You can almost see in the windup that he doesn't really want to throw the pitch you've called. Then he ends up hanging a breaking ball, the hitter takes it over the wall and all the second guessing starts. The pitcher wonders, "Why in the world did I throw that pitch?" and he loses some confidence in the catcher.

It's a working process, and the more you work with a pitcher, the more you feel comfortable with what he's going to throw. It becomes a smoother operation. When the pitcher and catcher are working extremely well together, that's when the fun starts. It's the most exciting thing in the game. It's a real challenge being in the heat of a confrontation. Setting up every batter is like a little skirmish in one battle of a 162-game war. The tougher the situation, the more fun it gets.

When Minnesota came into Toronto in April, we got into a really tight situation. We were up 2 – 0 in the top of the eighth, two outs, the Twins had the bases loaded and Gary Gaetti came up to bat. Gaetti's a tremendous hitter, a dead fastball hitter who can hit over 30 home runs a year. Tom Henke was on the mound, a fastball pitcher, so it was power against power. We've come to the conclusion that we're very successful throwing Gaetti nothing but off-speed pitches, the slower the better. So we threw him nothing but changeups.

We worked the count to 2-and-2 and I thought, "Okay, let's let him see the fastball. Nothing he can hit, but a fastball up and away and maybe he'll swing at it." He took it for a ball. Tom looked in and I thought, "Perfect timing." The runners would be going on the 3-and-2 pitch and from a pitcher like Tom, Gaetti would be thinking fastball all the way because a walk would bring in a run.

142

I have confidence in Tom Henke throwing any pitch he has at any time. I put down a changeup. Tom didn't hesitate. He wound up, threw the changeup and Gaetti had the bat around before the ball got near the plate. Gaetti was really hopping. He snapped his bat away and started screaming at Tom, "A big guy like you, you got to challenge a hitter."

But we'd won the skirmish, and that's when you feel really good. You've accomplished something and you think, "Wow, that was great." Of course, he could have hit a home run and then you'd think, "Shit, what did I call that pitch for?" That's happened a lot, too, and you have to learn to take that in stride.

Having an experienced pitching staff like we have on the Blue Jays helps a catcher who is just learning the job. They know how they want to throw to certain hitters and what they like to throw in certain situations. Working with them, Pat's pitch selection in most cases was very good. What was a bad situation, I felt, was that Pat caught the first two or three games that Todd Stottlemyre pitched. Here were two guys learning the game in the big leagues on a team that was supposed to win. It didn't work out too well.

Before the games, I'd sit with them off in a corner and try to help them out with a game plan, pointing out the hitters' weaknesses, telling Todd, "Your fastball's got good movement. Try not to pick the corners early in the count. Go right after the hitter. You try to throw the ball down the middle of the plate and nine times out of ten it's going to sail or sink off to the corner one way or another. So try not to be too fine and get yourself behind in the count. Strike one on the hitter, be aggressive. Utilize all your pitches." When the pitcher doesn't have big league experience, it puts an awful lot of pressure on the catcher to remember all the information he has to keep stored upstairs.

143

They'll work it out. They're learning and they'll give the Blue Jays a lot of good years. There's a lot of talent on this team and there's an awful lot of potential talent. It will just take some time to get the mesh right. It'll take time to get it right in the clubhouse, too, and that's something the team is going to have to think about. A team that gets along will win an extra five or six games a year because when you get out on the field, you're pulling for each other. You want competition on the team, yet you want that closeness, that pulling for the other guy. And that's something I didn't see this season. The camaraderie seemed like it was a lot better in the past. The friendships on the team aren't the way I'd like to see them.

We always used to get there at 2:30 or 3:00 and we'd look at videotapes of the opposing team, study the charts we have on every hitter, going back two years in some cases. We'd check box scores and see who was on a roll. We'd always have a card game going. I don't know the reason for it, but if we're supposed to be dressed at five, some guys now come in at ten to, leaving them just enough time to pull their uniforms on and get out onto the field. After the game, it's the same way. We used to sit around — and there still are a few guys who'll stay — and have a couple of beers and talk about what we did, what we could do to improve, certain pitches that were thrown, certain pitches that were hit, certain situations that came up and we didn't execute like we should have. That's the way it should be. Baseball's as much observation as skill and execution.

Now that's like a lost art. Guys just don't put an effort into it any more. It seems like they're there from five until whenever the game ends, and then it's a mad rush to the showers to get out of there and get home. There's no one hanging around the clubhouse any more, and that's where knowledge gets passed around.

In the minor leagues, we'd sit around and talk about the game until two or three in the morning, sometimes. The next day we'd get up and have lunch together, then **144** go to the ball park together. We all had the same goal and we were competing for the same chance to make it to the big leagues, but the minor league teams were closely knit with the players and even the players' families. We used to always have get-togethers where the players, their wives or girlfriends, and their kids would have a barbeque at one house one day then at someone else's house the next.

You can't expect to have the close-knit feeling in the big leagues that you do in the minors. There's more of a distant, business-like atmosphere and that's to be expected. Players are older, they're more involved with their growing families, they're concerned about investments and businesses they've got going. Players are busy, and I'm the same way, but still, you've got to get your priorities straight. And your priorities have got to be baseball first, before any other business.

The sad part is that it's the kids, the rookies just coming up, who are there at ten minutes to five just in time to get dressed. To me, they're not going to learn by doing that. It takes a great individual to be able to play baseball well without help from his coaches and his teammates, and there are not that many greatly talented people out there.

You can learn an awful lot just sitting around talking about the opposing team or what you would do in a certain situation. I've always believed that a smart player is a better player than a player with an awful lot of ability who doesn't use his head. A smart player thinks of what he's going to do in a certain situation before it happens. Then once it does happen, he has the ability to make a split-second judgement. It becomes instinctive. Sometimes the players blessed with great ability have that instinct naturally or are able to acquire it on their own, but not all the time. Having talent is not enough. Even naturals have to work.

But work ethics aren't the same as when I broke in, either. Then, if you were a rookie, you were the first one on the field and the last one off. You did work. There were lots of drills and you worked hard at them, giving **145** everything you've got. Now there are a few drills and the rookies seem to go through them at half motion. They do in spring training, too, and then wonder, "Why didn't I make the team?" The veterans sometimes aren't any better. People just don't seem to go about their jobs as hard as they should, and that's one of the reasons why both leagues have a few superstars and a lot of mediocre players.

Those kinds of new attitudes are changing the game, too. It used to be that if a player got a lot of hits, he'd expect to be brushed back from the plate or even be hit with a pitch. That seems to have gone out of the game. Now if a guy gets a couple of hits or a home run and the pitcher throws the ball inside on him in his next at-bat, he gets all upset and wants to fight. That doesn't make sense. It's crazy. I'm a firm believer, and always have been, that you've got to pitch inside to win. You have to establish the inside part of the plate. And sometimes it's necessary to hit someone, not to hurt him, but to deliver a message. It might be to protect one of your own players or to give a batter who gets hit after hit after hit a little something else to think about. It's a purpose pitch. I've never called for a pitcher to hit a batter in the head. I won't tolerate that. No player should tolerate that. You're talking about a life there. It's dangerous. But I have called for pitchers to hit a batter. A pitch in a guy's butt or rib cage is a bruise. We all get bruises.

I don't know why the closeness isn't what it should be. I just know I look at an organization like the Tigers, battling the Yankees for first place in June, and see that there's no way Detroit has a better team than we do. Yet the Tigers have a better record over the past five years, the only team in either league that does have a better record than ours over that time. The Tigers didn't have a better team in 1987, either, yet we lost to them when it came down to the last day.

No way they've got a better team, but they play with a lot of heart. They've got veterans, young guys, some cast-offs from other organizations who know they might be getting their last shot. They play with determination. I don't know whether it's Sparky's doing or Bill Lajoie's or the players' themselves. I just look at them and see a close-knit ball club, then I look at our ball club and it's just not there.

When we were in Boston, a few of us went out to dinner together. We had gone out once before in Chicago, too, just to spend some time together and talk about what we could do to pull out the rest of the season. It wasn't any one person's idea. It was just a bunch of guys getting together. It was relaxed and everybody had a good time, so we tried to institutionalize it a bit. I feel that the team that does some things together off the field will be a better team on the field. There's a greater feeling of unity, a closer feeling, if you associate with your teammates, and you lose something off your team if that doesn't happen. We used to have big dinners on almost every road trip, and we'd spend hours going over things or just having a good time in each other's company. In Chicago, we went out, ate, and were back in our rooms in a couple of hours.

Quite a few players were asked to come, but only six or seven did, which I guess was not bad, considering. It was hard to get something going.

The team just wasn't a cohesive group. It's a touchy thing to talk about, but in the clubhouse this year, there were the loners, the Latin guys, the black guys, and the white guys. Even saying it makes it sound worse than it was, because it's not that there was animosity or hostility between the groups. It's just that every clique hung together. There wasn't the easy mixing you have to have to make the team a team.

I don't know why these divisions emerged this year. Maybe they were always there and were just hidden because we were winning — winning makes the clubhouse a happy home — but I don't think so. I don't remember it being this way all the time that I've been with the club. Maybe some black players will say I'm wrong, but it never seemed to me that black or white made any difference. Whatever the controversy about blacks as managers or in the front office, among the players, everybody's equal, everybody's just as good, or as bad, as anybody else. You can't have it any other way in athletics. And I know that black players like playing in Toronto, where there's not a lot of the prejudice and intolerance that unfortunately still exists in some parts of the States.

I guess the Latins feel like they're in a different situation. They come into a new culture and have to learn a new language. They come into a league with old rivalries that they haven't grown up with. All that's got to be difficult. I can understand a little bit of what they must go through. I experienced for a few scary days in the hospital in Barquisimeto what they must go through every day when they first come into the major leagues. But there have always been Latin players on the Blue Jays, and I don't remember any barrier that segregated the clubhouse before. The newspapers and the fans and the Latin players themselves always emphasize how emotional they are and how they're so moody. I guess there's as much truth to that as there is to any stereotype. But it's

147

really become an easy way to brush off certain things that happen, and I think it does a real disservice to the Latin players and to the team.

Latin players just don't always conform to that simple view. Sure, George Bell is emotional, but he's easy to get along with as a teammate and he plays hard. Alfredo Griffin wasn't moody. He was the backbone of this club for years, a super individual. He was outgoing, happy-go-lucky and a real gamer. You couldn't ask anywhere for a greater guy than Alfredo. Tony Fernandez is the same way. He could get carried away with his emotions when he first came up, but he's become a mature man. He always has been an exceptionally hard worker, and he turned himself into an all-star player. You have to be strong up the middle to be a contender — pitcher, catcher, second, short, and centre — and Tony keeps the middle intact. He showed me a lot this year, playing hurt for a good part of the season. His knees limited his range and his elbow injury made his throws to first not as brisk as they used to be, but the fact that he was out there playing meant an awful lot to us.

Damaso Garcia was a different story. He was moody, no question. But he was an outstanding athlete, one of the most talented players you'd ever want to see. When he was healthy and wanted to play, he was the best second baseman in the game. But there were days when Damo simply didn't want to play. We're entertainers and people pay good money to come and watch us perform, and there's no excuse for not giving it all you've got for the three hours you're out on the field. There were times when Damo wouldn't do that. He'd just go through the motions.

He left badmouthing the organization, saying it was prejudiced against Latin players, suggesting that there was some sort of racial thing going on. I've never known that to be the case. Just the opposite. The Blue Jays have always done more to bring Latin players into the big leagues than any other organization. They have money invested in Epy Guerrereo's camp in the Dominican and do everything they can to keep up the Latin connection. Whether that's mainly because of all the talent there or because the organization doesn't have to give up any draft choices to sign the Dominican players, or both, I don't know. But the Spanish influence has been growing. I knew that when an interpreter joined the coaching staff in 1988 and when a Dominican left-handed batting practice pitcher joined up as an "instructor." I knew that when I overheard my boys saying "coño" instead of "shit."

I don't know whether the experience with Damo had anything to do with it, but the idea seems to have taken hold that no one should say anything critical to "moody" players or they'll quit on the team. In the big leagues that seems to mean the Latins, and I think that's wrong and unfair to them. I've played with these men. There's probably a Damo in every clubhouse, but they're from all racial backgrounds.

In the minors, the "moody" untouchables seem to include the cocky "bonus babies," too, wherever they're from. I have a hard time understanding that. By the time players get to AAA, they're not kids. They're over twenty-one, or at least close to it. By the time they get there, they should already have the skills to play. What they have to learn there is how to use those skills every day and learn what they have to do for themselves to be physically able to play every day. I believe that if grown men are treated like grown men, they'll act like grown men. If they're treated like kids or spoiled brats, they'll behave accordingly. I've talked with minor league instructors in the Blue Jay organization who've been told to go easy on certain players, no matter what they do. Just always use kid gloves. I've talked to a scout who said that at the A ball level, one of the Blue Jay teams is the most undisciplined, disoriented group he's ever come across.

I've been with the Blue Jay organization from the beginning and have always been treated extremely well. I respect the organization and I respect those in authority ahead of me. I want to finish my career with Toronto and

149

I would hate to do or say anything that would jeopardize that possibility. But if there's one fault the organization has had the last eight or nine years, it's that it's pampered too many players, from the minors right up to the big leagues. It's been a long-standing attitude that's created a monster the organization will now have to live with. Special treatment for anyone on a team doesn't work. It puts player against player and group against group and the team doesn't function as a team.

Everyone has to be treated the same, the rules have to be there for everybody, and if that means egos have to get bruised, that's the way it is. Baseball's a game for outstanding individuals, but it takes a team to win. It's very tough, maybe impossible, to win when a clubhouse is divided.

I don't remember any divisions in the clubhouse when the Blue Jays started to win consistently and to challenge **150** Detroit, New York, Boston, and Milwaukee for the leadership of the AL East. We all pulled together, worked hard. We played tough. In 1984, we stayed near the top of the division all year. In fact, we were in second place all year. We played good ball, but the Tigers had won 35 of their first 40 games and we could never overcome that lead.

Detroit's lead was impressive, but not insurmountable in the right circumstances. We could have caught up, the way we were playing, except that we had the same problem that year as we had in '83. It seemed like we were always taking leads into the seventh or eighth inning and then blowing those leads. Every contending team has to have a stopper in the bullpen, and we just didn't have one.

Joey McLaughlan had still been our main stopper in '83, going into 50 games for us. But in '84, Joey struggled early and ended up pitching only eleven innings in six games. After Coxy had put him in a few times only to see us end up losing, he swore he was not going to use Joey in a save situation again. But one Saturday afternoon in

Detroit, the save situation arose and Coxy brought him in anyway. Joey proceeded to give up a game-winning home run to Chet Lemon, hanging a pitch right where Lemon likes it. Before the ball was even over the fence, Coxy was standing on the dugout steps screaming, "I've got to be the dumbest motherfucker around. How could I do it? I said I wouldn't do it and I still went out and did it. I'm the dumbest fucking manager in the game. I've just got to be the dumbest manager around." That was Coxy. He was a treat.

I think it was in Cleveland not too much later when the Blue Jays gave Joey his release. Coxy hated that part of the game in which you have to send people down or just let them go. It's got to be difficult to tell a man he's no longer wanted. Naturally, Joey was upset, saying that he hadn't been given the chances. Coxy was so upset at delivering the bad news that he tried to forget the whole thing by heading for the nearest bar. He was in rare form that night, rare form.

With Joey gone, Roy Lee got into more games and pitched fairly effectively. Dennis Lamp was signed as a free agent and went 8-8 with ten saves. The reliever with no saves at all after one really funny appearance on the mound was Rick Leach. He came into the game when we were getting blown out by Cleveland. He looked in at me so intently I couldn't keep a straight face. He waited, but all I could do was motion to him as if to say, "You're expecting a sign? Are you serious? Just throw the ball in and let's get out of here." He faced three batters, walked two, then gave up a home run. He didn't stop hearing about that for a while.

The reliever who got into more games than anyone else was a rookie, Jimmy Key. He was good right from the start, although he still had to go through a learning process. He worked hard, and he still has to work harder than anyone else, because he's got to be precise with his pitches. He has to be able to hit the corners to be effective. He changes speeds well and has a real good sinker that drops right as it gets to the hitting zone. If hitters could lay off that pitch, it would be a ball because it drops out of the strike zone. But it comes in right at the knees and it's a tough pitch to lay off of. If it's hit, it's a ground ball to short. He's also got a good changeup and a good curveball. He isn't afraid to pitch inside, he's a good fielder, and he doesn't make that many mistakes. He doesn't beat himself.

He's always worked between starts on spotting the ball, practicing the location of his pitches. He can throw the ball consistently on the inside or the outside part of the plate. Doyle Alexander was the same way. His location was perfect. With the right umpire, a pitcher will get that first strike if he is consistently an inch or so off the plate. With both Doyle and Jimmy, we've had pitches called for strikes that were three or four inches off. The ball was consistently there, and the umpire would widen the strike zone. Umpires love to work pitchers who can throw the ball inside when the catcher sets up on the in-

152   side.

Jimmy did a good job his first year. He did a bit of everything and went 4 – 5 with 10 saves. But the total saves for the bullpen only climbed to 33, one more than we'd had in 1983.

We didn't get the pitching staff the runs we did in '83. The team average was off a little and there were fewer home runs and RBI. But some players had very good years. Rance Mulliniks really came into his own as a hitter. Rance has very sharp eyes, and his .324 average was the best on the team. Except for 1986, he's hit around .300 pretty consistently ever since.

Dave Collins was in his second year with the club, and he had an outstanding season. Dave was a sparkplug. He was an exciting player who had a lot of spunk and enthusiasm. He would motivate the team an awful lot. With the speed that he had, he could steal a lot of bases, 60 of them in 1984. He was the sort of hitter a manager loves to have in the lead-off spot in the lineup, because that immediately puts pressure on the defence. When a guy like Dave gets on base, the number two hitter then sees a lot of fastballs because the catcher wants to throw the guy out at second. Everything Dave did, he did hard.

I remember only one time when he didn't hustle. We were in Boston and losing 3 – 2. Coxy sent him in to pinch run in the ninth. The next batter hit a ground ball and Dave didn't run hard at all and didn't slide into second base to break up what turned into a double play. Coxy was fuming, and rightfully so. A manager has a right to be pissed off if a player doesn't hustle. We went into the locker room and Coxy told the security guard to keep the media out. We were having a meeting. He ripped into Dave, telling him, "It doesn't take much to go out there and hustle. You didn't hustle and you shortchanged yourself, you shortchanged the 23 other guys on this team, you shortchanged the coaching staff. I'm not saying you could've broken up the double play, but you could have given it an effort."

Dave turned around and said, "If you want a fucking pinch runner you can go get Matt Alexander." Matt was a pinch running specialist with Oakland at the time.

153

That started a whole new round of shouting. Dave took off his glasses. They were ready to go at it, but Cliff Johnson stood up between them and said, "Okay guys, that's enough. We'll carry on with it another time." The next day, it was if it had never happened. But that was Coxy's style. He'd say his piece, tell you exactly what he thought and then as long as you went out and busted your butt on the field, he wouldn't say another word about it.

It was kind of funny that Cliff had been the peacemaker in that confrontation. One thing I can say about the organization is that there's been a good mesh of players over the years. The personalities have matched up pretty well. But Cliff was different from everyone else. He'd say things that were off the wall, and we'd just look at each other and think, "What?" He was a good-old-boy who had a habit of saying things before his mind had worked out what he wanted to say. Everything was positive, but not everything he said made sense. We'd figure, "Ah, that's a Cliff Johnson statement. He doesn't mean any harm by it." But what made him an odd choice for peace-maker was that he got into one of the first fist fights between players that ever happened with the Blue Jays. Damo and Cliff had a running feud in 1984, and it finally erupted around the batting cage over who was going to hit next.

Cliff had a good '84 season, batting .304, with 61 RBI, and he set a major league record that year with his 19th pinch-hit home run. The year before, Cliff had been the platoon DH with Jorge Orta, and together they'd led the league for the DH position with 113 RBI and 34 homers. But Jorge was traded to Kansas City for Willie Aikens before the '84 season, and Willie wasn't able to match Jorge's numbers. They combined for 87 RBI.

The catching platoon did almost as well, with 83 RBI, even with pretty poor seasons by both Buck Martinez and me. I managed 15 home runs and 46 RBI, despite hitting .238 and despite being on the disabled list for the last half of June with a tendon injury I got in a collision at the plate. Buck had really hit his peak in 1983, his third year with the team. He'd hit .253 then, with 10 homers and 33 RBI, but his average dropped to .220 in '84. His RBIs stayed up there at 37, but he hit only half as many home runs.

But the second catcher should emphasize defence, and Buck was a pretty good defensive catcher. He called a good game and had a lot of experience, which is what you look for to handle a pitching staff. We got along well as far as communication and working together went, and I learned a lot from him. When he came over from Milwaukee, he came with a different view of how their pitching staff handled hitters around the league. We'd go over our notes on how the two teams worked different hitters, and if our notes were the same we knew we had a lock on the guy. Buck was never noted for his hitting, and if he got on base, we'd need three singles to score him. He was probably one of the slowest guys in the league, but catchers don't get paid for speed. We had

154

some good years together, and putting our offensive numbers together, we probably did better than any other catchers in the league. The organization got good production out of us.

We finished the season with 89 wins and 73 losses, the exact same record we'd had in '83. It was frustrating chasing the Tigers all year and never catching up. We went into September nine and a half games back. By the end of the season, we were still in second place, but had fallen 15 games behind. Yet, people were beginning to take some notice of us. We had spent five years in seventh place in the AL East and we'd managed to escape the cellar in '83 only by tying Cleveland for sixth place. But for the second year in a row we had shown ourselves to be contenders. We were getting some recognition as a team and as individual players. We started to become known around North America.

Recognition can sometimes be a hard thing to handle. Not so much for the team, because that's what the team wants. Maybe it puts a bit more pressure on players to perform, knowing that people have such high expectations, but that's not always a bad thing. For an individual, though, there are a lot of positives and negatives.

For me, I remember being singled out around that time in kind of a funny way. Chris found an article in some inflight magazine that said I was rated the most talkative catcher in the American League. I didn't think that was true, and I still don't. If I've acquired that reputation, it's probably because the people writing those articles ask the top hitters in the game and I know some of them pretty well. With most players, there's usually not much conversation, just the pleasantries, although if I think I can distract a hitter a little bit and break his concentration, I might say more than usual. I mean, I'm not going to say, "Batter, batter, swing batter" or anything bush like that, but I've kept up running conversations with more than a few hitters. I learned long ago that the very best of them can't be distracted, anyway. Their concentration is too good.

Catch

Guys like George Brett or Wade Boggs or Kirby Puckett are almost impossible to pitch to and there's no way their concentration can be disturbed. There's no one way to get them out. Kirby's a slasher. Pitch him high or pitch him low, he'll swing at it, and he loves to talk at the plate while he's doing it. This season in Minnesota, he robbed me of two home runs by crawling up over the fence, and when he came up to the plate he said, "Hey, how's it going, E?"

I said, "I'm not talking to you."

"Why not?"

"I'm hitting the ball hard and you're robbing me. I'm not talking to you."

"Oh, come on, E."

"No. I'm not talking to you."

Every time he came up to bat he tried to start a conversation, but I kept the act up until we played the Twins in Exhibition Stadium. When he came up then, I said, **156** "Okay. Now I'll talk to you. You can't climb over our outfield fence."

Most of the time hitters and I just talk about how's the family, where are you going on vacation, where's a good place to eat after the game. I know George Brett pretty well and know he's an avid golfer, so one time I asked him how his game was going. He started telling me about it and kept on talking while the pitcher was going into his windup. He said, "I'm swinging the club well. I shot an 84 on this really tough course..." *crack*. The ball went off the fence and George went in with a stand-up double. He looked in at me from second and all I could do was shake my head. I was sitting back there amazed.

In his next at-bat, I said, "George, I just can't believe you can carry on a conversation and still hit the ball like that."

He said, "Ah, I was just lucky that time."

He got set in the box and I said, "Do you do any fishing around here?"

"Yeah, I do a lot of fishing. There're farm ponds around that we catch a lot a bass in. Larry Gura's got a farm about half-an-hour..." *crack.* He made contact, but he popped out.

In his next at-bat, he came up and said, "Hey, Ernie, I don't want to talk about fishing anymore. Let's go back to golf." We started talking about how my game was going and again, right in the middle of a sentence, he got another base hit.

George usually hits over .400 against our ball club. We've tried to get him out in every fashion — throwing away, throwing in on him, changeups, curveballs. You can't sneak a fastball by him, no matter where you set him up. We've had most luck throwing off-speed pitches and letting him supply the power. He's amazing. He always says, "Yeah, Ernie, you're my favourite catcher," which starts me wondering, "Why am I his favourite catcher? Maybe he knows how I'm going to call pitches on him. Maybe these little conversations actually help." John Watham, who's now managing Kansas City, used to tell me the same thing when he was playing. He also hit very well against us.

157

Wade Boggs is another one we try to throw an awful lot of off-speed stuff to, and we try to make him pull the ball. He's an inside-out type hitter who likes to hit the ball the other way. If we throw him off-speed pitches, he has to roll his hands over and, hopefully, either hits a lot of ground balls or fly balls to right field. He's one of the best hitters in the game right now. It's very tough to strike him out.

In one game in 1984, we did have some success in distracting him. Boggsy's very superstitious and he has endless little rituals to help his concentration. One of them is always drawing a Hebrew letter in the dirt with his toe as soon as he gets in the batter's box. Many times when I'd run up the line to back up a ground-out by the previous batter or back up a pickoff play at first, I'd drag my foot through the box on the way back to the plate and wipe the letter out. Now he's used to my tactics and when I go up the line he stays in the box holding the bat across his body like some sort of shield to protect his territory.

Wade's got to eat chicken every day, which some people find hard to believe. But every time I've been out with him, he's had chicken and other friends have told me the same thing. His biggest superstition, though, has to do with the the number seven. Before a 7:30 game, he'll run out on the field at 7:17. If it's a 1:30 game, he runs out at 1:17. For a one o'clock game, he runs at 12:47. There has to be a seven in the minutes for him to get out on the field. In the game in '84, we decided to mess with him. Bobby Cox suggested that we call the scoreboard operator at Exhibition Stadium and ask him to stop the clock at 7:16 and start it up again at 7:18. Bobby made the call himself.

We watched from the dugout as the Red Sox took the field. All except Wade, who stood staring at the clock. We could see his disgust from across the diamond when the clock stayed at 7:16 for what seemed like forever. Boggsy was some kind of hot when he came up to bat. He seemed to think I was the one who did it and started screaming at me, "You're fucking with me, Whitt. You're fucking with me. I can't believe you're doing this to me." He went 0-for-4 that night.

Now we try the same routine at least one time whenever he comes into town, but it's only worked that once. Every other time, he's gotten a couple of hits.

It's a good feeling being singled out by your peers, no matter what the reason. There's not much of a negative side to that, unless you've got a bad reputation. But there are some negatives that go with public recognition. Chris and I remember how we felt the first time we went out to a restaurant in Toronto and someone came up and said, "Aren't you Ernie Whitt?" We looked at each other and we were so excited. It was like it meant that I'd come into my own. Now it seems like a very small world, where we can't go anywhere without someone interrupting whatever we're doing to say a few words or ask for an autograph. I almost always try to be obliging, but it's sometimes hard. I have a strong sense of obligation to the fans and I'd hate to brush by a kid wanting an autograph, but

158

it can get tiring and puts a strain on my family. Chris and the kids all know that sort of thing goes with the job, and they're very understanding.

Where Chris draws the line is at our home. That's our private domain and she cherishes that privacy and protects it. It's amazing what people will do when they think you're public property. When we first moved into our old neighbourhood, we turned in early our first night there, shut off the lights, and closed the drapes. A little later, the doorbell rang. A group of parents were down by the edge of the yard and had sent their kids up for autographs. People have come to the door of the home we're in now or stopped by if they spotted me in the yard. Sometimes when I've played in Detroit, and not in a pennant race or anything, just a regular game when there are lots of seats available, unknown friends of people I haven't heard of since high school have found our unlisted phone number and asked for 20 – 30 free tickets to the game.

Chris is very direct. She's not one to bite her tongue or sit **159** back and let things go by. She doesn't mind playing the heavy where our home is concerned. She screens the calls and guards the door and makes sure we have a private life. She holds the shield that keeps new people that we meet at a little distance until we can figure out whether they like us for ourselves or because I'm a baseball player. What is sometimes worrying is that, like most baseball wives, she's home alone a lot with the kids. One evening in 1984, we had a message on our answering machine that our house was going to be bombed that night. The police came and checked things out. There was apparently nothing to the threat, but it raised some concern with us. Now we're hooked up to a security system and, much as she hates guns, Chris keeps a small pistol handy.

She's a fierce protector, and I don't know what I would do without her. I count on her so much, not only for maintaining a home life and raising the kids single-handedly much of the time, but for her support and her good sense and the poems she writes for me on the opening day of every season. She keeps the negative side of major league life to a minimum.

The positive side really outweighs the negative, anyway. You can make or break any situation, and high-profile recognition can be put to good use. When I first came up with the Blue Jays full-time in 1980, I started looking for an organization that would represent me for endorsements. I had meetings with a few companies in both Detroit and Toronto, then chose a company in Toronto called Sports Administration. The endorsements didn't exactly fly in. After a year and a half of things not coming through as they should have, the company had a shakeup and a new president, Richard Box, took over. I struck up a good relationship with Richard and also with David Bedford, another officer in the company, and they came up with several endorsements and speaking engagements for me. They've continued to do so ever since, matching up my name with products or organizations in such a way that everyone benefits from the association. Over the years, I've supplemented my income substantially by making speeches and radio commercials and appearing in advertising campaigns.

I've been able to have some success with that because I've been with Toronto a long time and the fans have been very supportive of me and my career. I've drawn a lot of strength from the people of Toronto and of Canada, generally, so I've tried to give something back. If my name can be used to help out in some way, I feel I owe it. To me, baseball players are role models. Kids look up to us, and I feel that part of being a good role model is getting active in community and charity work and having a good time doing it. There's no reason why ball players shouldn't get involved. Hopefully, when people are aware that Ernie Whitt or Dave Stieb or Rance Mulliniks or Jesse Barfield is involved with a project, it might make them think that maybe they can get involved, too, and give a bit of their time or money.

I've done some work for MS, the 65 Roses Foundation, Variety Village. I've also been on the Canadian Cancer

Society as an honourary campaign chairman nationally for three years and for the Ontario division in 1988. I attend functions, speak on behalf of the Society, and get involved with the Terry Fox Run. That work has taken me all over Canada. It consumes a lot of time, but I don't feel that I can just sit back. I'm more than happy to get involved.

But when I first became well-known, I also wanted to do something in a big way with a specific charity on an on-going basis, so I asked Richard and David to develop a plan that could use my name to best advantage. For the charity, I wanted something to do with kidney disease because Chris's dad had died of kidney failure at a fairly young age. I never met him, but he was an avid baseball fan and he meant an awful lot to Chris. I also love kids and love working with them, so I wanted to have kids involved, too. They came up with the idea of helping Camp Dorset, a family camp for dialysis patients where both adults and kids could enjoy the summer months. To me, that fit the bill perfectly. It was also a charity that was hurting for money at the time. It was a brand new camp built by the Lions Club of Hamilton.

We thought the best way to raise money would be through an annual golf tournament that we called "The Ernie Whitt Charity Classic." The only way it was going to be successful was if other players participated, because what the people would be paying for was a good time and the chance to say they'd played golf with George Bell or Tom Henke or Lloyd Moseby. But I also didn't want people to drag the players down. We don't have many off-days during the season, and if the players were going to be asked to give up their day, then they had to have an enjoyable time. There'd be no pressure, the emphasis was on fun and everything was done in a first class manner. The first tournament in 1984 went over extremely well, and we've been carrying on ever since.

Tom Cheek, who's been part of the Blue Jays' radio broadcast team since the ball club began, has been the emcee at the tournament dinner every year. He's

161

a tremendous speaker, a really smooth professional who keeps everything moving along at just the right pace. Gordie Tapp has been a part of the tournament almost every year, too. He's a great gentleman who puts a lot of time into charity work without getting the recognition he deserves. He's very busy, always rushing to Nashville or somewhere, yet he's been very faithful and always very funny. John Candy came out for two years. He's another extremely busy individual who has always helped me out whenever he could to draw more people to the tournament. He's a very funny man, but so down-to-earth. He makes me play terrible golf because I'm always in stitches when he's around, yet he gives of his time.

It's been very successful. We know that because as soon as the tournament's over, we get requests for entry to the following year. We try to limit the teams to 35 so that it's not a long day, and we've had sell-outs in all five years. Our goal is to donate $25,000 to Camp Dorset, with the remainder of the proceeds going to a fund for Dennis Holmberg, a coach in the Blue Jays minor league system, whose wife and daughters were injured in a bad car accident in Syracuse several years ago. The kids came out of it okay, but Diane Holmberg was paralyzed and needed constant nursing care. Minor league coach isn't a well-paid position, and we felt we could help a friend, one of my teammates in a way, a member of the Blue Jay family, by easing his burden a bit. The tournament means an awful lot to Chris and me because we know there's a lot of people benefitting from it.

It means a lot, too, when players from other teams give of their time. What we try to do every year is get players from the opposing team to participate if they also have an off-day and are in our town. In June of 1988, the Red Sox were in Toronto, and Wade Boggs, Roger Clemens, and Spike Owen came out. With most of the Blue Jays on hand, including George Bell, it was really something to

162

boast that we had the only tournament with the American League's MVP, Cy Young Award winner, and batting champion taking part.

It was gratifying that the Red Sox participated. They didn't have any hard feelings about our sweeping them at Fenway at the beginning of the month. When they came into Toronto, they were playing only a little bit better ball than we were. They had 27 wins and so did we, but they had only 27 losses to our 32. New York and Cleveland were setting the pace in the division, and our two clubs were battling it out for fifth and sixth place.

We took the first two from them, making it six straight on the year. But then they found a way to beat us. They just let us play the way we'd unfortunately been playing a good part of the season. Errors, bad throws, routine fly balls dropped, poor covering of the bases. They took a 5 – 0 lead into the second inning and ended up beating us 8 – 2. The one bright spot was that Mark Ross, who'd **163** been called up from Syracuse, gave up only three hits in six innings.

Then the Indians came into town. After our sweep in Fenway, we'd gone to Cleveland and given a couple of games away, getting swept by the club for the first time since 1980. It sure was strange to see Willie Upshaw out at first in an Indians uniform, and it was surprising that his reception by the fans was so cool. I expected more of an ovation after all the good years he'd given to Toronto, but the fans seemed to have changed. They really weren't happy when Cleveland took a 6 – 1 lead into the seventh. The Indians beat us 8 – 6, but we came back to take the next two games, the last of the series a 15 – 3 blowout behind some of Dave Stieb's best pitching of the year. It was his eighth straight win.

Just before we went into Detroit on June 16th for our first series of the year against the Tigers, the trade rumours started flying. Of course, as far as some guys were concerned they had never stopped. There had been speculation about Jesse Barfield being traded right from the beginning of the season. That was hard on Jesse in a year he didn't need more problems.

Jesse's troubles really started back in 1986 when he led the league with 40 home runs and had 108 RBI. It's almost understandable that the fans might expect that kind of year to be repeated over and over again. It's not so understandable that the media and even the organization seemed to adopt the same attitude. In 1987, Jesse had 28 home runs and 85 RBI and everybody seemed to be thinking, "Gee, I guess he's had it, he's going downhill. He's not going to do anything anymore." But look around the league in 1987 and see how many outfielders put up the numbers Jesse did. You could probably count them on the fingers of one hand. He did not have a bad year. He simply didn't live up to the unrealistic expectations people had after his career year.

164
Before the 1988 season began, Jesse had surgery on his wrist and his knee. I've never had wrist problems, but other players who have had that kind of surgery have told me that it takes at least six months before you feel right again and can work your hands without pain or the fear of pain. And the hands and wrists are the most important tools a ball player has. Early in the season, Jesse said that his wrist was bothering him. I got the feeling that management didn't believe him and thought that maybe he was just complaining for the sake of complaining, that he was using the surgery as an excuse to not give a hundred per cent. A doctor looked at the wrist and said everything seemed fine and that it shouldn't be bothering him. But so what?

I've known Jesse for many years and I have never seen anyone work as hard in spring training, work as hard in practice, or work as hard in a game. He's an intense player who is very demanding of himself and who wants to win just as much if not more than any player I've ever met. If a man like that says his wrist hurts, his wrist hurts.

Instead of giving what he said the proper consideration, the organization turned up the pressure. The trade rumours never stopped from the first week of the season. He kept being told he couldn't hit the inside pitch anymore. I gather he was called into the office a few times and was asked if everything was okay personally, was everything okay financially, were he and his wife getting along — just playing mind games by throwing a lot of negative things at him instead of building him up positively.

Then the media joined in. When he was moved to the eighth spot in the lineup, reporters kept on him about how could he accept batting in that position. Of course, back in spring training, they all criticized George for not accepting the DH role and said a player paid good money should do what he's told. To me, they were talking out of both sides of their mouths.

All that has an effect on a player, and it was sad to see Jesse feeling so down. He used to be such a delight to have around the clubhouse and he'd still do some of the little instigator-type things he's been known for — his favourite is the flaming matchbook thrown in at a guy on the crapper — but for most of the season he seemed to stay by himself. He'd come in, do his work, go home.

165

But what was interesting to me about the trade rumours in the middle of June was that for the first time, my name seemed to be prominent. Most players don't like to see their names in the papers in trade speculation. At least, I don't. Some players welcome trades when they're not happy with management or the way they're being played or the relationships they have on the team. That's never been the case with me. I've made it clear to the Blue Jays many times over that I'd like to finish my career in Toronto.

But when teams are struggling, the talk heats up. In June, both Montreal and Minnesota were having problems but were not out of the races in their divisions by any means. Both teams were looking for a catcher and both, it was hinted in the papers, were interested in me. I always repeat to myself, "If you can't control it, don't worry about it." But you read it. It's there in black and white and somewhere in the back of your mind you think, "Geez, this could happen." Then you start wondering who else is on the team, what's the manager like, how will I get home from there, what will my family do?

I tried not to think about all that, but it was hard, especially when some of the players arrived at Tiger Stadium and told me that Greg Myers's name was on the rooming list at the hotel, along with outfielder Glenallen Hill's. Jesse and I looked at each other, thinking that maybe this could be it. But I asked Mike Mitchell, our travelling secretary, about it and he said the team used various names for booking extra rooms just in case they might be needed. It was just a coincidence that those particular names were chosen.

I did think it was unlikely that I would be traded. Greg had been out of the Syracuse lineup with a sore shoulder and, as it turned out, was about to undergo surgery, so I knew he couldn't be called up. But I also know that there comes a time in every career when the veteran has to step aside and let the kids take over. I was in the last guaranteed year of my contract and sometime over the summer I would chalk up ten years with the same major league team. Before that date, I could be traded anytime and anywhere with no say in the decision. Once I reached that mark, though, I could veto any deal. If the Blue Jays were going to trade me, it would be before then.

But I put the rumours behind me going into Tiger Stadium. I always like coming back and playing in front of my family and friends, and the first game of our series was made even more special because it was the first meeting between our two clubs since the last Sunday of the '87 season, when we lost our division to them. The match-up was Jack Morris against Mike Flanagan, and the last time they'd faced each other was in the Saturday game that year. They'd both been brilliant through nine innings in one of the best duels I'd ever seen. I had watched them from the bench. That was a game I wanted very badly to get into, but I had not been used.

This year, Mike pitched into the ninth again, looking for his first shutout of the season. He didn't get it, but his breaking ball was going for strikes and he had great location on his fastball. He had a cushion to work with. Jack Morris only lasted into the third inning, giving up seven runs, the last two on my triple off the right centre field fence. I added a two-run homer into the upper deck in the ninth, making it a 4-for-4 night for me, with 4 RBI. It was my best night of the season.

July

Whenever we seemed to be making progress this season, **169** we somehow always fell back. We split the series in Detroit against the Tigers, then came home and lost to the Orioles. And as June ended, we dropped two out of three in Baltimore. We were spared the sweep by the return of Jimmy Key, who we'd missed an awful lot. He had a strong outing, and with Dave and Mike pitching well, there was a lot of optimism about the second half of the season. Jim Clancy and Todd Stottlemyre were both pitching much better than their records indicated, and both deserved to see some breaks coming their way.

But Jimy's hands were really tied going to the bullpen. Eichhorn and Wells were both struggling. John Cerutti was doing well with whatever job he was asked to do — spot starting, short relief, middle relief — although it's difficult to have no set role. The only two who could do the job consistently for us in the late innings were Tom Henke and Duane Ward.

Tom wasn't getting many opportunities, though, which was tough to figure out, both for Tom and the rest of us. Duane Ward was getting a lot of work, and had really developed into an outstanding pitcher. He'd learned to control his arm and throw his fastball and curve for strikes. He still had a tendency to be a little wild, but when a guy's got a 94 mile an hour fastball with movement, it's not always bad to be wild. It gives the hitters something to think about. "Psycho," as some of the guys call him, did everything he had to do, and by the summer he had become a pitcher. He was just one pitch — something off-speed, maybe a straight 80 mile an hour changeup — from being a really, really good pitcher. He wanted the job of main stopper, but there's nothing wrong with having two good guys available to go out there, as long as they accept their roles.

There had to be some changes. Just before the All-Star break, Mark Eichhorn and David Wells were sent down to Syracuse. I was kind of sorry to see Mark go, but he had to work on a few things and Syracuse was a good place **170** to do it without having to work under a lot of pressure.

I wasn't surprised to see David Wells go down though. I thought he should have gone down long before. All through June, Jimy kept going to him in tight situations and he'd blow his chance time in and time out. He'd come in, give up an extra-base hit or a home run and either take us right out of the game or let the opposing team come back. At the break, he had given up homers in five of his last eight appearances. It got to be that when I saw David coming in from the bullpen, the ghost of Joey McLaughlin would start dancing in my head. He couldn't get his curve or changeup over for strikes. All he had was the fastball, and one-pitch pitchers don't last long in the big leagues.

David let some time get away from him. He had a good September in '87 and seemed to think he had it made, that he wouldn't have to worry about going down to the minors again. He's got the arm to be a very good pitcher, but he has to learn to take care of himself and he has to learn to pitch, rather than just throw. There are a lot of good left-handers around the league and on our own staff who can be studied from the bench, and that's where hitters and approaches to the game can be studied from, too. For a pitcher just learning, the time between starts can be as useful as playing time, if it's used constructively. David didn't use that time well.

With David and Mark gone, we expected that Jeff Musselman would come back up. We had missed him in our lineup almost as much as Jimmy Key the first few months of the season. We needed help from somewhere. At the break, we finished off with series with one of the best teams in the league and three of the worst. We'd dropped two out of three to each of Baltimore and California, one of three to Seattle, and three straight to Oakland. We were 42 – 46, eleven-and-a-half games behind Detroit. It was the first time in six years that we'd gone into the break under .500.

We had a reminder of better days when Dave Stieb was selected to pitch in the All-Star game, the only representative of our team. I felt very happy for Dave. He deserved the honour with the season he was having. Back in 1980, he was the youngest pitcher ever chosen to play in the All-Star game, and now he was off to make his sixth appearance.

171

Dave probably has the most natural ability of any of the pitchers on the team. I'd be hard pressed to find anyone better anywhere in the league as far as natural talent goes. In spring training, I was really hoping he could come back after a few rocky seasons, and he came back in a big way. He's matured a lot these past few years.

He's a very high strung individual. To me, he's been pampered a lot in his career and it's been hard for him to accept not being the top man on the totem pole. I thought Bobby Mattick spoiled him when he first came up. Bobby had his pets, and David was one of the main ones. There'd always be little things that sent everyone the message, like in spring training one year when everyone, including Dave as the starting pitcher, was supposed to be on the field at 10:00. But Bobby had let him go across the street to have breakfast because he'd slept in. Little things like that. Anything David wanted was okay with Bobby.

That kind of treatment didn't help the attitude problem he had. Like most young pitchers, he would try to lay the responsibility for a hit anywhere except on himself. If someone made an error behind him, he would stare at the fielder like he was saying, "What the hell are you doing? How could you miss that ball? Now you're making me look bad. You're making me throw to another hitter." There were times when he would show me up, too. I'd call a pitch, a guy would get a base hit on it and David would stare in at me with his "How could you call that pitch?" look.

Opposing players started to love facing him. As soon as someone got a hit off him, he'd throw the rosin bag up in the air and act like he'd just witnessed some incredible event. The players on the other team would scream out from the dugout, "You can't believe it, can you?" and all kinds of other things to try to rattle him. They'd give him a terrible time. Kansas City especially would really try to get him going. They had the knack.

I felt that his attitude cut down his effectiveness, yet he was still the dominant pitcher on the team and one of the most dominant in the league. When he first came up in 1979, he threw basically hard stuff — the moving fastball and a good, hard slider hitters had very little chance of hitting. Tom Underwood edged him out by one in the number of wins to lead the Blue Jays in 1979 and Jim Clancy did the same in 1980, but after that it was all Dave right through to 1984, when Doyle Alexander won 17 to Dave's 16. Dave worked his ERA down from 2.83 in 1984 to 2.48 in 1985, but Doyle still won more and lost less.

Dave was struggling and I think what happened was that while he was having a rough year, for him, he saw Doyle out there throwing lollipops up to the plate with little apparent effort and having a tremendous season. That seemed to show him that another style of pitching could be effective and he started experimenting. Here was a guy with a hard fastball and a slider that would knock your shorts off, and he was constantly throwing breaking stuff. He almost fell in love with throwing a changeup. He also started to work with an over-the-top curveball. When he wasn't successful with it, he tried even harder to pitch that way. I wasn't sure whether he did it because he wanted to take some stress off his elbow or because Al Widmar was constantly pounding on him to come up with an off-speed pitch. Whatever the reason, he got out of his own style.

When he threw the curveball, he would change his arm action from three-quarters to almost straight over top, which was as obvious to the hitters as it was to me behind the plate. Hitters started sitting on it, so that was another adjustment he had to make. In '85, '86, and parts of '87, he did have some success, but he wasn't dominating as he was in '83 and '84 and as he was this year.

In 1988, he came full circle, throwing basically the hard stuff. But he's also come up with a real good curveball, to go with the fastball and slider, that he throws out of the **173** same arm spot.

He's a tremendous competitor when he wants to pitch, and I emphasize "wants." There have been times when he just hasn't gotten himself mentally prepared. He'd wander around as if to say, "I don't feel like pitching." But if you work every fourth of fifth day, you have to be mentally ready to go out on the mound and face the opponent. The times when his head simply wasn't in the game were the times when he'd really struggle and get knocked out in the first or second inning.

In 1987, Jimy Williams took him out of the starting rotation near the end of the season, and I didn't blame Jimy for that at all. Before one game when he was scheduled to go out against Milwaukee, he told trainer Tommy Craig that he didn't want to pitch and what he said got back to Jimy. In the first inning of the game, he gave up some hits and a few runs and was shuffling around in a distracted sort of way, so Jimy went out and pulled him. Afterwards, he was wondering why and I told him, "David, your attitude stinks. I've seen you mope around the mound for years when somebody gets a hit off you, but now you're moping around like you've got an 'I give up' attitude. That's not like you. It's like you don't care. Here we are in a pennant race and you don't even seem like you want to be out there."

But this year, he put together a good season. The control was still not where I'd like to see it. He has trouble getting the fastball in on left-handed hitters. The only way he can get inside is with the slider. But his fastball's good and the curve and slider started really working for him.

And he turned things around mentally. Now, in most cases at least, if there's an error, he'll look back as if to say, "Don't worry about it. I'll pick you up. I'll get this next guy out." There are still times when the old attitude floats back. I've gone out when a hitter has driven one through a hole and David would say, "Where the hell are we supposed to be playing this guy?"

174 I'd say, "Look, you made a good pitch, the guy just hit it in the hole. He hit a ground ball, so what else can you do?"

There are still those little flare-ups, but he's matured a lot since '83 and '84. When his mind is set right, when he goes out with a positive attitude and doesn't let a base hit or an error or a misplay affect him, he is one of the best pitchers in the league. I wasn't the only one to notice. Some of the hitters would come up, David would throw one in and they'd say, "Wow, I haven't seen a pitch like that from him since '84." He was back on track and I'm glad Tom Kelly recognized that when he selected his All-Star from Toronto.

It wasn't surprising that no Blue Jay was voted to the team. Not that we didn't have players who deserved to make it, but Toronto fans don't vote. George Bell was elected to the starting team in 1987 after a real promotional push, with extra ballots printed in the newspapers, but he's the only one who's made it that way.

The players don't like the fan selection process much. It's become a popularity contest that doesn't seem to have anything to do with ability or a good season. It's got more to do with name recognition. I know that if Reggie Jackson had been on the ballot, even after his last few bad seasons, he would have finished high up in the balloting. It was funny on our team that Rance Mulliniks got more votes than Kelly Gruber for third base. Rance had only played a few innings at third because of his injury in the home opener, while Kelly was having the kind of year that would have gotten him into the All-Star game under any system that made any sense.

It's not that the fans don't deserve to have a say. They do. They pay their money to see the ball games, so they should have something to do with the process. But most players, I think, would like to see a system that divided the vote into thirds, with the fans, the players and the managers and coaches each making their selections. That way, two-thirds of the votes would be cast by people who are on the scene day after day and know who the best players are. The players would be honest. We know **175** who's having a good year and who's struggling. It's our job to know that.

In 1988, the ballot stuffing that goes on in densely populated areas like the Bay area in California was really apparent. Nothing against Walt Weiss, but when you think about all the good shortstops in the American League it seemed ridiculous that Weiss would end up third. And even Tony La Russa said that neither Mark McGwire nor Terry Steinbach, the starters at their positions, deserved to be there with the kind of years they were having.

Maybe I take it too personally, but I feel that if I'm not a better catcher than Terry Steinbach, I should hang up my cleats. I felt the same way about Terry Kennedy of the Baltimore Orioles, who was the fans' choice in 1987. He was hitting about .180 at the time and I was hitting around .270. It was some consolation that in a poll of the league's managers at the break that year I led the pack with six votes to Terry's one. It's satisfying to know that your peers appreciate your talents, even if the public doesn't. But I would dearly love to get into the All-Star game again. I made it once, and I have Sparky Anderson to thank for that.

Playing in an All-Star game had always been one of my goals, just like winning the pennant and the World Series. But it was the one goal I never thought would be a reality. The Blue Jays have always used me as a platoon player, and very seldom do you see platoon players in the All-Star game. They just don't get the attention or the publicity that everyday players do. Plus, playing in Toronto is a disadvantage. It's turned around some in the last few years, but Toronto players don't get the notoriety they would if they played in New York or Los Angeles or Chicago. To a lot of American fans and some of the media, if you play north of the border you might as well be on another planet.

176 But in 1985, we were in California playing the Angels when the starting team was announced. The next day, when they announced the reserves, I was sitting out by the hotel pool and Kenny Carson, our trainer and travelling secretary at the time, walked over to me and said, "You've been selected to the All-Star team."

"You're kidding."

"Nope. You've been selected and so have Jimmy [Key], Dave [Stieb], and Damo [Garcia]. And Bobby's going to coach. You fly out Sunday."

He gave me the flight numbers while my mind was just racing. I was so happy and excited. To achieve a goal is always satisfying, but to accomplish something I wanted so much but thought was out of reach gave me an amazing feeling. I ran in and called Chris in Detroit and through all the tears of joy we worked out the arrangements for meeting in Minnesota.

Other players and players' wives told us before we went that a lot of things would be going on and that we should try to take them all in and enjoy ourselves. Even if we felt tired, we should push ourselves on because it might be a once-in-a-lifetime chance.

We took their advice. The whole atmosphere was electric. There were parties, dinners, all kinds of events, constant activity everywhere. If you wanted to, you could be involved in something every second of the day. And we tried to be involved in everything.

There were presentations. Chris got a corsage before the game. Each player received an oil painting of himself. I got the ring that I'll always cherish. Chris got the All-Star program book, looked through it and then really felt like crying. She found my name, but it was underneath a picture of Jeff Burroughs, our DH that year. We were mistaken for each other an awful lot.

For me, it was nice that the starting catcher was Carleton Fisk, with Rich Gedman as the other backup, all three of us products of the Red Sox organization. And it was thrilling to be in the clubhouse and look around the room and see Mattingly, Henderson, Molitor, Yount, Trammel, Winfield, all the others. I thought, "I belong here. There's no reason why I shouldn't be here. I should have been here before."

177

But the most thrilling moment for me was lining up before the game and being introduced on the field. I still get goosebumps thinking about how they played the Canadian national anthem while the cameras focussed on Jimmy, Dave, Damo, and me. I guess I've played in Toronto so long I feel part Canadian now. I travel a lot in the States, but always to the same cities. In Canada, I've been all over the country from Vancouver to Newfoundland, speaking and meeting people in places everywhere in between. When they played 'O Canada' I stood there with a lot of pride, thinking, "God, we're representing a whole country." I could imagine a bit what it must be like for an Olympic athlete winning a gold medal.

After all the excitement, the game itself was a little disappointing. I caught half an inning and was due up to bat, but the National League brought in left-hander Fernando Valenzuala and I never got the chance to hit. I was in pretty good company there. Wade Boggs and Ben Oglivie didn't get the chance to bat either.

At the big dinner and dancing bash after the game, Boggsy and I kept griping about how frustrating it was to not get up. But Chris and Debbie Boggs kept things in perspective, saying, "Why be down? Sure, you wanted to play more. But you were here. You were in the All-Star game. How many guys get that chance?"

Not many do get that chance. I was proud to be there, especially as part of such a large Blue Jay contingent chosen by the manager and the league. It was recognition that we'd really arrived as a team.

Something else made the experience gratifying to me. I had no incentives in my contract. The Blue Jays didn't have to reward me in any way for my selection to the team. But it's a mark of the way the organization treated its players that when I got back to Toronto, Mr. Hardy called me into his office and handed me a cheque for $10,000.

178　This looked like it was going to turn into a near perfect year. After appearing in the All-Star game I had three goals, and I really believed that I could achieve them all in one year — division title, pennant, World Series. At the break, we were in first place in the division. It was tremendously satisfying to feel everything positive, just all going in the right direction, especially since the first part of my season in '85 had been spent under a terrible cloud.

It's not uncommon for players to get hit with paternity suits. You hear about it all the time, but you never think it can happen to you. It's part of baseball life, and the effect is devastating for the player and his wife. I know that from first-hand experience.

I've heard stories about players being approached while they're on the field or in a crowd of fans, being asked their names, then handed legal papers. I was saved at least that embarrassment. The district attorney in Roseville is a friend of mine, and when a suit with my name on it crossed his desk during spring training in 1985, he phoned to give me warning and said he'd deliver the papers personally in Dunedin the following week. A woman in Milwaukee was claiming that I was the father of her baby girl.

That just floored me. Absolutely floored me. I told him I didn't know any women in Milwaukee. I didn't know this woman's name. I hadn't been fooling around with any woman in Milwaukee. But he said, "Well, she's claiming you're the father, so the papers will have to be served."

I went in immediately to see Pat Gillick and told him the situation. He called a team lawyer in Toronto who got onto his contacts and found an attorney to handle the case in Wisconsin. I couldn't believe this was happening to me.

Then I had to go home and tell Chris. When I got there, she was just going shopping with her friend, Esther. I said, "I've got to talk to you."

"Let's talk later. We're just going out."

"Chris, I've got to talk to you now."

She looked at me funny, a little fearfully, I guess, thinking that maybe I'd been traded or something. Esther went on alone and I told Chris what had happened. Her knees just about gave way, it hit her so hard. I told her there was nothing to it, that I hadn't done anything to be ashamed of in Milwaukee. I know she believed me. But the mind does tricky things, and Chris has always had a very active imagination. There was a lot of friction between us. Whenever we hear of similar suits now, Chris's heart always goes out to the wife. The man, she feels, at least knows one way or the other if anything happened. The wife has no way of knowing for sure and becomes an outsider, looking in on maybe something, maybe nothing between her husband and some stranger. It was a trying time for us.

On an off-day during the season, we both flew to Milwaukee and met with the attorney. He asked again if I knew the woman, if she maybe could have been from another city where something might have happened.

I said, "Look, I don't know this woman. I'll do anything you want me to do. I know that this is not my child."

179

We went to the blood centre, where they took my picture and drew out the blood samples. The woman was supposed to be there, too, but she never showed up. That was probably just as well. I know that I would have wanted to strangle her. Chris felt more along the line of ripping the lips off her face for starters, then going for the jugular. She was appalled at the selfishness of someone who would put her own small child through a series of blood tests, her own family through uncertainty, and other, innocent people through so much heartache and trouble. We couldn't figure out why she would do such a thing. We thought that if it was just for the money, there were a lot of players making more than me. If someone had used my name to get with her, why didn't she drop the suit? She must have found out the truth at some point. We couldn't understand. Chris gave the attorney a package to pass on to the woman, containing birth control information and a Bible. She considered underlining certain scriptures, but figured the woman would probably need to read the whole thing.

180

We had got the notice in March, and it was May before the issue was finally settled. The blood test proved I wasn't the father, and our attorney went before a judge to get the suit dismissed. We discussed counter-suing. We couldn't put a price on the humiliation involved in going through the tests or on the strain the whole episode put on our marriage. But we thought we should be compensated for at least the financial expenses involved. We had to pay for the flights to Wisconsin, the legal fees, even the blood tests themselves. But the attorney said that we'd be as likely to get blood from a turnip and we should just forget about it. It was better not to make a scene.

He said the case wasn't unusual. Similar things had happened to a couple of Brewers, Green Bay Packers and Milwaukee Buck players. My friend in Michigan, too, said the case wasn't anything out of the ordinary. He told me it happens a lot in the entertainment business and it happens a lot in sports. It's unfortunate, but people in the limelight are subject to that sort of thing. I had the certainty that there was nothing to it, but it was still very traumatic for us. It was such a relief when it was over and we could get back to more positive things.

The Blue Jays had always said that if the team was one or two players away from being a contender for the division title, those players would be acquired somehow. After we finished in second place in 1984, still without a consistent reliever to close the door in the late innings, the club traded Alfredo Griffin and Dave Collins to Oakland for Bill Caudill. Everyone was sorry to see both Alfredo and Dave go. They were solid players who were well respected and liked an awful lot by everyone on the team. But the trade made a lot of sense, and not only because we got one of the premier relief pitchers in the American league, a guy who had 36 saves in 1984. But Tony Fernandez and George Bell couldn't be kept back any longer. The shortstop and left field positions had to be opened up.

About six weeks later, Gary Lavelle, one of the National League's best, came over from San Francisco in exchange for Jim Gott and two minor league players. I didn't know much about Gary at the time, but I found him to be a real gentleman and very competitive on the field.

We started the season with high hopes of winning the division. We thought having Bill and Gary would put us over the hump. But in the first half of the season they both struggled. Gary had some arm problems and was very inconsistent, although he pitched some good ball games for us. He had good velocity on his fastball and he hid the ball well because of the high leg kick that he had.

But Billy blew a lot of save opportunities at the beginning of the season. Some people thought that maybe his huge contract put a lot of pressure on him and it affected his concentration. I thought the main problem was the way he was used. When he pitched for Seattle and Oakland, he was used almost every day. He'd pitch two

181

days in a row, get maybe one day off, then come back for another three days straight. That was the sort of pitcher he was. That was his style. He had to pitch that often to be effective.

When he came to Toronto, he didn't get nearly the same amount of work. That was partly because in a lot of games we'd be up or down by three or four runs and wouldn't need to bring the short man in. But I felt that the Jays were also trying to protect his arm a little bit because of the big investment they'd made in it. Billy got out of his groove. He never adjusted to pitching one day then having three or four days off. Whenever he came back after a few days rest, he'd lose a little sharpness off his fastball. The location wouldn't be there. When he didn't capitalize on the save opportunities, Coxy would go to someone else, usually Jim Acker, and Billy gradually fell out of Coxy's good graces as the stopper. It was unfortunate. I have the highest respect for Billy. He always wanted to do what he could to help the team. He wasn't one to just sit back and collect his pay without giving an effort.

182

We were still doing well. We were in first place the beginning of May and by the end of that month we had a lock on first that we never gave up the rest of the season. But by the All-Star break we weren't getting the results we all expected from the bullpen, and at that point the Blue Jays called up Tom Henke from Syracuse. We had just picked Tom up from the Rangers that winter as compensation for Cliff Johnson going to Texas as a free agent and I thought he had pitched well enough in spring training to make the team then. But with all the money invested in Bill and Gary, there was no way Tom was going to make the staff as a reliever.

Tom had, and still has, an overpowering 94 – 95 mile an hour fastball and an outstanding changeup that he throws like a forkball. His fastball has good location and he comes back with tremendous arm action on the changeup. It looks like a fastball on the release and the hitters are usually way out in front of it. When a pitcher can throw that hard and has command of the two pitches

Tom has, it's very hard to get a hit off him. He finally joined the team in July of 1985. To me, he's why we won our division. He had 15 save opportunities and converted 13 of them. We finally had someone consistent who could come in and nail down those games in the last innings.

That he had games to save was because the rest of the pitching staff put everything together, too. Dennis Lamp had been moved to middle relief and ran up an 11 – 0 record, one short of the major league record for consecutive wins by a reliever. Jimmy Key had been moved out of the bullpen to the starting rotation and pitched very effectively. Jimmy was the first left-handed starter for the Blue Jays who had won a game since 1980, when Paul Mirabella beat Boston. Stieb, Clancy, Tom Filer, Ron Musselman — all had good seasons. We had the arms to win.

But I guess who sticks out from that year is Doyle Alexander, who had come over from the Yankees in the middle of the 1983 season and pitched extremely well for us for the next two years. Doyle wasn't then and still isn't the sort of pitcher who immediately impresses anyone. He's not a power pitcher at all. But he's probably the best student of the game I've ever seen. He's been around so long that he knows all the weaknesses of the hitters and he can execute against those weaknesses. There are a lot of pitchers who just sit on the bench between their starts and don't pay attention to what's going on in the game. Doyle watches everything, studying every hitter so that he has a game plan for each of them. Not only does he change his speed with his fastball, curve and changeup, but he changes his arm action from over top to three-quarters to sidearm. He gives a hitter three different looks with three different pitches, making him very tough to read.

In the clubhouse, he was a very quiet man. We never talked much. He'd call me an old fart and I'd call him one, since we were the senior citizens on the team. We went fishing once or twice, but there was never any closeness off the field. We kept things on a professional level. I

183

respected him as a pitcher and I think he respected my ability to call a game.

He basically kept to himself, except that he found a friend in Jim Acker. They stuck together all the time and it was funny to see a change come over Jim. Doyle was very anti-management and anti-authority. That was in his nature. If management said one thing, Doyle would say the opposite just on principle. When Jim Acker first came over, he was a happy guy. Nothing bothered him and he never complained, but the more he hung around Doyle, the more he became like him.

The two of them were good to have around the clubhouse, though. They'd hang around just like about seven or eight others — Buck Martinez, Clancy, Rance, Dennis Lamp, the coaches, me — and we'd talk about what had happened that day and what might happen tomorrow. We took our game seriously. We wouldn't have had it any other way, and neither would Coxy. We knew we could win this thing.

184

I think it was in August when Cliff Johnston was quoted in a paper saying that we didn't have the stuff to win the division because the team was run too much like a country club. We were in Minnesota at the time and Coxy called a meeting. Everyone filed in and we all sat there, then Cliff looked around and said, "All right, I guess we can start the meeting now."

Coxy looked at him real hard and said, "Sit down and shut the fuck up."

Cliff just stared at him. "What?"

"You heard me. Sit down and shut the fuck up." He glared around the room and said, "There's some low-rent cocksucker on this team who says we don't have the makeup to win this thing. He says it's too much like a country club. Moseby! Did you bring your golf clubs on this trip?"

Lloyd was really startled. "No, Skip, I didn't bring any golf clubs."

"Upshaw! Did you bring a tennis racket on this trip?"

"No, Skip."

Toronto Blue Jays

(Photo: Courtesy of Ernie Whitt)

(top)
Bobby Cox about to be ejected by Drew Coble, 1983.

(lower)
Dave Stieb (left), Jimmy Key, and I help celebrate winning the division championship, 1985.

Canapress Photo Service

McConnell/Toronto Star

The Globe and Mail

(top left)
After a long night in Cleveland in August, 1986. I homered in the
twelfth inning to win the first game of a doubleheader and also
homered in the second game to help get the sweep.

(top right)
In the wee hours after re-signing with the Blue Jays, January, 1987.

(lower)
Waiting with Dave Stieb for Willie Upshaw to make the play.

(top)
Handing out awards in Whitehorse, Yukon. *(Photo: Courtesy of Ernie Whitt)*

(lower)
At the Ernie Whitt Charity Classic. *(Photo: Courtesy of Ernie Whitt)*

Jim Wilkes

McConnell

(top left)
Taylor checks out a high fly ball. *(Photo: Courtesy of Ernie Whitt)*

(top right)
Ashley is escorted to the mound to sing the national anthem at
Exhibition Stadium. *(Photo: Courtesy of Ernie Whitt)*

(lower)
EJ runs a bat back in Dunedin. *(Photo: Courtesy of Ernie Whitt)*

(top)
Jimy Williams passes judgement on Joe Brinkman's call
in New York, 1987.

(lower)
Putting the tag on Alfredo Griffin, August, 1987. *(Photo: Courtesy of
Ernie Whitt)*

Mike Slaughter

Tony Bock

(top)
Scoring the winning run as Jack Morris rolls in the first of seven
games against Detroit, September, 1987. (Photo: Courtesy of
Ernie Whitt)

(lower)
Trying to swing without pain at Tiger Stadium, September, 1987.
(Photo: Courtesy of Ernie Whitt)

Toronto Blue Jays

(Photo: Courtesy of Ernie Whitt)

"Well, there's some cocksucker in here that says we've got a country club going. He says we don't have the ability to win this thing."

Cliff said, "Now, Coxy, are you going to let this drive a wedge between us?"

"Sit down and shut the fuck up." Coxy's veins were just popping and his eyes were bulging. If Cliff hadn't sat down and shut up, Coxy would have ripped into him with more than words. "Well, that same son-of-a-bitch is the guy who came up with double vision on a Sunday afternoon in New York with a left-hander throwing, the guy who was out running hard and drinking Scotch all night long, and now he's got the balls to come here and say that we don't have the nerve or the talent to win this thing."

He just ripped Cliff to shreds, going on about how he owed all of us an apology. Cliff kept saying he hadn't meant anything by it, he'd been misquoted or misunderstood. The screaming and yelling went on for ten minutes. But in that afternoon's game, Cliff was in the lineup as DH and everything was forgotten. I think he even had the game-winning RBI that day. That was Coxy's style.

As it was, we struggled the last week of the season again. We went into Detroit and dropped all three games, which brought the race down to the final weekend series against New York.

We were so determined to win it. We had to win it. We were going to win it. Even the Friday night game didn't shake our confidence. We had the game won in the ninth before Butch Wynegar tied it up with a home run, then lost it in the tenth when Lloyd dropped a routine flyball. It didn't matter. We were going to win.

Doyle went the distance in the Saturday game and gave up only one run to the Yankees. It must have been even more satisfying for him because New York had given up on him and George Steinbrenner was still paying his salary. Against Joe Cowley, Willie homered, Lloyd homered, I homered. We took the game 5 – 1 and ran

185

out onto the field. We mobbed Doyle and carried him back and celebrated in traditional style in the clubhouse, getting soaked to the skin in champagne showers. We had won 99 games. It was so thrilling after so many years of being out of it to see everything come together and to win the toughest division in baseball. We had to struggle, but we did it. The city went mad, the partying kept on until the wee hours of the morning. It was a great time.

Sometimes I wonder whether we didn't become satisfied with achieving that goal. We had set so many other goals before and had come close, but had fallen back so many times that I think we were a little astounded that we'd actually achieved this one. Maybe we didn't go into the playoffs hungry enough. We wanted to win more than anything in the world, but maybe we were missing just a little edge. I don't know. Maybe we became too complacent and eased up after the first two games went **186** our way. It's hard to say what happened, except George Brett.

In the first game of the championship series against Kansas City, Dave Stieb shut the Royals down. They got only three hits through the first eight innings. Tony and I drove in two runs apiece and we were up 6 – 0 in the fourth. All Kansas City could come back with in the ninth was one run.

The second game was tense. We were down 3 – 1 going into the fourth, but came back to tie it in the sixth. When George Bell hit a sacrifice fly in the eighth, we went up by a run, but then Pat Sheridan came in to pinch hit in the ninth and hit one over the wall. The Royals went ahead in their half of the tenth, but Al Oliver, the pinch-hit specialist we'd acquired for the stretch drive, lived up to his reputation. With two outs and two on, Al singled in the tying and winning runs. He had more heroics in the fourth game when Charlie Liebrandt stopped us cold while the Royals went up 1 – 0 in the sixth. We tied it in the top of the ninth, then Al came in to pinch hit again and doubled in two more runs.

A big part of our strategy in the whole series was to try not to pitch to George Brett. We really didn't want George to beat us. Anyone but George. But there were situations where we had to pitch to him, and when we did pitch to him he beat us. He really got his team going with two home runs and a 4-for-4 day in the third game to beat us 6 – 5. That was a game we should have won. Jesse and Rance both homered for us, the only home runs we hit in the series. In the sixth game, when we should have been wrapping it up, George broke a 2 – 2 tie in the fifth with another home run.

Then in the final game, the Royals beat up on Dave Stieb in the sixth and went up 6 – 1 on Jim Sundberg's triple. That nobody could believe. It was such a lazy flyball, an easy out that drifted and drifted in some jet stream right out to the top of the wall. It shouldn't have happened. But then, we shouldn't have walked Steve Balboni, of all people, to load the bases for Sundberg in the first place.

187

I remember going back to the hotel in Toronto and sitting there quietly with Chris, saying, "How could we have lost it?" People all over the city were probably asking the same question. To me, we had a better team than Kansas City. They had great players like Brett and Frank White and Hal McRae, but I felt there was no way they could match up with us. The one thing I could never understand about that series is that Jim Clancy had been taken out of the starting rotation and moved to the bullpen for long relief. We went with Doyle, Dave, and Jimmy Key in the series, but Doyle and Jimmy had struggled against Kansas City all year while Jim had pitched the Royals effectively. He always has.

How could we have lost it? I have to look at it in the sense that we just weren't meant to win it that year. We had them 3 – 1. St. Louis had them 3 – 1 in the World Series, too. Kansas City did the same thing to the Cardinals and came out of it as the World Champions. It was like somebody upstairs was saying, "Look, the Royals are going to win this thing and that's all there is to it."

About a week after the final game of the pennant series, Bobby Cox announced that he was leaving. It wasn't a complete surprise. We felt that he was being put under a lot of pressure. He was the type of man who liked to do things his way. He didn't want to be dictated to and we felt that maybe he was being pressured by the organization to play certain players or do certain things he didn't want to do. Instead of having that hassle, he had the opportunity to go home to Atlanta with the security of a five-year contract, something Toronto wouldn't offer. I think another reason he left was that he and Pat Gillick were real good friends and their friendship was on the edge. But even with his family in Atlanta and the security of the contract, I think he might have stayed if the Blue Jays had offered him more than just a one-year deal.

He was the best manager I'd ever played for. All he ever wanted was a player to go out and give everything he had on the field. He accepted that physical mistakes were going to happen, but believed that mental mistakes come from lack of concentration, and there's no need for that and there's no excuse for that. He was a fighter, and he had the respect of all the players because we knew that he wasn't going to take any bullshit from anyone, whether it was from management, an umpire, or a player on the team. He proved that many times over. I was sorry to see him go.

We picked up after the 1988 All-Star break with a two-week road trip, the longest trip of the year, beginning with four days in Oakland. We'd played well against the western division in 1987, but this year we hadn't done well at all. We'd dug ourselves a big hole with those teams while having a winning record against the AL East.

We usually have a team meeting to start the second half, but this year the meeting schedule was a little different. Jimy had some things on his mind, so he first asked Pat Gillick, Paul Beeston, and Peter Hardy to fly out to the coast to re-evaluate the first part of the season and, I guess, to talk about some of his concerns and clarify some of his thoughts. It was good he could talk with them. Jimy seemed to have aged ten years. The pressure was getting to him and he was really looking bad.

The players didn't know that the brass had been in town. I think they just flew in, met for a few hours and flew right back out again. But Jimy told the whole team he had met with them and had told them he wasn't going to take any more bullshit and was going to start fining and benching players.

I was happy to hear that. There had been a lot of incidents all through the year when I thought some disciplinary action should have been taken, and I don't mean over disagreements some players expressed about some of Jimy's moves. That's always going to go on. That's part of baseball. That's the nicest thing about the sport, all the armchair quarterbacking, the talk around the donut shop the morning after the game of "How could he pull the pitcher?" or "Why didn't he call for a bunt?" Players like to do that as much as anyone. And I doubt there's any business anywhere in which the workers think that the boss is doing everything right all the time. Why should baseball be different? Players are entitled to gripe about management as much as any other group of employees.

But the boss is still the boss and deserves both respect and an effort on the part of his people. If he's going to keep that respect, he's got to set down some rules about the way his group operates and he's got to make sure the rules are followed. When they're not followed, then he's really got to lay down the law. The rules are there for everybody and if any player screws up, it's a fine. Automatic. Cut and dried. No questions asked.

All year, we had players wandering in at 5:15, the time when everyone was supposed to be out on the field. Some players wouldn't show up for infield when everyone was supposed to be there unless he had clearance from Jimy. Players would show up late or not at all for team functions. Guys weren't wearing collared shirts on the road. They were wearing T-shirts at home. Except for Rick

Leach being fined for wearing jeans to Tiger Stadium, nothing was ever done. To me, that's when a person in authority loses respect. That's when the second guessing goes from the normal disagreements with moves to questioning every move a manager makes, because people are always looking over his shoulder and thinking, "How come I have to do this and not him? I guess I can get away with that because nothing happened to this other guy." If the team is supposed to be someplace at a particular time and if we are in fact a team, then the team better be there. The whole team.

It's not in Jimy's makeup to assert his authority all the time. He's a good guy who'd rather go a different route. That's just his personality. He tries to treat his players like men, believing that if they have respect for him and for the organization and for the game, they'll go along with the rules without him having to stand over every player's head all the time, saying, "You've got to do this" or "You've got to be on time." He'd much rather ride along without rocking the boat, which is fine. But if there are players who take advantage of a manager's good nature, he has to draw the line.

190

I felt all year that Jimy was trying to pamper certain players. I felt that he was afraid to discipline some players because he thought they would quit on him. That's a bad way to go about things and it creates a bad feeling in the clubhouse. There's no reason why a manager shouldn't demand obedience to the rules and demand hustle on the field. If a player doesn't run out a ground ball or make an effort on a fielding play, the manager has every right to say, "You're on the bench. You don't want to play, sit down. I'll get someone who'll give me a hundred per cent." And it doesn't matter whether the player is a rookie or the most valuable player on the team. That sets the tone, just as Joe Morgan did in Boston when he took over the Red Sox and benched Jim Rice. It doesn't matter who the player is. It matters who's the boss.

A manager has to be a disciplinarian, but he also has to understand the players. Players want to be treated like men. They want to know they have a role and are expected to play it, and they also want to be able to express concerns without fear of repercussions. Jimy went out of his way after the All-Star break to hear what the players had to say and to improve the communication on the team. He called six of us in — George Bell, Lloyd Moseby, Mike Flanagan, Jimmy Key, Kelly Gruber, and me — to talk about what we needed to do over the last half of the season. We were going to be a kind of liaison group with the rest of the players. He felt we needed an attitude adjustment, but said that management hadn't given up on the team, he hadn't given up on the team, and that we shouldn't give up on ourselves either, even if some of the fans and the media had already written us off.

He asked us all for our opinions on changes that could be made on the field, and as we went around the table there seemed to be a consensus in three areas.

We were concerned about the emphasis on youth when we were expected to be a contender. When we left spring training, we left with rookies or second-year guys at first, second, third, the outfield, the mound, the bullpen, and behind the plate. It had worked out well with a few, like Kelly, Freddie, Pat, and Duane Ward. But it was tough for Sil Campusano, for example, who will be a tremendous player some day, to learn the job at the major league level while we were supposed to win. The same went for Nelson Liriano, who has great ability and very good work ethics, the best among the rookies, but was still learning the game.

191

We also expressed our feeling that Jimy was not using Tom Henke enough. We realized that the organization was grooming Duane Ward, and the playing time Duane got helped him change from a thrower to an effective pitcher. But when there's a horse like Tom out in the bullpen, he should be utilized. There had been many situations that had arisen when we thought Jimy could and should have gone to Tom but didn't.

Our other concern was Jesse Barfield. We felt that management would just have to accept that Jesse is a streak hitter. He's the sort of player who can look terrible at the plate for a week solid, but who can carry the team for a week or ten days when he gets hot. He was that way even in the year he hit his 40 home runs. He'd go two weeks sometimes and do nothing, then would turn around and tear up the league. He's never going to hurt the team defensively, so he just has to get out there every day.

Jimy said that as far as he was concerned, Jesse was going to have to work himself back into the lineup. We felt one of the reasons he wasn't in the lineup was that he hadn't listened to some of the things Cito had told him to do and had said that he would work on things himself. Talking to Jesse, I know it had been a frustrating year for him. He knows he's a streak hitter but he found that every time he'd get his stroke back he'd be given a few days off so he could work on his hitting in a "positive" frame of mind. All that ever accomplished was that he lost his rhythm and timing all over again. The man just wanted to play every day.

192

I think the attitudes did change after that meeting. We weren't going to just play out the season. We were going to fight to win as many games as possible because in this game anything can happen. We knew first-hand about that after being four-and-a-half games in front the last week of the 1987 season then losing the division to Detroit.

Some individual players came alive, too, especially Manny Lee. When his attitude is proper, he's a tremendous athlete. He's more of a slap hitter from the left side, but he's got some pop from the right. Ever since he had come up, he'd wanted to play shortstop, which was unlikely as long as Tony stayed healthy. After the All-Star break he seemed to finally accept his role at second base and started playing more aggressively. His attitude really changed and he started making plays I couldn't remember other second basemen making.

Oakland had beaten us eight straight in April and May, but we took three out of four from them in July. Flanagan, Key, and Stieb all pitched really good games, and while

Dave didn't win, we had our chances to score and didn't do it.

About a week after the meeting in Oakland, we were in Seattle when Jimy called us all in again. In the game the night before, Jimy had benched George because of the horrendous road trip he was having defensively. There are defensive slumps as well as hitting slumps, and George was going through a big one. The bus had arrived when Jimy came out and said, "George, we'd like to have you in here at our meeting."

In front of all the other players, George said, "No, I don't want to go into the meeting."

I didn't think that was a class act at all. Jimy had gone out of his way to show his confidence in George and to treat him as a leader on this club, then George just turned his back and refused to have anything to do with something that was supposed to help the team turn things around. That told me that George was only thinking about himself. But, again, when George has his mind made up about something, no one can change it.

193

I was disappointed by what happpened and I'm sure Jimy was, too. The group of six went to five then never met again. I also felt that maybe Jimy had it in his mind, "All right, you showed me up in front of the players. I'll pick my time and show you up someday."

A few days later, we were in Minnesota. We had a two-run lead with Twins at first and second. There was a hit to left and George charged the ball, but then he threw past the cut-off man to try to get Kirby Puckett at the plate as he ran in from second. I jumped as high as I could, but the ball was way over my head. Kirby scored and the runners advanced to second and third, wiping out the possibility of a double play on the next hitter. When George came into the dugout, Jimy said in front of the players, "You've got to hit the cut-off man."

George exploded and started mouthing off to Jimy and the two of them got into a very heavy shouting match. They were angry enough and close enough to each other that it looked like they were going to come to blows, but some players and coaches moved between them to stop the confrontation. I know some players were hoping they would come to blows to get their conflict settled one way or another. It had never stopped simmering since it had boiled over in spring training.

I was far enough down the dugout to not hear what they had said to each other, but I was told later that George had said it was my fault the runners advanced because I hadn't tried to catch the ball. That bugged me. Chris and the kids were on the road trip, and that night Chris and I stayed up into the wee hours talking over whether I should just let the whole thing roll off and leave it as a "George will be George" sort of thing. But I had to confront him with it.

The next morning, I asked him, "Did you say it was my fault that the runners advanced and that I should have caught the ball?"

"Yes."

194   "George, you give a hundred per cent on the field. I give a hundred per cent. No one plays harder than you and me and that's what I appreciate about you. But you've got to be a man and stand up and say you messed up. Admit it. You mess up, you mess up and that's all there is to it. If I throw a ball into centre field to get a guy trying to steal, it's my fault. I threw the ball away. I take the blame. And, George, you threw the ball away last night. It was a physical error and a mental error. You had no business trying to throw Kirby Puckett out. You wanted to keep the double play in order."

He said, "Ernie, I'm sorry. This whole year has not been a good year. Nothing has gone right for me this year."

We looked at each other, but there didn't seem to be anything left to say, so I just walked away. We didn't speak for over a week. George became very reserved and wasn't his usual self for about ten days after the incident before he came around again. Frankly, I thought both George and Jimy were at fault, George for his mental error and Jimy for confronting him in front of his peers. That's the old Billy Martin style that doesn't have a place in the game anymore. No one likes to be embarrassed like George was in Minnesota, or like Jimy was in Seattle for that matter. If you've got something to say to a man, call him aside, take him down the runway and say it. Nothing more has to be done.

As I went back to the dugout, one of our radio broadcasters, Jerry Howarth, said, "Ernie, I'd like a drop-in for the show on George."

I was still in a pretty sour mood from talking to him, so I said, "I have no comment. I don't want to talk about it. I'll talk to you on Friday."

I walked on and Todd Stottlemyre said, "What have you got no comment on?"

"About my retirement because I'm sick of all the bullshit." I smiled at him, Todd smiled back, I walked on.

We played the day game in Minnesota, then flew to Toronto, so we were back early to the house we had rented in Mississauga for the summer. Chris and I were watching the ten o'clock news. When an item came on about my impending retirement and the plans for a statement Friday, Chris looked over casually and said, "The least you could do is tell me when you're leaving the game."

195

I couldn't believe it. By the eleven o'clock news I wasn't just issuing a statement, I was calling a press conference. It reached all the newspapers right across Canada and got picked up by the media in the States. Friends from all over the continent started calling and asking me what was going on. I had no idea such a big deal could be made over nothing. The best I could do was try to make light of it, saying, "How else is a guy who's hitting .230 going to make some headlines?"

Needless to say, I took a lot of ribbing around the clubhouse. Mike Flanagan came up to me with a look of real concern and said, "What am I going to do with your retirement present? Boy, I hope I can take it back."

I was glad when all the fuss died down. When it did, I could think about the western road trip with some satisfaction. It had been a good trip both personally and as a member of the team. Personally, because Jimmy Key had been sabotaging my locker all year, cutting the bristles off my brush and doing other sneaky things. He never owned up to it, but I had witnesses. In Minnesota, I finally managed to get into his locker and snip his new shower shoes. My only regret was that he didn't walk out of them. As a team, we could take some satisfaction because we came out of it okay, even though it was rough. We had some big early leads and ended up losing. We took leads into the ninth and gave the game away. We blew some games. But we were 8 – 6 on the trip. I felt we could have been 12 – 2.

August

We started the month three games under .500, which
seemed to be a real barrier for us. We'd get close, then fall
back again. What we didn't need were injuries to compli-
cate things for us, but Lloyd Moseby's back pains put him
on the disabled list for a couple of weeks and Sil Campusano twisted his ankle. Rob Ducey got the call up from
Syracuse to take over in centre field.

Doug Bair, a veteran right-hander, got the call, too,
when Todd Stottlemyre was sent down. It was a good
move for Todd. We hadn't scored many runs in his starts
and I think he looked at his record and lost a little confidence in himself. He had a really hard time against left-
handed hitters. They were batting around .370 off him,
while right-handers were only batting around .190. He'd
bear down too much when a left-hander came up.

With younger pitchers, they get ball one and you can
see their face get tight with tension. Ball two, and they
look like they want to rip the hide off the ball and tear out
the stuffing. Then they bear down and start throwing
harder and harder, rather than just relaxing and letting
everything happen. That's when the catcher has to go out

and say something. It might be a joke or some remark about a nice looking woman in the stands. If the guy's getting hit pretty good, I might tell him we have to move the married infielders back since they still want to have children. Anything to relieve the tension. Learning to relax in those situations is one of the hardest things to do, but pitchers have to learn that if they're going to stay out of trouble.

Todd would get into trouble when he tried to do more than he was capable of doing. When he stayed within himself and let everything flow naturally, he had a better curve and better velocity and movement on the fastball. After George and Jimy had their altercation in Minnesota, he came into the game and walked three straight hitters. I think he threw only one strike. But in a situation where he got behind on the count and there was nowhere to put the batter, he started worrying about laying one in there that the hitter could take out for a grand slam. He tried to aim a little more, and when a pitcher tries to aim too finely, he misses even more and loses velocity off the fastball. He was trying to throw strikes, but he just couldn't do it that night. That's the way baseball is. Some nights everything goes right, some nights everything goes wrong.

Any pitcher wondering how to stay on an even keel could do worse than to look at Jim Clancy. He keeps everything inside. He's the type of pitcher I don't have to go out and pump up or calm down. He's on an even keel, whether he's getting ripped or he's in control. He never lets anything bother him, at least he doesn't show it. The most emotion I remember him ever showing was in '82 when he had a no-hitter going against Minnesota. It slipped away with two outs in the ninth when Randy Bush had a broken bat single over Damaso Garcia's head. When he lost it, Jim stepped off the mound and looked briefly up in the air.

Jim and I go back since Day One. We're the last of the original Blue Jays taken in the expansion draft of 1976. I remember when he came into camp that first year, a tall, lanky right-hander who threw hard. He was a power pitcher, but a very quiet individual. He never said much then and he still doesn't. He's a good guy to have around, though. Quiet as he is, he's usually in the middle of the practical jokes and pranks in the clubhouse or the con- frontations we always get going on the bus. I'm known as something of an instigator on the club, and Jim's always quick to jump in. I remember him really getting worked up over a bet we had on how long it would take our bus to get from Seattle airport to the Warwick Hotel down- town. Jim and I had $100 riding on it — I said 20 minutes, he said 25 — and we both got our supporters screaming at the bussy to slow down, screaming at him to speed up. Run the red lights. Get going. Jim gets very animated in that kind of situation. (We made the hotel in 19 minutes, 57 seconds.)

We've stayed pretty close, not only as teammates, but as families. We've lived close to each other in Mississauga and our kids have played together. Chris has remained good friends with Jim's wife, while they're going through a separation.

199

He's really easy to work. His control is there most of the time, although he goes in streaks where he gets into trouble. He's still a power pitcher, a fastball-slider type, but he's been working on an off-speed pitch the last couple of years. He's developed a changeup or a split- fingered pitch, and his curve has come a long way. He went out against Milwaukee this year, basically a fastball hitting club, and threw his curve 50 per cent of the time. I think it was a three-hitter. That will help him, because sometimes he falls in love with throwing the fastball.

With Jim, if you can get him through the first inning, he'll settle down and do well for six or seven more before he tires. He's the sort of pitcher the catcher has to work with early to find out what's working for him. He likes to establish his fastball the first couple of innings, then goes to the slider. If he doesn't have the overpowering fastball, we move to something else. Usually he has at least one pitch working very well for him, but it takes some time to find out which one, and it usually takes a couple of innings to get all of them working. But he's flexible enough to be able to change quickly. In one spring training game against Cincinnatti, he threw nothing but fastballs and got beat up pretty bad. The bases were loaded with nobody out and Eric Davis was coming up to bat. We switched to nothing but sliders and struck out Davis and the two batters after him.

He's a workhouse who can give the team 240 innings a year. He'll never complain about anything and accepts whatever the manager does. He really struggled this season, with a pretty brutal first half. When Jimy took him out of the rotation and moved him to the bullpen, Jim was the first to admit he was having a tough time. Some pitchers would have complained and asked to be traded, but he just said, fine, he had some mechanical things to work on so he was happy to get the time.

200	He goes about his business, preparing for each game by playing Top 40 tunes on his guitar. That's kind of changed over the years. It used to be that the pitcher of the day had precedence in picking what kind of music we listened to in the clubhouse, and everyone accepted that. With Jimmy Key, it didn't really matter, but when Doyle Alexander was pitching, it was country music. With Dave Steib, it was nothing but hard rock and Clancy would bring in the Top 40 tape he wanted to listen to that night. Now most times everyone has his own cassette. Dave still listens to the hard, hard rock, but he does it over on his seat with the headphones on. Dave's also a collector of guitars, and a lot of times he'll sit in front of his locker with an electric job hooked up to headphones so that only he can hear what he's playing, which is fine with us. But the day that Jim pitches, he takes his guitar back into the weight room while everybody takes batting practice.

Jim worked hard while he was in the bullpen, and in the second half of the season, he was one of our better pitchers.

By the middle of the month, we finally went over .500 after series with New York and Kansas City. We had put some distance between us and Cleveland. We were now solidly in fifth place and closing in on Milwaukee, but we still had New York, Boston, and Detroit to get by. As always, rumours of trades for the stretch drive were floating around the league, and prominent names seemed to be Jesse Barfield and Dave Stieb, who had both asked to be traded. It was unfortunate, but another player who let it be known that he'd be willing to go to another club was Tom Henke.

The whole year hadn't been going well for Tom. He'd converted almost every save opportunity he was given, but he didn't feel there were enough of them. He felt that maybe the Blue Jays were getting back at him for taking the club to arbitration in the off-season. I couldn't believe that was the case, although every arbitration case seems to end with bad feelings. Tom had been upset that he'd had to go to arbitration in the first place, and even more upset that the arbitrator didn't see things his way. But, for his part, I think he'd gotten over that by spring training. Tom's not the sort of man who holds grudges. He could see the experience as something to learn from, even saying that every player should go through it at least once to toughen him up.

201

I'd go along with that. Negotiating for big dollars is quite an experience for ball players. Most don't come from very wealthy backgrounds and scratch along at pretty poor pay in the minors. Then suddenly they find they're dealing with figures that can go up into the millions. I guess that's when agents become really helpful, although the longer a player is in the game and the more business experience he gets, the better he can handle negotiations himself. I took that route in 1986, and it was a real education.

Bargaining with the front office was something I thought would be an easy thing to do. I felt that the relationship I had with the Blue Jays was a good one — and I still feel it's a good one — so I figured that once we got into the negotiations it would be very cut and dried. Basically, all

I was looking for was parity with the other catchers in the league. I'd always had an agent before, but it didn't seem right to pay someone five per cent of my money just to get a contract. I was prepared to do it myself. I wanted to do it myself.

Chris and I thought we would get the numbers on what catchers were making from the Players' Association, take my standings from the Elias Bureau, which is known throughout baseball and used by both clubs and players, find out my rankings, put the numbers together, and it all would be quite simple.

I guess the reason we were a little naive in thinking that was because of what happened in spring training in 1986. I could become a free agent at the end of the season. I was playing out the option year of a three-year contract that paid me $175,000 in 1984, $175,000 in 1985, and, if the club exercised its option for 1986, which it did, a base salary that year of $275,000, with deferred money. The deferred payments of $41,000 for ten years starting in 1990 added another $410,000.

In the spring, I sat down with the Blue Jays Administrator of Player Personnel, Gord Ash, to talk about a deal. I looked at the first proposal that he put on the table and I couldn't believe it. The way he explained it, I'd be making a million dollars the first year, a million-two the second year, and a million-five the third. I looked at him and said, "Is this right? Is this for me? Or is this for Bell or Barfield?"

"No, this is it."

I took it home right away and Chris and I looked it over and said, "Gee, this is unbelievable." We were really excited about it, especially since we thought if they were offering this in the first proposal, what were they going to do if we negotiated a bit. They always start at the bottom line.

As soon as I walked in the next day, Gord said, "I didn't explain something to you yesterday. Those numbers are what the total value of the contract would be after a certain number of years, under certain conditions"

"Excuse me, Gord, run that by me one more time a little bit slower."

What it came down to was if I deferred taking a lot of money, the contract would be worth a million dollars after ten years. What they were offering me was actually $450,000. I said, "This is totally unacceptable to me. All I want to do is talk total dollars now. I'm not worried about what it's worth ten years from now, I want to know what the total dollars are going to be for 1987 and 1988." Finally, I said, "Gord, can you and I sit across the table, reach an agreement, shake hands, and we've got it?"

He said, "No, I'd have to get it okayed."

"Well, nothing against you, Gord, but I personally would much rather sit across from someone who, if we strike a deal can stand up, shake hands, and we've got it. I don't want to have to wait a couple of days down the road to get an okay." He said he understood and that's when I started talking to Paul Beeston and Pat Gillick. Paul and I spoke during spring training, but nothing was accomplished. The numbers never got higher than $500,000. I'd had real good seasons in 1983, '84, and '85. I was ranked up among the top three catchers in the league all those years. So when I saw other catchers making $800 – 900,000 and even over a million dollars a year, I looked at the $500,000 and said, "No thanks."

Paul said, "Let's put it this way. If you go out and have a good season, we'll open the bank doors for you." I thought, fine, I'll take my chances. I wasn't really concerned about going through the season without having a contract at the end. That's just part of baseball. I took him for his word on it and played through the '86 season going on what he had said. All along I thought, "This is going to be a piece of cake. I go out and perform, I'll be compensated for it."

It was a tough situation for our ball club in 1986. We were coming off winning the division, but we'd lost the playoffs and we'd lost our manager. All the players had really liked Bobby Cox, which made it an especially

203

tough situation for Jimy Williams. No one really knew what kind of manager Jimy would be. We knew he was knowledgeable about baseball and that he'd had managing experience in the minor leagues. He'd been with the team since Bobby Mattick took over in 1980. He was always approachable and had a good relationship with a lot of players, me included. Relationships with most of the coaches improved after Coxy moved their changing lockers from out near the manager's office to into the clubhouse with the players. Coaches still ride a separate bus with the manager and the press, but their lockers are still in the clubhouse.

Everyone had liked Jimy as the third base coach. I thought he was one of the best third base coaches I'd ever seen, and that's an important position, the key position on the coaching staff. The pitching coach is critical, too, and good batting instructors are worth their weight in gold, not so much for going over the mechanics of hitting as for talking about what a pitcher is going to do in certain situations. The bullpen coach works with the catchers and evaluates whether pitchers are ready to go into a game. The first base coach is mainly there to work with the fielders in practice and remind runners on first in a game situation how many outs there are, what the pitcher's pickoff move is like, whether a fielder is sneaking in on a play. That's why a lot of first base coaches are guys just starting on their way up or guys putting in the years to get their pensions.

But a third base coach in a game situation has to relay all the signs from the manager to the hitters, sometimes very quickly, like when there's a pitch-out and the runner's got a quick take-off. He has a lot of split-second decisions to make. How fast does my guy run? He may be the fastest man on the team in a straight forty-yard dash, but how well does he run when he has to make that turn every ninety feet? Does he loop around, which costs time, or does he make the proper turn to go home? How is the opposing outfielder's arm? Can he make the throw? Is it worth the chance to send the runner in? Who's on deck?

Is he hot? Is it better to hold the runner and see what the next batter can do?

Jimy was very good at making those decisions. He's a fundamentally sound baseball man. He evaluates situations and players well. He's good at handling game situations on the field and he's a super instructor. He sticks up for his players, to the umpires and to the media. But to go from the third base coaching box to the manager's office is a hard transition. As a coach, you're changing in the same locker room as the players and it's all buddy-buddy. You have to listen to the players' complaints and try to help them out. You don't have to show any authority, because that's the manager's job. Then, all of a sudden, you're the manager and it's not buddy-buddy anymore. You still have to keep an open-door policy and listen to the players, but you've got to separate yourself from them and make decisions and show that you're the boss.

Getting the right balance is tough for any new manager **205** coming into the big leagues, whether he's promoted from within the organization or not. New guys always have to feel their way around, and it's become even tougher the last few years since managing styles have had to change. The old-style manager is fading from the game. You still see the same names coming up all the time — Dick Williams, Chuck Tanner, John McNamara, Dallas Green, even Billy Martin for one last kick at the can. These guys seem to float between teams, always getting rehired whatever their record on the last team they managed. But the players are different now, the business is different, and sometimes the style doesn't match up too well.

A guy like Billy Martin would be awfully hard to play for. Talking to some of the players who've been with him, if you ever made a physical mistake he'd jump all over you. It's difficult to play with that kind of pressure hanging over your head. From what I understand, he'd always second guess the catcher, too. If the catcher put down a fastball and the guy hit it, Billy would wonder why the dumb son-of-a-bitch didn't put down a curve. But if you told him it was a spitball, then Billy would never yell at you. He and Art Fowler, his pitching coach, were always teaching pitchers how to throw wet ones, blowing out a few good arms in the process.

Always getting on a player's case and intimidating umpires by screaming and yelling is just not an effective way of going about things anymore. New York loved Billy Martin because the fans there love to see battles and they knew they'd get one every time Billy stepped onto the field. They don't call it the Bronx Zoo for nothing. There's always something going on in Yankee Stadium. There are the animals out in right field with the conga drums, the cans, and bells, getting the Latin beats going and getting the crowd motivated. There's always a fight breaking out someplace. You always see security guards running. You always see the guards grabbing people who've jumped out onto the field, dragging them through our dugout, beating the hell out of them down the runway. There's no place as bad as Yankee Stadium. It's the one place I've never wanted Chris to see a game. It's dangerous.

It was funny the first time we went to the city as tourists. We went down before Christmas one year and I told her, "These people are so rude. They'll cut you off, push you around, let doors slam in your face. The people of New York are the rudest people in the world." But everything I said went right out the window. Everyone was unbelievably polite and considerate. We ended up out on the streets at four in the morning, singing "New York, New York" and having a great time.

But something seems to happen in the summer. People seem to turn crazy. Yet you can't get away from the feeling that Yankee Stadium is a special place. When I'm not playing, I like to sit out in the bullpen visualizing Mickey Mantle and Babe Ruth and Roger Maris and all the other great players, imagining what it must have been like to play with them and against them. I'm sure kids down the line will wonder what it was like to play on the same field as Mattingly, Winfield, and Henderson. Yankee Stadium

206

is so traditional, yet such a madhouse. The fans almost demand not only a team of superstars, but a manager who's fiery and intense. I thought Lou Pinella was a good choice to replace Billy when he got released for the last time. Lou was an intense player and he manages the same way, but he stayed close with his players and he manages people very well.

The key is utilizing all your players, not throwing the same nine guys out there all the time, keeping the team fresh. Tom Kelly has done a tremendous job that way in Minnesota. Sparky Anderson's done the same with his group of overachievers in Detroit. The newer guys like Tony La Russa or John Watham are the same way. They're good at people management, not only handling each of the 24 guys going out individually against the pitcher, but putting a whole team out there on defence, a team that really functions as a group as well as a collection of players. It comes down to a manager taking charge of a ball club, and that's not always an easy **207** thing to do.

That kind of thing takes time, and when Jimy took over the Blue Jays he didn't move quickly to really get control of the team. He let things slip away from him more than he should have. We got off to a terrible start in 1986, winning nine games and losing eleven in April and going 14 – 15 in May, but it wasn't until the middle of May that Jimy had his first meeting to air some dirty laundry. From that time on, we made a nice surge back into the race. We were in seventh place, ten games back at the beginning of June, then played well over .500 ball — 17 – 11 that month, 15 – 11 in July and 18 – 10 in August. By September, we were in second place, only three and a half games behind Boston.

We got off to a fairly strong start on the stretch drive, then came the incident I mentioned before. We went into Boston with the Red Sox needing to win one game against us to clinch the division. Joe Johnson had shut out Boston for eight innings only the week before, but he was pushed back in the rotation to pitch against the Yankees. Duane

Ward would be making his first major league start. We found that so puzzling. We were in a situation where we had to play full out. We had to win every game, day by day, and not think ahead to some future series. All the players were wondering, "Why in the world would they make a move like that? Why would they let a rookie start a game of such importance?" The only answer seemed to be that management had written us off. They were saying, "Well, we've blown this season so let's forget about it and see what the young kids can do."

That was so disheartening. It was like a physical blow to our pride and intensity. When we lost the game 12 – 3, the "let's forget about it" attitude spread. We were out of the race and just playing out the time. We ended up in fourth place, nine and a half games back.

It had been a mixed year, maybe understandably so with Jimy getting a feel for both the team and the manager's job. The bright spot was Jesse Barfield leading the league with 40 homers and he and George Bell both driving in 108 runs. Jesse and Tony Fernandez also became the first Blue Jays to win Gold Gloves for their work in the field. And Mark Eichhorn just blew hitters away with his sidearm delivery. He won 14 games, saved ten, and finished the year with an ERA of 1.72.

Personally, I had a good year. I've never been a flashy player. I might hit three home runs in a game or get a grand slam on an exceptional night, but I feel that my strength is consistency, year after year. I'm out there every day with the gear on, ready to do what I can, and I usually hit between 15 and 19 home runs, average .250 or .260 and drive in 50 or 60 runs. In 1986, I hit .268, with 16 home runs and 56 RBI. I thought that record was "a good year," good enough to get the bank doors open, anyway. Then the contract negotiations started.

In the middle of October, Paul Beeston called and said he was coming to Windsor to talk. I crossed over the river, met him for lunch and was offered roughly the same numbers he'd presented to me in the spring — $500,000 a year on a two-year contract with a third-year club option. They were not going to give me the three-year contract I wanted.

Needless to say, I was a little upset with him. "Paul, I thought you said that if I went out and had a good season, you'd open the bank doors for me."

"Well, we feel this is very fair for you."

"But I want parity with the other catchers."

"What's parity?"

"I think we're talking $850 – $900,000 a year. That's not overpay. That puts me right in the middle of the catchers, and that's getting rid of the Gary Carter contract." Carter had signed when the owners were just giving money away, so Chris and I didn't even include his contract in our calculations. We were talking about Carleton Fisk, Rich Gedman, Lance Parrish, or Ozzie Virgil and Jody Davis in the National League — catchers who caught 125 or 130 games and had decent numbers offensively. Putting their numbers together with mine and comparing where they ranked to where I ranked during the past few years, we thought $900,000 was a very fair number. There were a few catchers, not including Carter, making over a million dollars a year, and there were five or six others making about $700,000. So we kind of averaged them out.

Paul said, "Yeah, I understand where you're coming from. I'll take it back to Pat and we'll talk about it."

All through the negotiations the Jays said they only wanted to give me a two-year contract. They had come up with a policy where there would be no three-year contracts, although if they absolutely had to agree to one, it would be with younger players they knew were going to be around for a while. All along they also said there'd be no more incentive clauses in terms of the number of games or innings played. They had recently had a problem with Dennis Lamp over incentives in his contract that would guarantee the following year if he played in a certain number of games. He had filed a grievance that the organization had kept him out of some games because they didn't want to guarantee that last year. So the only

209

incentives would be of the award type — All-Star selection, Golden Glove, Silver Bat, MVP of the league.

That position cut off some negotiating room because if you get to where you're only $100,000 apart, you can always bridge the gap by throwing in incentives. And that can be good for the ball club and good for the player. If the player performs, then he should be rewarded.

After that meeting in Windsor, I thought, "Now what do we do?" They were at $500,000, I was at $900,000 and we were not closing quickly. Through October it kept going back and forth. They would call, I would call, nothing would change. Then Pat and Paul flew into Detroit and met with Chris and me for about an hour at the airport. Still nothing had changed. At the end of the meeting, I took a baseball out of my sports coat and tossed it over to Beest. On it, we had written "The ball's in your court." They got a kick out of it. But that was the way the negotiations went. We got along fine. There were a few snide remarks snipped in here and there and I'd throw a couple their way, but nothing hostile. It was very cordial, but nothing was accomplished. We seemed to be meeting just to say we were meeting. The whole process seemed to be more for the press and the people of Toronto who were interested in what happens in baseball in the winter time.

When I was going through Toronto's airport in November, I called Pat to see if there'd been any movement on their side.

He said, "No, we haven't changed our position. If you feel you're worth that kind of money, why don't you test the free agent market."

That kind of caught me off guard. I thought, "Here's an organization that says they want to keep me, yet they're telling me to go out and test the free agent market?" To me, that didn't make sense unless they really didn't care whether I stayed with the team or unless they knew there was no other team out there that was going to touch me or offer me more money than the Blue Jays were offering. That told me right there that there was a little collusion going on between the clubs. When he told me that, I knew I was going to be in for a long road. It upset me. I mean, you play your whole life to get to where you can make some good money, then you find the ball clubs all sticking together to bring the players' salaries down and there's no bidding going on for your services.

There was a deadline in early December for announcing that you were a free agent and another date soon after for filing for arbitration. If you accepted arbitration, you didn't lose your free agency, but you were considered signed to the ball club for one year and had until your arbitration date to try to reach an agreement.

I went into the free agent market.

The most common complaint in baseball is that there aren't enough veteran catchers. Here I was, 34 years old, with almost ten years experience in the major leagues. I'd spent my career with one of the elite teams in the game and had been ranked consistently among the top of my profession. Not one team called me. But I called about ten ball clubs, all in need of catchers and all American League teams, except one. I contacted the Atlanta Braves and spoke to Bobby Cox. Coxy said he already had two over-priced catchers on his hands. If he could deal one of them, he'd be more than happy to have me, but he couldn't see anyone picking up their contracts.

Only one team showed any interest at all, and that was the Oakland Athletics. Sandy Alderson, the general manager there, said to send a proposal, but also said they didn't give three-year contracts.

I talked with the Yankees. Woody Woodward, the general manager at the time, said he'd get together with Lou Pinella down in the winter meetings in December to re-evaluate their talent and would get back to me afterwards. I knew Lou Pinella liked me as a player, so I figured things might work out in New York because they were looking for a catcher. They never got back to me.

I talked with Bill Lajoie in Detroit. He said the Tigers were going to put all their eggs in one basket to re-sign Lance Parrish. I could accept that. He also said that even

211

if they didn't retain Lance, the Tigers have a policy that they won't sign free agents because they wouldn't want to give up their first round draft picks as compensation. So there went my chance of playing for Detroit, the only team I'd really want to go to if I couldn't play in Toronto.

But at least Bill Lajoie was very good about it. He was going down to the winter meetings, too, and said, "I'm getting back on Friday, I'll call you Saturday morning to let you know what our people think." Bill Lajoie and I have had our differences. He had said way back when how he felt that I would never make it past AA ball. That kind of motivated me a little bit then and it still does when I go into Detroit. I still want to prove him wrong, even though I have long ago. But he was good enough to get back to me when he said he would. The other clubs didn't bother.

Ten different ball clubs, and only one that showed any interest. I really didn't want to go to Oakland to play anyway, so that limited me to one team and that was the Blue Jays, which was fine because I really felt that sooner or later things were going to work out. Toronto was the place I wanted to play.

The deadline for filing for arbitration was around mid-December, but I had already told Pat that I was not going to accept arbitration. I wanted more than just the one-year deal arbitration could give me. The deadline for an organization signing its own free agents was January 7th or 8th, which left us about three weeks to negotiate after the arbitration deadline passed. And with Christmas, the holidays, and people away on vacations, the whole last half of December was gone. We were really down to the first week of January to make a deal, yet there was really no concern on the Blue Jays' part. But then they knew there was no other team out there bidding on me. I never let them know that, but they had confidence.

We met once more in December before the winter meetings. Pat and Paul booked a suite upstairs at the Renaissance Centre in Detroit where Chris and I joined them. Paul had a briefcase with all the material he felt he

212

needed and said, "Okay, we're going to get down to it today. Now, tell me where you're getting your numbers from."

I explained the procedure I'd used — the Elias ratings, the numbers from the Players' Association, my conclusion that $900,000 would give me parity with other catchers.

He said, "That's not what we have."

"Well, tell me what you do have."

"According to this Elias ranking, that's not the way it should be."

"Wait a minute. You're looking at the wrong rankings."

"Oh no, it's right here," and he showed me the page.

"That's not it. Turn the page and this is the final rankings right here."

He got up and called Tal Smith, who handles arbitration for the Blue Jays and other ball clubs. Tal said I was right.

After 20 minutes to half an hour studying the numbers and rankings, he said, "Okay, I see where you're coming from now. We have no problem with it. We'll work with it. I'll tell you what we'll do. We'll offer you a two-year contract at $700,000 a year."

"We're still $200,000 apart. That's not what I'm looking for. $700,000...I mean, not to take anything away from it, it's a lot of money, but it still doesn't give me parity with other catchers."

"Well, this is our offer to you. We'll give you two years at $700,000 a year and we'll have a third year option that we'll throw in at $800,000."

"It's not acceptable."

"Think about it. This is our offer to you right now. $700,000."

All through this process, Chris would throw in supportive comments, saying things like, "Here's someone who's been very loyal to your organization, has done everything you've asked him to do. He's gone away in the winter time to help promote baseball all over Canada, to help promote your organization, and the numbers are right here in black and white. We're asking for parity with other ball players and you're saying yes, we see that it's fair, but you're not going to give us the numbers. Why is that?"

They had no explanation, but through the whole process Paul Beeston would often say "the pendulum swings both ways." The pendulum had been on the player's side for a number of years, and now the pendulum was on the management's side. He said, "We know you're worth that amount of money. Two years ago you would have gotten that amount of money. You would have gotten a lot more. But this is the way it is right now. This is what we're going to pay you."

It still wasn't acceptable, so we shook hands and wished each other a Merry Christmas. Then Chris and I gave them a present she had prepared that we felt they would probably deserve—a little stocking full of coal.

214 It was frustrating. The whole process was such a serious thing for me, doing it myself for the first time and thinking that it was going to be easy because I wasn't trying to get a huge contract. Needless to say, I spent many a sleepless night, especially towards the end, trying to think of ways of how we could bridge the gap. Every time I'd come up with a brainstorm, they'd veto it. During the last week before the deadline, we talked maybe once a day. Had they changed? No. Had I changed? No. And every day more and more media people would call.

"Has anything been accomplished?"

"No, nothing's been accomplished."

Three days before the deadline, Paul called to say he and Pat would fly in with a final offer two days later, the last day before the Blue Jays would be unable to sign me back until May. They came to the house and handed us a hand-written proposal — $750,000 for 1987, $750,000 for 1988, and a club option for 1989 at $800,000 a year that would be exercised within 48 hours after the last game of the World Series. There were some incentives — for

MVP, Gold Glove, Silver Bat, World Series MVP, league playoff MVP — and a $250,000 interest-free loan that would be paid back in 1990 if the Blue Jays didn't exercise their option.

We sat there. We talked. We went around and around the same arguments. Finally, I said, "No, this is not acceptable to us. You know, I thought we were going to get something done here. Well, let's at least eat."

Chris had made her famous porkchops, and after dinner we went back into the living room for coffee and a little more discussion. But they wouldn't budge. Paul said, "You knew we were going to give you our final offer. This is our final offer to you and we're not going to negotiate any more. This is it. It's take it or leave it."

"Well, I'm going to leave it."

It was only 7:30, but they got up to leave. And Chris and I started thinking something was wrong. They knew the last plane had already gone. They had to spend the night in Detroit, yet they were leaving at 7:30. Maybe they were really not concerned whether they signed me or not. As they left, Pat said, "I'll call you tomorrow to see if you've changed your mind."

"Fine, you can call me, but I'm not going to change my mind. This is not acceptable to me."

The final day arrived and all the newspapers started to call. I told them, "Nothing's happened and nothing will. I'm not going to sign with them. They said that was their final proposal. I gave them my final proposal. I was willing to negotiate, but they left. They didn't want to negotiate, so as far as I'm concerned I won't be a Blue Jay."

The whole day went by with never a word from Pat. Finally, about quarter to six he called. "Have you thought about our proposal any more?"

"No, I haven't thought about it. Why should I accept something like this?" I was mad. I was angry that they had left at 7:30 unwilling to try to work things out when they had to spend the night in Detroit anyway. I didn't know whether they wanted to get their beauty sleep or what, but it was very frustrating to me. And I was mad

215

that this was the first word I'd heard from the organization all day.

The call turned kind of nasty. I said, "How do you guys sit down when you agree with my numbers, you have no problems with my numbers, you know I'm not trying to rip off the organization, you say you see where I'm coming from, yet you go way below my market value?"

He said, "Look, you're just a platoon player. You can't hit left-handed pitchers. You're lucky to be getting what we're offering you."

I kind of snapped. "It's not my idea to be a platoon player. I've told you, I've told all the managers I ever played under that I want to play every day. And if you look at my numbers, I do quite well against left-handed pitchers."

He came up with a number and said, "You had your chance the final month of the season in '85 and you didn't hit."

216   "Pat, do you remember I almost broke my shoulder the final month of the season? Most of your players wouldn't even be playing the final month if they had an injury the way I had an injury. But we didn't have a catcher that could do anything."

"That doesn't matter. You still only hit .185 the last month."

"I was playing hurt. I went out there for the team, for the organization. I wanted to win that thing really bad and I was out there playing hurt the whole last month of the season."

"Well, you're still only a platoon player. And you can't hit against left-handed pitchers. And that's all that we're going to pay you. No more."

"Well, you're not going to pay me anything because I'm not going to play," and I slammed down the phone.

Chris's mouth just dropped after all the screaming, and she couldn't believe I had slammed the phone down in his ear without saying goodbye. But I was furious.

I said, "I'll never play for the Blue Jays again. We'll take our chances. We'll go on to other places."

I was very bitter about what he had said. He knew the whole left side of my body was black and blue, and for him to say I didn't perform, it was like he had no respect for me whatsoever. It hurt. I mean, it really dug deep into me. Then I said to myself, "Wait a minute, maybe it's just a negotiating ploy. They're just trying to get under my skin. I'm not going to let that happen." But it still really hurt.

The whole evening, phone calls came in from the media. I told them negotiations had broken off. I would not be a Blue Jay. I had to tell the same thing to the photographer for one of the Toronto papers who was camped out on our driveway.

Paul Beeston was giving a speech in Sarnia that night, but in between courses of the meal he must have called Pat to find out what was going on because about 9:30, he called and said, "I hear you and Pat had a problem."

"That's an understatement. Yeah, we had a problem. I **217** just cannot understand why you guys agree that my numbers are fair, but you won't accept them. I'm not saying that $750,000 is not a good salary because it is. I mean, anyone in their right mind would accept that. But I'm going by what the market value is."

"We understand that, but it goes back to that pendulum. The pendulum is on our side and we don't have to pay you that."

I dropped down to $800,000 with incentives and the loan, but still they wouldn't budge.

Paul said, "Look, I can't increase the numbers. What I will do is increase the loan. We'll put it up to 350 but that's the most that we can do for you. Think about it. I'll call you back in about half an hour."

I called John Boville, my financial planner, and asked how much the change increased the value of the contract. He figured that with what we could do with the interest free funds, it was worth at least another $25,000 each year, which would bring the numbers up a bit. "It's not bad," he said. "Not bad."

Catch

At 10:00, Paul called back. I was in the mood to play some hardball, too. "I just can't understand that you're going to let a guy go who's been good for the organization over a matter of $50,000."

"Ernie, we just can't do it. We've reached our maximum of what we're entitled to pay you. As far as we're concerned, we've stretched it because we do want to keep you, but we're not going to go any higher."

I told him I couldn't accept that. He said he understood and wished me the best of luck. At 11:15, Pat called back, saying, "I'm going to have to put out a press release to say what we've offered you and probably say some negative things because of what you made last year and the fact that what we were offering you was a good pay increase."

"I don't give a damn what you do. You go ahead and do what you want. I'll have my own little press release. I understand what you have to do. Please understand what I have to do. It's unacceptable and that's just the way it's going to be."

He said okay and we both hung up.

Chris and I sat around in silence, just watching TV. The midnight deadline was getting closer. Chris flipped through the stations around 11:30 and landed on the "Dating Game." We didn't say a word. I started getting agitated. Things were getting tense.

"Chris, we've got a big decision here. Do we pass up this kind of money and take a chance on what we don't know lies ahead of us? I mean, there's uncertainty out there. Look what happened in the '85 free agent market. What's going to happen here?"

"I don't know what we should do."

Quarter to twelve and I said, "Chris we've got to make a decision. Do we accept this or don't we? It's not what we want, but it's definitely a big increase. I mean, we never dreamed we would make that kind of money. How can we give away a certainty for an uncertainty, when we're talking that kind of money? We'd be set for life by accepting this contract. We know there's collusion going on out there. We know we'll have a grievance through the Players' Association. If I'm worth what we feel I'm worth, we're going to be compensated down the line. Maybe we should just take it and let the Association follow up."

"Yeah, I guess maybe we should."

"We've got to make a decision."

"You'd better call them then."

Ten to twelve, and I called Pat Gillick. His line was busy. What the hell do I do now? We've got to get to the Association by midnight. It had been made very clear that there would be no extensions. I called the Association and spoke to a representative. "Look, I've called the general manager, his line is busy. I want to accept their proposal as it stands. Okay?"

"That's fine. As long as you've notified us, we'll notify the Players' Relations Committee [the owners' organization] and it's a set deal."

Five minutes to twelve. I called Pat again. He answered the phone. I said, "Okay, we've got a deal, except that you know it's a 350 loan, not 250."

"The 250? No, no. It's an advance on salary."

"What? Wait a minute, I've got it right here. It says a $250,000 loan and you knew Beeston increased it to 350."

"Oh, I think it's an advance on your salary, not a loan."

"Pat, we've been negotiating this for two days and this is the first time you've ever come up with an advance. I think we've got a problem because I'm not going to accept it as an advance on salary."

We had another problem because the only person who could clarify the situation was Paul Beeston and he was on the highway somewhere between Sarnia and Toronto. Pat called the owners' organization and I called the Players' Association and read the guy there the contract as I had it. It was 11:58. The Association's man hooked up a conference call with Pat and me to see if we could straighten things out, but Pat wouldn't make any commitment until Beeston got back to Toronto around one o'clock. The way we left it was that if the contract read

219

Catch

750, 750, 800, with a 350 interest free loan, it was a deal. If not, I was a free agent.

We waited. The phone kept ringing and every time it did I'd jump up thinking we'd finally have a decision. But every time it was another reporter asking if the deal had been done.

About 1:25 AM, I got the call from the Association. Paul had just arrived and clarified the issue. "It's an interest free loan. You're signed with the Toronto Blue Jays."

Pat called to confirm the contract and said he'd call back in the morning, although it was three days later before I spoke with anyone in the organization, and that was Paul Beeston. Again, the phone was ringing off the hook and we sat up until about five in the morning trying to unwind and relax. We were exhausted, but happy that the whole long process was finally over.

There's no question it was the most nerve wracking thing that I'd ever gone through. It was fun in a way, but it was frustrating, too. I always said I'd only take on doing it myself if I could deal with anything harsh that was going to be said. I really didn't think there would be too many negatives flowing out of the negotiations, and there weren't until that six o'clock call. But that got under my skin and I still feel it today. It's a bad feeling when the organization doesn't seem to recognize a gamer who wants to play every day and who plays injured, especially when there are an awful lot of players out there who won't play if they have a hangnail, players being paid premium dollars. To this day I wonder if they really respect me for the type of player I think I am. I don't know if I'll ever know the answer to that.

Other than that doubt, the experience didn't have any negative effect on my relationship with the organization, at least not on my part. It had kind of a surprising effect on the way I feel toward Pat Gillick, though. Pat is a neighbour of mine down in Dunedin, Florida. He's always been very nice to my family. He's helped Chris carry groceries or offered to take her and the kids to the ball park. But to me, he's always been kind of distant, not

220

the type of person to look someone directly in the eyes. I still sense that he's not really happy with the way I handle myself or the way I go about my chores. There's just not a warm feeling there. I never really see him that much around the condo in spring. He runs every morning and I might see him as he's coming in when I'm out walking the dogs and it's a "Hi, how are you doing" type of thing. There are players he seems to feel more comfortable around than me. I think in some cases he gets too emotionally involved with some of the players. I've never really felt that close with him, but oddly enough I think since the contract negotiations I've felt more comfortable with him than ever before.

Looking back, that was a good time, not a bad time. I filed a grievance, along with a lot of other free agents that year, and Chris and I both testified at the arbitrator's hearings in New York. We won our case and were happy to hear the arbitrator's finding of collusion among the owners. We expect to be compensated somewhere down the line, but there's no hard feelings on my part against the Blue Jays or the owners, generally. From the start, I looked at the negotiations as a challenge. It was a business experience that was something different in my life. It was something that I had never done before and something that I really wanted to do. It always helps to play against the best, and I learned an awful lot from playing hardball with the Jays.

I have to give the Blue Jay organization credit. It set out with a plan to build a successful franchise and it accomplished that goal. It certainly must be the most successful expansion franchise ever. To think what we've accomplished in only twelve years in a tough division puts things in perspective.

The organization has always taken the long-term view, and that's as it should be. It has to make sure that there's always going to be a team that plays good enough ball every year to draw the crowds that will help turn a profit. As a businessman, I can understand that. The organization's been very good that way. We've got some good scouts who Pat Gillick's relied on to get talented players who were left unprotected on the rosters of other teams. There's been a lot of talent developed within the organization.

An organization can't just throw a talented team out on the field and expect it to win, though. Talent's the foundation, and we've had a pretty good foundation for a long time, but if there was one thing we showed in 1988, it was that we have to get a winning spirit back, a winning desire, that positive flow of things through the organization. That was really missing this year, and I think there's got to be a change in the philosophy of some of the people in the organization to get it back. I guess there always has to be a balance between the long-term view and the short-term view. Thinking ahead, in a game or a season or over five years, has its place. But there also comes a time when you have to say, "What'll happen next inning or next week or next year is all well and good, but there's something we have to do right now if we're going to win this thing."

If one of the goals of the organization is to win a world championship, then it has to do the little things necessary to win. It's got to look for overachievers, not underachievers. It's got to make some of the players appreciate the fact that they're in the big leagues, and make sure they don't forget how good it is up here and how rough it is down in the minors. It's got to go with the best players and not play options and numbers games.

Players are never taken into management's confidence about what the thinking is. The organization's intentions are sometimes hard to read, so players always look for little clues. The best is the shifting around between the majors and the minors, which sends a message to the players. It tells them something. That's why there's always a lot of speculation about who'll be called up in September.

When we went into Arlington for a series against the Rangers at the end of August, the call-ups were the main

222

topic of conversation around the clubhouse. It didn't seem the same to be in Texas without having a bunch of Upshaws running around.

There was speculation about Geronimo Berroa, a left-fielder who was having a good year, just to have another right-handed bat coming off the bench. There was speculation about infielders like Alexis Infante or Eric Yelding, who had a great year at second base in Syracuse. There was speculation about Todd Stottlemyre and Pat Borders coming back up.

It was interesting that Pat's situation worked out so nicely from the organization's point of view. Sal Butera had come up after Pat had pulled a rib muscle around the All-Star break. He'd been on the disabled list for awhile, then stayed with the Chiefs. Sal was catching well and the pitchers seemed to enjoy throwing to him, but Pat was doing a great job down in Syracuse and could have come back sooner. I'm sure his bat would have helped in August, but he'd been left down until September. I don't know whether it was just a coincidence, but a player needs three years of major league service, with 172 days in each year, to be eligible for salary arbitration. By being in Syracuse until September, Pat would wind up the 1988 season with 169 days of service, meaning he'll have to play almost four solid years before being able to go to arbitration. Maybe I'm reading more into the situation than I should, but that seemed a convenient way for management to get the upper hand and hold a gun to his head for an extra year. In a business sense, I guess that's what you have to do, but it's unfortunate that that sort of "numbers" thing has to happen.

It's always interesting to speculate on the rookies, especially wondering if there'll be any sign of humility or appreciation for being up in the big leagues. It used to be that rookies were seen and not heard, but now they generally talk back to the veterans and act as if they think, "Yeah, I'm up here and I got it made. I'm as good as you are." The veterans don't like it very much.

223

There are ways of welcoming rookies to the game. When I first came up, I was a victim of the "three-man lift," which is too complicated to explain, but the rookie ends up pinned in the middle of the clubhouse with his pants down while the other players toss anything from tobacco spit and baby oil to atom bombs, cola, and powder onto his crotch. That kind of thing sets the tone for the pranks that usually go on in the clubhouse, like the sliced-off pant leg, the flaming fire-bomb, or, my own favourite, the bucket of cold water on the guy in the crapper. I've also been known to use a hose.

There are all kinds of variations we use to get even with the rookies for talking back, and it's usually on a getaway day when all the clothes and shoes are packed and on their way to the airport. What quieted Lou Thornton down was a long, embarrassing walk through the airport in Baltimore wearing funky yellow shoes with three-inch heels. After Rob Ducey had popped off a few times, some

224 players got into his locker around the eighth inning of a game and spread some Capsolin in the crotch area of his pants and the armpits of his shirt. Capsolin's a very hot substance, and the heat intensifies when moisture is added. As Rob danced around the bus on the way to the airport, he vowed never to talk back to veterans again. The same treatment was handed out to David Wells and Jose Nunez, with the same result.

At the end of the month, the organization sent Doug Bair down to Syracuse and brought David Wells back up. It was a puzzling move, bringing Wells back with only four days to go before the September call-ups. Maybe a trade was in the making. But what made it a shocking move to the players was that Doug had been doing a good job for us, doing everything he had been asked to do. In eight games, he'd come in with 12 runners on and had stranded every one of them. When David went to Syracuse, he complained and threatened to file a grievance against the club for sending him down with a sore arm. He spent two months with the Chiefs and pitched only five times. He got into a game in Texas on August 26, and nothing had changed with him. He was still throwing the ball, not pitching. He couldn't get his curve over, the pitch he was sent down to the minors to work on. It seemed so unfortunate, as it had all season. Here was a guy with a tremendous arm who just hadn't matured enough to become the real good pitcher he could be.

Other than speculation, everything seemed to be on a slide. Most of the players were talking about the end of the season, as if they'd already written off the year.

On August 27, we played an exciting game that we gave away. George Bell was kicked out. He had argued after Tim Welke called a strike on him while George was about ten feet away from the batter's box, so Joe Brinkman ran him out of the game. The defence wasn't there, we couldn't turn a double play. The attitudes really started to crop up. To me, there were too many fingers pointing in the wrong direction. Everyone had some excuse. The talk on the bus was "That was Jimy's fault" or "Jimy should've done this" or "If we had a real manager." Stuff that I hadn't heard since Bobby Mattick's and Roy Hartsfield's day. On Jimy's record alone over the three years that he's managed the club, third best in the game, he deserved better than that. I hadn't always agreed with everything Jimy had done either, but he had also made some correct moves that just didn't pan out. If a player doesn't do his job properly, there's nothing a manager can do about it. And if the organization doesn't come across with the personnel to work with and who will match the manager's style, it's very hard for him to win.

There was just too much complacency. We had too many players making good dollars who were in the comfort zone. The incentive and the initiative seemed to be gone. There are certain players you can give high salaries to and they'll continue to go out and bust their butts and try to do better. They won't become complacent with themselves. There are other players you can't. To me, the organization has to know the personnel, know what each player is like before they hand out contracts like that.

225

Players were pretty much giving a hundred per cent during the games, but there weren't many who were willing to put out that little bit of extra time and effort that has to be put out to win. We have extra hitting every day at home and almost every day on the road, and all year it was always the same people coming out. Rance Mulliniks was always there, Nelson Liriano, Rick Leach, me. It doesn't have to be much. Even five or ten minutes a day would be fine, just to work on things and fine tune the instrument. Jesse and Lloyd had come out around the beginning of August and their numbers had started climbing up. Even in the early part of the season when averages were around the "interstate line" — I-95, I-96 — too many players, both rookies and veterans, didn't take it upon themselves to say, "Geez, you know I'm not feeling that good at the plate. I better do something about it."

The team was going through a tough time. The attitudes were bad and tempers were short. I made my own contribution on a team photo shoot. We had a day game to play, but we had to be out on the field in uniform at 10:30 for the photo session. The photographer waited five or ten minutes to see if everyone might show up, then went ahead anyway. Fifteen minutes later, one of the missing players wandered in, so the photographer started again. A few minutes later, another latecomer arrived, so it was back to square one. When he said he had to change cameras yet again, I said, "Bullshit. Everyone was supposed to be here at 10:30. I was here at 10:30. Most of us were here at 10:30. We've been standing here half an hour and you want to start all over again? Well, I can be a rebel on this fucking club, too." I walked off. No one was fined.

Everyone seemed to be saying, "Let's finish up the 30 days and go home." It's easy to go to the ball park and perform when you're winning. It's exciting to do that. When you're losing, that's when you've got to kick yourself in the butt and say, "Okay, I'm getting paid to go out and perform and I'll do the best I can." You've got to take some professional pride to finish the job you were hired to

226

do. It's difficult, but that's when a man shows what kind of ball player he is.

There were too many guys riding out the storm. That was the feeling I got from the coaches, too. Even from the manager. Jimy hadn't said anything to the players for three weeks. The whole staff seemed to be feeling the pressure of knowing they might not be back. Their minds all seemed to be somewhere else, maybe wondering if they might be on the unemployment line in 1989. It affected the whole morale of the club.

227

September

The last month of the season began with a meeting in the clubhouse on September 1. We had just come back to Toronto from Texas and Milwaukee. Al Widmar had joined the club again after missing part of the season because of surgery, and he had been watching our games from up in the stands in Arlington.

Jimy opened the meeting and basically said, "Gentlemen, we've got one month to go in this season. We can turn it in or put out an effort and prove to ourselves that we're a better ball club than we've shown this whole season. We're not out of the race yet. We've still got a month to go and as badly and as poorly as we've been playing, we're only ten-and-a-half games out. We could still sneak in the back door on this, but we've got to play good ball and we've got to go out and bust our asses and do everything we haven't been doing the last five months."

Al Widmar spoke, too, talking about personal pride and about how September was a 'salary drive' in his day as a player and still is today. The idea is that whatever a player does in September always helps out in negotiations for the following year because what a player does in

September is what people remember. He said that from his viewing in the stands in Texas, and the scouts with him felt the same way, it just looked like Toronto wasn't ready to play. We'd walk to our positions between innings, there was no fire under anybody. Like Jimy, he said we had to put fires under our butts, use the last month as a salary drive if we had to, but that we could put a scare into a lot of people if we had a good month. He said, "This team's very capable of doing well, and you never know what can happen."

We could see what was happening to the other teams in the division. Boston's pitchers were hurting, Detroit's pitchers were hurting, and New York's pitching was a disaster. Whatever we lacked in hitting, hustle, and execution, we had a strong pitching staff. It became even stronger when Mark Eichhorn, Todd Stottlemyre, Doug Bair, and Frank Willis were called up from Syracuse, along with Infante, Campusano, and Borders.

230 We left the meeting and took the Rangers 5 – 1. Jimmy Key kept Texas to six hits. I'd been hitting well, .314 since the All-Star break, and took one of Charlie Hough's fastballs over the fence to lead off a three-run fourth, then doubled and scored in the sixth. Jesse had two singles and a walk and Rick Leach got the game-winning hit. The only thing that marred the game was that Tony got thrown out after saying something in Spanish to the home plate umpire, Joe Brinkman.

We took the next three from Texas, too, getting 14 hits in the third game of the series. I singled, George got a couple of singles, Jesse doubled twice, and Freddie, Tony, and Rance all homered. We were back at .500 and seven and a half games behind Detroit.

We moved on to Tiger Stadium. In the first game of the series, Fred Lynn put the Tigers up 1 – 0, but Tony cleared the bases with a double off Jack Morris to put us ahead. They tied it, but Tony put us up again, only to have it go to extra innings tied 4 – 4. I was due up to lead off the top of the tenth, but Willie Hernandez, a left-hander, had taken over for Morris in the ninth, so I figured I was out of the game. Much to my surprise, though, Jimy left me in. I don't know why. I'm sure if it had been the inning before and George had got on base, Jimy would have pinch hit for me. Leading off the inning, maybe he felt, "Give him a shot." Before I went up, Cito said, "Look for the fastball on the first pitch, and if it's in the zone, don't wait for anything." The first pitch was a fastball, but not in the zone I wanted. The next was a fastball, too, that I took for another ball. Now I had Hernandez in the hole. He didn't want to walk the leadoff guy and I very seldom face left-handers. He'd have to come with a fastball. He threw one high and I hit it into the upper deck. With that, the Tigers dropped out of first place. We were now six and a half games behind the new leader, Boston.

We picked up the next game 7 – 3, with Jimmy Key up against Doyle Alexander, and started thinking "sweep." But the third game didn't turn out as well. It was a critical game for us. We could have made up some ground. New York, Boston, and Milwaukee all lost that night. But **231** we always have trouble hitting against pitchers who throw us a lot of off-speed stuff, and Frank Tanana beat us again.

We had been down, but battled back and tied it in the ninth. In the Tigers' last at-bat, Chet Lemon hit one to left, and I have to give him credit. Ever since I've known him, Chester's hustled right from the swing of the bat. He's always gone full out from the box, and that's where doubles are made. You don't make a double by jogging down to first then turning it on going into second. If he hadn't been a hustler, the hit was a routine single, a solid two-hop line-drive right to George. He didn't have to range to his right or left. He figured it was a routine hit, nonchalented the ball, looked up, saw Lemon driving for second and made the throw, but too late. Alan Trammell came up and singled in the winning run.

It was so frustrating to lose a game on a play like that. You can't take anything for granted in any game, especially not a critical game like that and especially against the Tigers, who seem to have won half their home games in the bottom of the ninth. But George didn't think he had done anything wrong and nothing was said to him, to my knowledge. I think Jimy had just grown tired of approaching him because he knew it would lead to a confrontation. It's unfortunate that George, this year anyway, felt that anyone who said anything critical was picking on him. No one likes to be criticized, but people are paid to point things out to you if you make a mistake. If I make a mistake, John Sullivan lets me know about it. I may not like it, but I have to accept it. It's part of his job to say what he has to say, and it's part of my job to listen.

We had seemed to be back to our winning ways, but then we went into Baltimore and dropped two games to the Orioles, leaving us seven and a half games back as we went home to Toronto to meet the Tigers again. After they scratched out a win in the first game of the series, we were back to .500 ball.

232   We came back to win the next two, though, the last of the series on a couple of hits by George and some hustle from Lloyd in the first to beat out a potential double play throw to second and then to beat out a throw to the plate. He was back on second in the third inning, with two out and Freddie McGriff on first. George hit a single and Lloyd headed home. Freddie started going to third. I was in the on-deck circle, waving Lloyd on because I could see there was going to be a play at third for the last out. But Lloyd eased up on the way to the plate, and didn't score before Freddie was tagged out.

When he got back to the dugout, there was a little confrontation like the one with George in Minnesota, only this time Jimy called Lloyd into the runway to talk to him quietly. I couldn't hear what they were saying, but I gather Jimy asked him why he didn't score and Lloyd reacted badly, taking the defensive and saying it wasn't his fault, that Jimy should be yelling at McGriff because he was the one who had the play in front of him. Freddie had committed a cardinal sin by making the third out at third base. But Lloyd did slow up coming home. They yelled at each other for a while, then Jimy just said, "Get out of here." Lloyd left the ball park.

To me, Lloyd is very moody. He's always one of two people. He's either joyous and joking or he's complaining about how tired he is or how his back's hurting him. He was a very cocky young man when he was rushed up to the big leagues, the same way some of the rookies are now. No one could talk to him and he had no respect for the veteran players. He was very confident and very sure of himself, yet it was still on-the-job training for him. But he's been a solid outfielder for the club. He's made some good plays out there, although I don't know whether he's ever thrown anyone out at the plate. He doesn't have a great throwing arm. Yet, offensively, he can make a lot of things happen. He's got speed. He's got power. He's made a tremendous contribution with his bat and his base running. When he hustles, he can be a real sparkplug.

He had given us the first run by hustling, but the next time he got on first, Jimy didn't give him the green light to steal whenever he got a good jump. That's why he didn't hustle on the way home and why he was mad at Jimy when he came into the dugout. I found out later that Lloyd was sulking over at first and was only taking a one-step lead-off. I mean, you can't do that. If I had the speed, I'd like to get the green light, too, but I'd have to figure there was a reason the manager hadn't given it to me.

To me, that was typical of what went on this year. Little things add up, even though they don't show up in the box scores. That's the way a talented team squanders its opportunities. It's the way we started to play even before this season.

We got off to a slow start in 1987. By the middle of April, we were playing .500 ball and were tied for fifth place, six games back. But we turned that around pretty quickly and stayed in first or second place most of May, June, and July. We even had an eleven-game winning streak in early June, a record for the club.

Through the whole season, we had some really hot bats. Fred McGriff ended up setting a rookie record with 20 home runs. Tony and Rance both hit over .300. Then there was George, having a career year, carrying the team offensively.

The starting rotation ran up good numbers. Dave Stieb had an off-year, but still went 13 – 9. Cerutti went 11 – 4, Clancy went 15 – 11 and Jimmy Key showed himself to be one of the best left-handers in the league. Tom Henke had a tremendous season, leading the league with 34 saves, and Jeff Musselman was very effective in his first full season.

We had the arms and the offence to do it all. I was really confident that this was our year. We had a better team than we'd had in '85. We worked and we hustled and could see that it was going to come down to us and Detroit. Juan Beniquez joined the team after the All-Star break to give us a little extra pinch hitting power off the bench. But as we headed for the stretch drive, we still needed some pitching help.

The first attempt at getting it didn't work out so well, when Phil Niekro came over from Cleveland. He was a class guy to be around, a quiet, serious man with a dry sense of humour. I'd look at him and think about his 300 victories and all the teams he'd played for, and I'd think that here was something I could tell my grandchildren about. I'd played with a guy who I'm sure will be in the Hall of Fame. After home games, I always sit in the whirlpool and Phil would come in and sit in the other tub, always in his hat, and we'd talk. He really had a thing about his wig. He was always the last guy to shower and he seemed to never take off that hat. I tried to get him to do it once, but he said, "Oh, no. Can't do it. Just can't do it."

He was only with us for a month or so and I only caught him one game. I didn't catch too many of his pitches, and that wasn't because of his knuckleball. It was because most of them were hit. I'd caught knuckleballs in the minors, so when Phil offered me an oversized glove I

234

turned it down. It seemed very heavy. I just used an old, very loose, flimsy glove of my own that was actually smaller than the one I usually use. I feel that I have quick hands, and the key to catching a knuckleball is to stay relaxed, let the ball come to you, then reach up and snatch it when it gets to the hitting zone. If you tense up and follow the ball in right from the mound, moving your glove up and down and from side to side, you'll be worn out by the second inning and be in for a long night. It was neat catching Phil, though. I really enjoyed it, and I was sorry to see a man of his stature go after only 21 days.

But we still needed a pitcher for the stretch drive and we were fortunate enough to get just what we needed. Mike Flanagan arrived in Toronto at the last possible moment before a September 1st deadline would make him ineligible for post-season play. Flanagan's a pleasure to catch. He's a thorough professional who always gives his best and never complains. He's a great guy to have around the clubhouse, a World Series and Cy Young winner who can help keep things in perspective. He keeps us laughing. He's quiet, yet he's off-the-wall, with a dry sense of humour and a deadpan delivery. In one game, I came in to catch when Mike was rolling along, no problem, 6 – 1 in the seventh. The very first sign I put down went out for a homer. The next sign did, too, and when I went to the mound, he just looked at me with a blank face and said, "Are you on my team?" Mike did a good job his first month with the Blue Jays, going 3 – 2 with a 2.37 ERA in '87.

235

We hadn't played the Tigers for almost three months when they came into Toronto in late September, but both our clubs had pulled away from the rest of the division. We'd been close for over a month, never more than one and a half games between us. When our home series started, we were up by half a game.

Flanagan pitched against Jack Morris in the first game, and we won it 4 – 3 in the eighth when Morris threw a wild pitch and I came in from third. It was great to win, but in the third inning Bill Madlock had tried to break up a double play by sliding wide of the bag at second. He got Tony in the knee and sent him flying. Tony came down hard on his elbow right on a piece of wood that marked out the second base area. His elbow was broken. We were upset with Madlock's slide, but when it comes down to a pennant race, a player has to play hard. It was an aggressive slide I've seen other players make, and if we had been playing on a natural surface Tony probably wouldn't have come out of it with anything more serious than a bruise.

In the second game, Manny Lee took over for Tony and ended up tying the game for us in the ninth with a triple down the right field line. Lloyd put it away by driving Manny in.

We had to come from behind the next day, too. The Tigers jumped all over Dave and built up a 9 – 4 lead that looked insurmountable, but we worked it to 9 – 7 going into the ninth. We got the bases loaded with no one out, then Juan Beniquez tripled. We were three and a half games up.

We should have finished things up in the fourth game. Doyle was trying to keep his consecutive win streak going for Detroit, but he gave up a run in the first and the 1 – 0 score stayed that way right up to the ninth. It looked like a sweep, but Kirk Gibson hit a clutch home run off Tom Henke to tie it up. Tom felt that it was as good a pitch as he had thrown all year, and it was. Good hitters can hit good pitches, especially someone like Gibson who seems to specialize in heroics in tight situations. He came back in the thirteenth inning to drive in the winning run. It was a hard loss to take, but we had to be happy winning three out of four from them. We had a two and a half game cushion that we felt we could maintain until the following weekend when we'd go to Tiger Stadium. We just had to hope that Baltimore wouldn't roll over against Detroit and that we'd have some success against Milwaukee.

The Brewers had always battled us, though, playing tough in 1986 and 1987. They're a good, young, ball club and we lost the Monday night game to them, the first of the three-game series. We were losing the Tuesday night game 2 – 1 in the fourth inning when I got a base hit. Jesse Barfield came up next and grounded one to third. The ball was bobbled, which gave me at least the chance to get to second base and try to break up the double play.

I slid hard into second in a kind of block situation where my arm came above my head, opening up my whole ribcage area. Paul Molitor was playing second base at the time, and as he jumped to protect himself, his knee hit my ribs. As soon as we hit I knew something was wrong. I knew it was more than just the wind knocked out of me. With all the collisions behind the plate and all the football games in high school, I'd had the wind knocked out of me many times, but I had never experienced that kind of pain before.

Tommy Craig, the trainer, and Jimy Williams came out. They kept saying, "Are you okay?" I couldn't say anything. I was just moaning and grunting. It hurt. Finally, I told them to give me a minute to gather my thoughts and slowly I picked myself up and walked through the dugout and into the trainer's room.

237

The team's doctor, Ron Taylor, was there. He looked at my side and said, "You could have a couple of cracked ribs and you might have punctured a lung. Let's go get an X-ray." But I'm hard-headed and wanted to play, so I told him I was fine. I guess I was hoping the pain would just be temporary and I'd end up with a bruise. I put the catching gear on and went behind the plate. I was catching the ball and throwing it back to the pitcher fine, but when I tried to throw to second base, I couldn't do it. I walked off the field.

We went to Mount Sinai Hospital and, sure enough, I had two fractured ribs and a little stream of air was escaping from a puncture in the lung. But the doctors said they'd keep me at the hospital overnight, talk to a couple of specialists and maybe get me back in a game by Friday. That put a bit of optimisim in my mind. But on

Wednesday morning I was in a lot of pain. Never having had cracked ribs before, I found it amazing how all movement seems to come from the upper body. It's very difficult to do anything, starting with breathing, without involving that area. For two weeks after the injury, I slept sitting up because it was just too painful to lie down.

On Wednesday afternoon, I came back to the ball park and dressed in uniform. I wanted to be with the team, at least on the bench, and try to root the guys on. But Juan Neueves threw an outstanding game for the Brewers. They had beaten us three straight.

Thursday was an off-day, and we went into Detroit on Friday having to win one of the three games to assure a tie and a playoff game the following Monday. We were still one game up. While we were playing Milwaukee, Baltimore had beat Detroit two games out of four, which we thought was fantastic. If Detroit had swept them we would have gone in with our backs against the wall. With the Baltimore split, we had the advantage.

238

But somehow, we didn't seem to feel that way. I don't know why. I think losing the game on the Sunday in the thirteenth after Kirk Gibson homered to tie it up in the ninth had something to do with it. It kind of set us back. I mean, it hurt. No one wants to lose an extra inning game, yet we had to be happy because we had won three out of four. But then after we lost the three games to Milwaukee it was like we just didn't have the fire or the drive anymore.

I don't know how much the injuries to Tony and me had to do with that. Tony is very strong up the middle and I feel I'm very strong behind the plate. I think the pitchers all have confidence in me as far as calling the game goes, as well as handling the defensive duties. But I don't think the injuries hurt us too much defensively. I thought Manny Lee did a good job of filling in for Tony, probably doing a better job defensively than Tony could at the time because Tony's knee was hurting and his range was limited. Manny made some plays that Tony probably couldn't have made then. And Greg Myers did a good job behind the plate and worked well with our pitchers. We have a very experienced staff.

Offensively, though, I think the injuries did have an effect. I've said before that pitching and defence wins ball games. We had great pitching and a good defence, but the Tigers had both of those, too. We were pretty evenly matched in those two areas. Every game against Detroit came down to a one-run margin and what we needed was timely hitting to drive in some runs. Five Blue Jays had over 60 RBI in 1987 — George had 134, Lloyd had 96, Jesse had 84, I had 75 and Tony had 67. Losing two of the top five run producers had to hurt.

Tony's .322 average was the highest on the team, and he was also batting in the third spot in the order, followed by George and me. Whenever the number three hitter and the number five hitter are taken out of the lineup, it's going to affect the team unless there's someone swinging a hot bat who can be put in there to protect the cleanup man a little bit. The opposing pitchers knew that they didn't have to pitch to George. They didn't give him much to hit at all, and he got frustrated. He started going out of his strike zone and swinging at some bad pitches. He wasn't patient and getting the walks. He was getting himself out. He wanted to do so well, he wanted to win and carry the team as he had most of the year, and I can't fault him for that. He tried to lift the team single-handed, but couldn't.

239

Coming into Detroit on Friday, I wasn't feeling any better at all, yet there was that bit of optimism the doctors had given me and the determination to give it a shot. The team doctors had brought all kinds of stuff from Toronto with them and started out by trying to wrap my ribs. That didn't work. So they said that with batting practice going to start at 6:00, they'd start giving me injections to numb the area about 5:30. We went down to the first-aid room in Tiger Stadium about that time and the doctor proceeded to give me five or six or seven shots in different areas, wherever I had any pain. I felt like a pin cushion. I got off the table and made some movement. I could still

feel pain but I figured it just took a while for the anaesthetic to take effect. I went back into the locker room, put
on a flack jacket and went out and tried to throw. There
was no way, but I thought that if I could swing a bat,
maybe I could DH or pinch hit.

It was cold, wet, and windy that Friday night. A tarp
covered the infield, so a centre field cage had been set up
for our batting practice. The only way to get to the cage
was directly across the field, and when I came out of the
dugout the field was just swamped with reporters and
cameras. It seemed like all the attention was on me, with
everybody calling out, "Are you going to play? Are you
going to play?" I just kept wishing that everybody would
go away. I understood they had their stories to do, but I
was feeling bad enough as it was. There we were in a
down-to-the-wire pennant race, two wins away from
getting to meet the Minnesota Twins, a team we'd owned
all year. And there I was on the field of Tiger Stadium, out

240 between the left field bleachers, where I'd spent so many
Saturday afternoons dreaming of playing in the big
leagues, and the right field upper deck where I'd hit so
many balls. I was right where I wanted to be, yet all the
attention seemed to drive home the feeling that I wasn't
going to get the chance to perform in the most important,
most perfect situation of my career. It would have been a
nicer evening without that walk from the dugout. As it
turned out, I never even got in the cage. The anaesthetic
was just not taking effect. I turned around and walked
back in deep frustration.

The lineup was posted and, of course, I wasn't on it. I
sat there watching the game, very discouraged, yet still
optimistic that maybe tomorrow would be a better day.
Maybe there'd be nicer weather, maybe we could get
more dosage in me and I'd be able to go with it. It looked
like we had assured ourselves of at least a tie when
Manny Lee hit a three-run homer into the upper deck to
make it 3 – 0. But the Tigers came back with four runs and
Doyle shut the rest of us down. David Wells did a tremendous job in relief, going six innings after Jim Clancy

was taken out. But we could never get the tying run. Very close, but we lost it.

I came to the ball park early on Saturday, and instead of going to the first-aid room, which was half-way around the stadium, I said, "To hell with it, let's just put up a sheet in the training room to keep the reporters from looking in. Let's do it right here." It was sunny and warm that Saturday, not hot, but a nice fall day. We went through the process again and this time I felt that the doctor hit all the right spots. I still couldn't throw, but I could pivot my upper body without pain and told Jimy I felt I could hit. He had already done the lineup and again I wasn't on it, but I said, "Give me a chance, let me see if I can swing in batting practice and see what happens." And I did swing the bat fairly well. I always enjoy batting practice in Tiger Stadium because you can see where the ball goes. They always try to go into the upper deck, anyway, and I hit a lot of balls there that day. But Jimy had his mind made up.

241

What made his decision even more frustrating to me was that Jack Morris was pitching for the Tigers and I'd always done well against him, with a lifetime average of around .350 or .360. Jimy said, "We don't want to hurt you and hopefully we can win this thing and you'll be ready for the playoffs Tuesday."

"But if we don't win here, there's not going to be a Tuesday for us."

He finally said he'd use me as a pinch hitter "if we need you."

The doctor had watched me take batting practice and asked how I felt. I said, "It feels good. I think we've got the right dosage. I think we're going to be okay."

He said, "All right. We'll come back in about the fifth inning and re-do the whole thing."

So in the fifth, it was back to the locker room, another round of shots and back to the dugout hoping to get the call. I was glad to at least be in the dugout because what was happening on the field was a great baseball game. Mike Flanagan and Jack Morris were just awesome, battling each other right through nine innings. Morris left after the ninth, but Flanagan pitched an incredible 11 innings.

For me, in the ninth, the novocaine started to wear off a bit, so we went back in again for a couple more shots as the game went to extra innings. Still I didn't get into the ball game. When Alan Trammel came up in the twelfth with the bases loaded and hit a hard shot that skipped between Manny Lee's legs, I suspected that I had seen my last chance vanish. On Sunday, the last day of the season, the Tigers would try to extend their one-game lead with a left-hander, Frank Tanana.

That Sunday, I went through the same routine — shots in the morning before batting practice — and I was feeling even better. Before the game and again in the fifth, the doctor came down. By this time, my whole side was black and blue from the needle marks. But Tanana pitched a good ball game and Detroit never did bring in a right-handed pitcher. Jimmy Key pitched a tremendous game. He held the Tigers to just three hits, and none of them should have been a problem. But Larry Herndon's lazy fly to left in the second got picked up by the wind and carried into the stands. The 1–0 score never changed.

242

When Garth made the last out there was just total frustration.

The picture of that last game that sticks in a lot of people's minds is George Bell standing on the dugout step almost alone as the rest of the team went back into the clubhouse. George was going through a lot of depression at the time. He had had a tremendous year, but he's a team-oriented player and it hurt that we didn't accomplish our goal. But he was no more depressed than the rest of us.

Jimy usually has the security guard hold the reporters out for a few minutes. After that game, they had to stay out a little longer than normal. A kind of shock set in over the team knowing that we had this right in our hands and we'd let it get away from us. There was no yelling or screaming, no throwing of helmets, no slamming of bats, very little cursing. It was like being in a morgue for a few minutes afterwards. Just total silence. Everyone was in his own thoughts. Everyone felt complete disbelief that it had happened to us. All that final week, we'd lose a game and we'd come back in and say, "Hey, we'll get 'em tomorrow." It was tough when it sank in that there were no more tomorrows.

The reporters came in and, of course, you have to answer their questions. They've got a job they have to do. But that's not the easiest time to talk with all the thoughts going through your mind — what could have happened, what should have happened, what didn't happen. Playing 162 games and accomplishing second place is like kissing your sister. It's nothing. It's frustrating. I can't think of any other word that describes the feeling. And when you're feeling so frustrated, you have to be very careful about what you say. There were a lot of things I think some players wanted to say, but didn't.

For me, I thought there were a couple of times in the Saturday game that Jimy could have used me as a pinch hitter. I was more than a little pissed off that I had gone through all the agony of trying to numb the pain, getting myself ready to pinch hit, showing him in batting practice that I could swing the bat and then not get used in a situation where I thought I could have helped. I had to bite my tongue a few times to not wonder out loud why he didn't send me in. But at times, you have to bite your tongue for the good of the team. Jimy gets paid to make those decisions. I don't always agree with him, but that doesn't matter.

243

A lot of people criticized Manny Lee for the Saturday game when Trammel's hit skipped between his legs. It was a hard hit ball in a do-or-die situation. The infield was in and, yes, you've got to make the play, but it was a tough play and you can't fault Manny for it. Errors are going to happen.

What you can fault players for are mental mistakes. There's no excuse to miss a sign, there's no excuse not to advance the runner with less than two outs and a guy on second base. There's no excuse for many of the little things we didn't do the final week of the season. I said all along that last week that the pennant was ours for the taking. We didn't have to worry about anyone else if we played the type of ball we were capable of playing. If we did that, then we would win it. We simply didn't play well the final week of the season. If you don't execute, you don't win. We didn't execute, so we lost.

A lot of people say that we choked, but that's not the case. We had great pitching the final three days. You couldn't ask for more from Clancy, Flanagan, and Key. They pitched their hearts out. If people want to say we choked, then fine, let them say that. We didn't choke, we just didn't execute. There's a difference.

We never threw in the towel, although we didn't go into Detroit with a lot of confidence. We should have. We had the advantage, yet it seemed around the clubhouse like Detroit had the advantage. We put more pressure on **244** ourselves than we should have. If there's a man on third base with less than two outs, the pressure shouldn't be on the hitter. The pressure is on the pitcher. He's got to try and get the hitter out, and if he doesn't then that's a run in. The hitter has to stay under control, stay within himself and do the things that he should be able to do if he's playing in the big leagues. You're not always going to get a runner in from third, but the feeling then was that there was more pressure on us than on the pitcher. That shouldn't have been the case.

The Tigers seemed very loose. There's no question they had some advantage by playing in their home ball park. You have to give their pitching staff credit, too, but it seemed like the whole team was more relaxed than we were. Maybe that had something to do with them winning the World Series in '84 with a lot of the same players. Darrell Evans is a very good person to have on a team, a leader others look up to and who's able to relax a lot of the younger players. And Alan Trammel had a tremendous year, George's main competition for the MVP award. Those two guys were key to their winning the series. But there's no reason why we should have lost three games to them. No reason at all.

I said afterwards that I thought it was a wasted year. There's no question we played good, entertaining baseball for the people of Toronto and across the country. Our pitching staff had given up fewer runs than any team in the league. Our defence had been the best in the game, giving up only 50 unearned runs.

Personally, I had a good season. Offensively, I matched the career high 19 home runs I had in 1985. My 75 RBI surpassed the best numbers I'd ever had and my .268 average was my best since Winston-Salem. When the Elias numbers for the season were released, I was ranked the number one catcher in the American League. Yet all that wasn't gratifying to me. It never will be gratifying because we didn't win our division or come close to achieving our ultimate goal of playing in, and winning, the World Series.

We had the team that was capable of doing it. With the **245** type of team we had, there was no reason why we shouldn't have won it all. It was great winning 96 games, the second best record in all of baseball. But the Minnesota Twins were the World Champions and they won 85. It doesn't make sense, but it's the luck of the draw being in the division we're in. We had our opportunities the final week and we didn't capitalize on them. Nobody took the title away from us. We gave it away ourselves.

The seven games we played against Detroit that last week of the season was like a mini-World Series, all one-run ball games between the two best teams in the game. I really feel the series took a lot of starch out of Detroit. It was so intense. Minnesota had a good team, but with really only two quality starters in Frank Viola and Bert Blylevan. When you have days off like you do in the play-offs and the World Series, though, you can basically go with two pitchers and maybe throw a third starter out there for one game out of the seven. Detroit was a better club than Minnesota, but our series took a lot out of them. They had nothing left when they played the Twins.

I didn't go to any of the playoff games in Detroit, but I did some analysis for the CBS station in the city. I'd do a six o'clock analysis of what I thought was going to happen in the game that night, key figures to look for, the lineups, the advantages to each team. At eleven o'clock, I'd do a recap of the key points of the game.

It was difficult for me to watch the playoffs, especially seeing Minnesota win it when they had beaten us only three times all year. It made me start wondering about putting some mini-playoff system into effect, with the two wildcards with the best records, no matter what the division, going at it for the chance to play against the winner of a series between the division champions. I wouldn't want to get carried away like the NHL, because that's ridiculous, but it's difficult to play 162 games and have only two winners in the final.

I had to watch the playoffs, but I passed on the World Series, watching only a bit of the seventh game. Like a lot of players, I think, unless I have a few good friends on the field I want to get away from the game for awhile when October comes around. The seasons are long, and another season is always coming up soon.

We really came to play during the last half of September. We played series against Boston, Baltimore, Detroit, and Cleveland, and we kicked their butts. We played with a lot of intensity, and I couldn't help but look back and wonder, "Where's all this intensity been the whole season? What would have happened if we had played like this all year?" We would have run away with the division.

We still had a few problems cranking up the drive for the last two weeks. When we beat Cleveland 4 – 3 in extra innings on September 16, we went four games over .500 for the first time all year. The next day, the Indians blew us out 12 – 3. That knocked us eight and a half games back, but Boston was coming to town the next day.

We took the first game 5 – 4, but Boston came back the next night to get only their second win against us all season. They got 16 hits and ended up winning 13 – 2. One of those hits was Wade Boggs's 200th of the year, making it six straight years he'd reached that mark. That was really something, a modern record. He's amazing, a pure hitter, the best I've ever seen. We know where he likes to hit the ball, and in that game we played our third baseman and shortstop no more than eight feet apart. Kelly and Tony were right together and Wade hit the ball between them.

I just look at him and say, "How does this guy do it?" There's something extraordinary about him. There's no one way to pitch to him. We'll make a great pitch, and he'll bloop it over the infield for a single, consistently. He almost never swings at the first pitch, although we've thrown him a fastball on the first pitch and he has hit it. He usually fouls off a lot of pitches and works the pitchers to 3 – 2, so our philosophy has been to pitch it down the middle of the plate and just go strike one with him. If he swings and hits it, fine. That's five pitches you don't have to throw to him. That saves wear and tear on the pitcher's arm. It's funny, though, that he's gotten his 200th hit of the year off Jeff Musselman two out of the last three years.

We went to Cleveland while Boston headed off to Yankee Stadium for the final showdown with New York. We were still on edge, I guess. There were some incidents between players. It was just that time of year when you're tired and frustrated and don't take as much as you usually do. Kelly Gruber and I got into it on the bus from the hotel in Cleveland. Kelly's got this head-butting thing he likes to do, and when he asked me a question and I didn't answer him, he put his head on my forehead. Four times I told him to leave me alone. He still kept his head on mine, so I threw him off me over to the other side of the bus, got on him, and told him again to leave me alone. I went back and sat down thinking that would be the end of it. He had hit the back of his head and saw a few stars, but when he recovered a few seconds later he came over and gave me a really hard head butt. I jumped up and

247

grabbed him, but the other guys held us apart. It was
unfortunate, but we apologized to each other at batting
practice. I told him that of all the guys on the team, he was
the last one I'd want to fight, and he said the same about
me. He's a good kid. There were no hard feelings.

That night, Dave Stieb went out for us and threw a
super game. He had a great curve, a great slider, a good
fastball, and we mixed the pitches well. He went into the
ninth inning without giving up a hit. We got the first two
batters out and worked Julio Franco to 1 – 2. Franco
fouled off a couple of really tough pitches, took ball two,
then hit a breaking ball to second base. It was a routine
ground ball. But it hit a rock and bounced over Manny
Lee's head.

I couldn't believe it. I walked out to the mound wanting to cry. We were obviously going to win the game, but
I felt like we'd lost the World Series. It would have been
the first no-hitter in Blue Jay history. I put my arm around
him and shook my head.

248

He said, "It's just my luck. I can't believe it."

"Well, let's just get this next guy out and we'll cry
about it later."

To me, he did pitch a no-hitter. It was an easy ground
ball that just happened to be hit in a terrible stadium that
somebody should blow up and convert into something
useful, like a parking lot.

The next day, we lost 4 – 3 and were officially eliminated from the pennant race.

We didn't really talk about it much, but as we headed
into the last week of September there seemed to be a
general agreement in the clubhouse that if we couldn't be
the guest of honour, we didn't want to go to the party this
year. For three years straight, we'd been featured in high-
light tapes and films for clinching the American League
East. In 1985, it was us jumping up and down on the
mound. In 1986, it was Boston celebrating while we
looked on from the dugout. And, being from Detroit, I
had seen Darrell Evans running to hug Frank Tanana
after tagging Garth Iorg for the last out of the '87 season

over and over and over again. We were just fed up with that and started playing with a lot of the drive we should have had all year.

We were still working. Jimy was out every day pitching extra batting practice to the young guys and a few veterans, as he had been all year. With the kids from Syracuse, especially Rob Ducey, the extra work paid off dramatically.

It was good to see people out. At this level of competition, the talent's about the same. Everyone's good. The difference between winning and losing is just that little competitive edge every player has to have, a willingness to go out and give of himself, sacrifice himself if he has to, for the good of the team. It may be laying down a bunt to move the runner over, it may be coming out early for extra practice if he's in a slump so he might only go 0-for-8 instead of 0-for-20. All hitters know when they feel good at the plate and when they don't. And if they don't feel good, that's the time they should make sure the coach throws them extra batting practice. It will help them quit worrying about fundamentals or work on anything they do think is fundamentally wrong. Even a few minutes a day will help a player get back in a groove again, of seeing the ball and hitting it.

249

I had found my groove. I'd been hitting well since the All-Star break. I was being selective at the plate, and you can do that when you're swinging the bat well. That borderline outside pitch that you might foul off or hit for a weak ground ball, you might take for a strike when you're going good. Or maybe the umpire will call it a ball. You try to hold off and put the pitcher in the hole so he has to come over with a strike. When you're ahead of the count, you look for a zone you can handle where you can pull the ball and hit it hard. I feel I'm good from the middle of the plate in, so if there are two balls and no strikes on me, I'll try and cut that plate in half and say, "I'm looking for one in that zone, thigh high. If it's there, I'll swing at it. He can throw me a strike on the outside corner, but I won't swing."

Catch

The hitter at 2-0, 3-1, or 3-0 is a much better hitter than he is when the pitcher's 0-2 or 1-2, and when you're going good, it always seems that the pitcher gets behind in the count. When you're not, it always seems that he's ahead. When you're not going good, he seems to be constantly 'painting the black' on you—throwing a hard sinker, about knee high, an inch or two off the black rubber on the outside edge of the plate. As Durwood Merrill would say, "It's a Hall of Fame pitch," one of the toughest pitches for anyone to hit, and it sometimes seems that the pitcher will throw you three of those in a row. That's when the ball looks very small.

When you're in a real good groove, the ball will look an awful lot bigger. You won't swing at bad pitches. The guy might throw you a breaking ball and even if you take it for a strike, that's fine because you've still got confidence in yourself. You'll say, "That's okay, I wasn't looking for that pitch. I was looking for a fastball and he threw me a curve. So what?" I'll just spit on it and think, "I know he's going to throw me a fastball." And, sure enough, when you're going good, the pitcher will always throw that fastball in your hitting zone and you hit the ball hard.

That's the groove, the feeling that you get into when you're swinging the bat well. The confidence is just flowing and you know you're going to have a good at-bat

We went into Fenway Park the last week of September, still determined not to watch any Red Sox dancing on the mound. The first game was a romp, 11 – 1. Rob Ducey went 4-for-5, with two doubles. Nelson Liriano drove in three runs and I drove in two with a double off the fence.

In my first at-bat the next night, the pitch came up and in on me and I hit it hard. I was a litle concerned if it was going to go out or not. In Fenway, just to the right of the 380' sign is a tunnel known as "dead man's alley." I've seen a lot of balls just crushed there, but the outfielder would make the catch at the warning track. Hit it ten feet on either side and the ball will carry. I hit it right to the alley, but the wind was blowing across from left field, pushing the ball away from the sign and over towards the line. It went three or four rows deep. Three runs scored.

In the next inning, Dennis Lamp was in for Boston. I've never had much success against Lampy, even when he was with the White Sox. He fell behind in the count, 2 – 0, and threw me a fastball down the middle of the plate. It went into the seats to the left of the 380' sign for a two-run homer.

The next time up, I fouled a hard tip off the foot of Boston's catcher, Rick Cerone. The Red Sox trainer came out, along with manager Joe Morgan.

Joe said, "Ernie, where'd all this come from? What are you doing to me?"

"I've got some power, Joe. I've always had power."

"Yeah, but all in one night?

"I'm just doing what you taught me back in Pawtucket."

"Okay, but you're not supposed to do it against us."

We swept the series at Fenway, the first team to sweep a whole season against Boston at home since the Yankees did it in 1980. The Red Sox' magic number still went to two as Baltimore beat New York and Cleveland took Detroit. But at least they weren't going to clinch the division against us.

251

October

We finished the year in third place, tied with Milwaukee, **253** two games behind Boston. The Tigers finished in second, one game behind the Red Sox. New York finished three and a half back. It looked like a close race to the wire, but that's just because Boston played so poorly the last ten days. We were never in the race. I suppose we could take some consolation from the fact that we weren't the only team in the AL East to have a disappointing year. For Boston to take the division with only 89 wins was unheard of. But I don't see any consolation in that. I expected more from the Blue Jays. The fans expected more. Everybody did.

What can I say about the season, other than that it was total frustration? Personally, I had a pretty good year. A lot of people wrote me off when I was struggling in the early part of the season, saying that maybe I was over the hill and should retire. To me, the easiest, simplest thing to do when you're going through a bad time is to quit. But I never gave up on myself. I knew I was hitting the ball hard. I knew things would fall into place and I'd start getting my run production, my home runs, my average back up. And I finished right on average, right where I've been the last seven years — .251, with 16 home runs and 70 RBI. What was important was that I didn't lose confidence in myself. I never have lost confidence in myself.

I think a player can tell if he's really struggling because he starts wondering whether he's lost the edge players need to be competitive at this level. I never felt I lost that edge. As long as I feel that I still have it and can contribute, as long as I still enjoy the game, and as long as I still haven't achieved my goal of winning the world championship, I'm going to continue to play as long as I can.

But what can I say about the season for the team? What went wrong with the Blue Jays? It's a pretty short list.

Lack of concentration. We did little things that don't show up in the box scores — missing the cut-off man, throwing the ball to the wrong base, not advancing the runners — all mental mistakes. Things like that add up, and when you don't execute properly, losing is what happens. We messed up simple bunt plays this year. I mean, on a bunt play you have to at least get one runner out, but there were times when we screwed those plays up. It shouldn't have happened.

Lack of respect for authority. We had a lot of guys who had no respect for authority at all. The more people I talk to, the more I find that that's the way it is in society generally. I talk to business people and others in different lines of work, and from what I hear the respect for authority just isn't there any more. It's unfortunate. On our club, people were always questioning what the manager was doing and why he was doing it, rather than saying, "I'm paid as a player. I'll go out and perform and look after my job. And if I do my job I won't have to worry about anyone else's." There were too many finger pointers, most of them pointing at Jimy. I've always believed that if you point a finger at someone, there'll be three more fingers pointing at you. Or, as Chris puts it, what goes around, comes around. A player has to look in the mirror and say, "I'm the one who screwed up that play." There were too many players trying to put the blame on anyone but themselves, and Jimy was a convenient scapegoat.

Not much camaraderie. There was more fighting and bickering on the team this year than in any other year I can remember. Guys wanted to fight each other, and it was usually over absolutely nothing. Little things would build and build, materialize into something and then explode.

Too many groups. We had a Latin corner, a black corner, and a white corner. Instead of everyone mixing and mingling, it was almost like the clubhouse was segregated.

Too much turmoil. There's a feeling you can get on a team, a feeling that everything's going to go right and everybody's pulling for each other. That feeling wasn't there this year, right from the start. People didn't accept their roles or their jobs. We had pitchers who thought they should be the stopper and couldn't understand why Jimy would go to Tom Henke in save situations. Guys said, "I should have the ball in that situation," rather than realizing that they had to get some experience and earn the right to have the ball. To me, we had players pulling against their own teammates and that doesn't make for a very good feeling on the team.

But in all the 12 years the Blue Jays have played, there have always been differences at some time or other between the players themselves, between players and management, between the team, the fans, the community. Everybody gets crabby every once in a while when things don't work out the way they should. There'll always be some differences and disagreements, but there's no reason to dwell on them. We all just have to learn from the experience and push on with it. Tomorrow's another day and next year's another season.

It was good to get home, settle in, and relax for a while. I decided not to take on too many commitments right away. I had to have a few meetings to finish up the book I'd been working on since the winter. I was booked to ride in the Oktoberfest parade in Kitchener, Ontario, and visit

255

my restaurants there. And, after a month or so, I did have to check out an investment opportunity in Ottawa and spend some time in Toronto with the Blue Jays' office, my publisher, and my business partners. But I tried to avoid travelling. I turned down invitations to banquets in the States and to golf tournaments in Florida and the Dominican.

I just wanted to stay put and rest. In my house, that means I had to get to work. Chris keeps a "honey do" list all year of jobs for me to do around the house. We've never been much for living high. Chris has always insisted on looking after the kids and the house herself. She wouldn't let a nanny or even a maid service anywhere near our home. A few years ago, we did decide to hire someone to keep the lawn trimmed in the summer, but that's about as far as she'll go. I've been trying for years to get her to agree to hire a window washer. I hate washing windows. But she just says, "Look, big boy, I want to see you being a leader off the field as well as on. You gotta do something around here."

But I took my breaks, as always. I didn't do much pheasant hunting, but I thought I'd take my dog Erica out to the woods, maybe for the last time. She's come a long way since that bus ride from Pawtucket to Syracuse. She's pretty much a house dog now, and she's getting old and slow in her movements. But I took a week to go deer hunting and enjoyed the silence in northern Michigan.

We also started building an addition to the house, and that took up a lot of time. It kept us both close to home. I had asked the Blue Jays if I could get an advance on the following year's contract to save me going to the bank for a loan, talking to both Pat Gillick and Paul Beeston. Paul and Pat went into their good guy-bad guy routine. Paul's always the good guy and he told me that if he had his way, there'd be no problem. But there's been a policy the last couple of years that they were not going to advance money any more. They had started feeling more like a bank than a ball club. Paul said he'd work on Pat while they were out at the World Series and see if he could get an okay.

I wasn't home long before some team news started circulating. The first announcements were about contract extensions for Jimy and some of the coaches. During the season, I was never sure whether Jimy would be rehired or not. I never got a feel for which way it would go. But I was glad he was signed back for another year as manager. I've always gotten along well with him. I haven't agreed with every move he's ever made, but that's what makes the game so great. You can always sit around and discuss things and feel that you could have made a better decision. Jimy took a lot of criticism this year, most of it undeserved. People like to judge a team by the manager, and that's baseball, but it's not fair. Jimy's a good baseball man. He's a great instructor and as far as motivating people went, I thought he did a fairly good job there, too. It's just easier to blame one man than it is to blame 24 guys, so he took the heat. It's unfortunate that he had to suffer through that.

257

A lot of people just see Jimy as he is on television, standing in the dugout, very serious, with a concerned look on his face. They don't know the real Jimy Williams. He's a caring individual, very family-oriented, and a very good natured person who'll goof around a lot. People outside the team rarely see the fun side of him, but he has all kinds of routines that are hilarious to see. He'll mimic people he sees walking down the street or in the hotel, really getting their movements down well. In batting practice, he'll take out his false tooth, pull his hat down sideways so his ears are sticking out and grab an old glove that he can bend almost inside out. He gets in his old-style, country-boy character and makes like he's pitching. In the dugout, he gets a kind of musical chairs version of the rally caps going, moving around until we get something going on the field. Then it's "everybody back to the same seats." A lot of people can't imagine him doing stuff like that, but that's closer to the real Jimy than the grim guy trudging out to the mound.

He can be very strong, too, as strong as he feels he needs to be. He had to be very strong this season. If a team's winning, the manager just has to put out the players and utilize all 24 guys on the team. If a team's not winning, the difficulties come and he has to make changes and try to get some winning combination out on the field. There has to be some experimentation, and some good moves just don't work out sometimes. A manager might make a pitching change, the reliever gives up a home run and the manager's a bum. If the reliever had better location and spotted the ball half an inch in another direction, the batter would pop up and the manager would be a genius. The margin between success and failure can be that small, but a manager's got to keep on trying and not let the criticism and the booing get to him. Jimy stood up to all that pretty well, taking the heat because the players didn't do their jobs. But I also feel that he was a little tardy in asserting his authority. If he would **258** have asserted his authority more strongly and sooner, like in the spring, I can't help but think it would have been a different season.

More news came when I got a call from a Toronto reporter saying that Pat Gillick had been on a radio talk show and had said that in 1989, the Blue Jays would be carrying three catchers — Pat Borders, Greg Myers and me — and that I would be primarily the designated hitter. I was a little surprised since, at the time, I wasn't even signed. The club hadn't told me whether they were going to exercise their option for the third year of my contract.

I guess I was a little surprised about DHing, too. The organization is caught up in a youth movement, and that's fine. Greg has to get the opportunity to play sooner or later. But I was ranked second among American League catchers in 1988, and for me to split the DH role with Pat Borders while Greg catches most of the games didn't seem to make a lot of sense. Of course, I didn't know whether that was just a story or if there was any truth to it. In 1989, I hope to catch as much as I have in the past, 130 or 135 games, but it's not my decision. I'll express my opinions to Jimy and Pat, but I just signed a player's contract, not a contract to catch. The organization can play me wherever they want. If they want me to DH, I'll DH and do the best I can. I won't be happy about it, but I won't walk out of camp over it, either.

The report made me wonder, though, what the plan was for Rance Mulliniks. What would they do with a guy hitting over .300? Then I heard he was going to play more third base, while Kelly Gruber would platoon at third and see spot duty at second. After what Kelly accomplished at third in 1988, getting the rhythm of the position and making some outstanding plays, that seemed crazy to me. To get the best out of a player, he's got to play one position. Some players can adjust to moving around, but it's hard. Second base is an entirely different position than third, with different throws, different ways of charging or playing back on the ball. Kelly turned himself into a fine everyday defensive third baseman, and it would be foolish to mess with him by having him float between second **259** and third.

Any move along that line seemed to indicate that maybe a trade for Manny Lee was in the works, which would make sense. He was marketable. But the team would probably have to get a veteran second baseman in return, along with maybe another outfielder or a pitcher. If the right deal comes along, anybody is tradeable. I wouldn't be surprised to see George or Lloyd traded. Something will have to be done about George and Jimy. Jimy was always very good about congratulating and encouraging George, but there's an awful lot of friction there, and as long as it is there, it's like being on a keg of powder that could blow any time. I would be surprised to see Jesse traded, even though after all the mind games he suffered through during the season he's the one player who seemed to desperately want to be traded.

But that's another great thing about the game. You can sit down and make all kinds of different lineups. It'll be interesting. There's obviously a plan in the works. Rob Ducey swung the bat really well in September, so maybe he'll get another chance in '89. I'm sure there'll be some other shifts. But we're solid for the future with players who came into their own this year, like Kelly, Pat Borders, and Freddie McGriff. You could build a franchise on guys like that.

Freddie probably has the best potential of any Blue Jay, past or present, to make it to the Hall of Fame one day. He's young enough to have a long career ahead of him and if he keeps making the strides he did in 1987 and 1988 and performs consistently over ten or so seasons, he's got a chance.

You can never know what might happen, but the only other candidate I can think of right now would be Tony, if he stays healthy. In 1987, he was the best shortstop in the game, hands down. You can see it on videotapes, but you have to play with him every day to really appreciate his anticipation. He has the best sense of where the ball's going to be than anyone I've ever seen and he has the quickness to react and make plays that are awesome. In 1988, with his knee giving him trouble and his elbow still recovering, he didn't have the range or the strength on his throws to first that he'd had the year before. But he can come back and dominate at the position again.

It'll be interesting to see what the plan is as it unfolds. But I was shocked and disappointed to see one piece of it fall into place when Rick Leach was given his release after five years with the club. It's too bad Toronto fans couldn't have seen more of Bone. He never played enough for them to really appreciate the sort of player he is. He was a real entertainment to watch in the dugout. He tried to keep everyone loose and keep himself occupied by doing off-the-wall stuff. He's very loud, with the booming voice of the college quarterback he used to be back in Michigan, and he'd get things going with peanut vendors, calling "Peee-Nuuuuuts" back and forth, then getting the crowds into the act. He'd make sand and Gatorade mud pies in Milwaukee and fire them at the bullpen car as it came around the track. The fans would get on him and he'd get these gestures going with them. When the music played, he'd start dancing in the dugout.

On the field, he was the type of player I like to see out there with me. He'd go through a brick wall for the team. He was never an everyday player, just a pinch-hitter, fourth-outfielder type, but he was a blue collar worker who wasn't afraid of getting his hands dirty. He always ran hard when he hit the ball. He wasn't afraid to dive for balls in the outfield. He'd try and take a fielder's kneecap off if he had to avoid a tag. When he did get the opportunity to play a lot, he showed what he could do. In 1986, he got into 110 games and batted .306 with 39 RBI. He was always hoping to get into more games and worked very hard every day to be ready if he did.

He was the sort of player the Blue Jays need more of and the sort of player Toronto fans appreciate. Toronto people are very conservative and very forgiving people. As long as you're giving the effort, they'll stand behind you. Toronto is the only place I've ever seen a player, Dave Collins, get a standing ovation for running hard to first on an easy groundout.

I feel I've been very well received by Toronto fans, and I think that's because they know that nothing's ever been handed to me. I had to work hard to get here, and the good work habits I created I take onto the field with me. I'm out there every day with the gear on, year after year. I may not always do as well as I'd like, but I think the fans realize that I'm doing my best. And I know parents don't want their kids looking up to a guy who doesn't carry himself well or curses on the field. I've said my piece more than a few times to umpires and players, but I don't do it where the fans can hear me, especially the stuff with the umpires. I try to do my best there, too, and the fans have been very supportive.

What I regret about the way we played in parts of the 1988 season is that we seemed to have jeopardized the close feelings fans all across the country have felt towards us over the past few years. Wherever we go in Canada, Blue Jay players are well received and made to feel really welcome. A lot of people think of us as Canada's team, not just Toronto's. It took a while for that affection to grow, and it's a pretty fragile thing. I'd hate to see us, or the fans, do anything to put it in danger.

The fans in Toronto, who backed us even in our first few terrible years, lost patience this year, to say the least. We've heard booing before. We've all heard some hard things said from the stands before. It happens all the time in rain-delayed games. In Toronto, there practically has to be a hurricane blowing to get a game cancelled, and players hate those games because we know the fans will be irritated and into the beer. It will be total abuse night when we get out on the field. But I've never heard so many boos and insults being screamed at us in Exhibition Stadium as there were this year. They booed Jesse, they booed Lloyd, they booed Jimy, they booed me and, most of all, they booed George.

Nobody likes to be booed. It's no fun. Nobody likes to be yelled at. Ball players, just like anybody else, like to hear positive things, they like to hear chants and cheers. You expect to be booed on the road, but you don't expect it at home. Not on this club.

Booing maybe goes with the game. It's a tradition and as long as it stays reasonably good natured, players will just have to live with it. But this year, some fans went way beyond booing.

One day in the summer we went to warm up for infield. Toronto's a late crowd arriving, so there weren't too many people in the stands. Over by the home bullpen, about half way up, there was this older guy, over 65, a real grandfatherly type. As soon as he saw George, he started screaming, "Hey, Beeelll. I'm gonna dooggg you, Beeelll. Go back where you caaame from. You stink." At first, it was like a joke. We all laughed, including George, who jumped up on the tarp and motioned for the guy to come on down. But the guy never stopped. A security guard came and told him he had to stop, but he yelled, "I don't have to be quiet. I paid my money. I can yell at Bell if I want to. Hey, Beeelll. You're overpaid. You stink."

262

The California Angels were all walking around and looking at us like, "Is this the way it is here? This is unbelievable." I felt a little embarrassed, because I know players love to come to Toronto to play. It's the city umpires love to bring their families to.

George finally got upset and yelled back, "Why are you doing this? What do you want to embarrass me for?"

Then two policemen came over and told the man that if he wanted to stay for the game, he'd have to keep his mouth shut. I had never seen that happen in Toronto before. I've seen it in parks all over the States. In some places, the police are kept really busy. Tiger Stadium can turn very ugly sometimes and Yankee Stadium is a zoo. But that was a first for Toronto.

I guess I'm in two minds about it. We're basically entertainers, and the fans pay good money to come and see us perform. If we don't perform well, then they have a right to say whatever they want. But it's getting hard to convince myself of that.

263

In another game in the summer, I tried to throw a guy out at third and the ball sailed into left field. It was a dumb mistake. The runner had a real good jump and it cost us a run. In the seats behind the plate, a few rows up from where Chris and the kids were sitting, some guy started hammering me. He went on and on and on. Players' wives learn in the minors not to say anything in that kind of situation. I don't think Chris has mouthed off to an abusive fan since Muzzy Field in Bristol, where she thought she was going to get drenched in beer for her trouble. But after a while, she'd had enough of this guy and told him to put a sock in it. She turned around and heard another player's wife say, "Oh, EJ, don't do that." Chris asked what and found that our son had flipped this guy the finger. That was it. Unacceptable. Grounded for a week.

EJ said, "Please don't tell Dad."

She told me that night, and I said, "Chris, we can't ground him for that. Sure, it was wrong. Sure, he shouldn't do that again. But he's nine years old and people are yelling and screaming at his dad. He just wants to stick up for me."

EJ and I went off to a room, and when I said that Mom had told me, the tears started coming a bit. I said, "I know you were upset that the guy was yelling at me. But that's the business your father's in. People can cheer you and they can boo you. You know, I'm sorry I threw that ball away. I didn't mean to throw it away, but that guy was upset with me and I know that got to you."

"Yeah, it did. I hate it when people yell at you."

"I know. Even though you hear it, you just have to let it go through and not let it bother you. But it does, I know, it bothers me, too, and I understand why you did what you did. But don't let it happen again, and I'll try not to throw the ball away again. Then maybe no one will want to yell at me."

A lot of times, players will sit on the bench and talk about finding some of these abusers in the stands. We **264** think about following them to work and watching what they do and calling them all kinds of names in front of their friends. We'd stand there and scream at the top of our lungs, "Hey, you missed a screw on that car. What's the matter with you? I'm paying to have you fix that thing. I'm paying your salary. Can't you do anything right?" Or maybe we'd pull up a chair next to some guy's desk and scream, "What? You haven't answered that memo? Are you crazy? Where are your brains? You're getting old. Hang it up." I'd pay $10-15 for the chance to see these guys work and to scream back at them. It's only fair.

This is our work. We may have bad days — everybody has bad days — but we're good at what we do. We wouldn't be here if we weren't. Back in the '70s, when I was still trying to get into the game, Chris cut out some statistics she'd found and pasted them into the front of the first scrapbook of my career. We believe you should know about the obstacles ahead because, if you believe in yourself and your abilities, knowing will just make you try harder and work with more determination. The statistics said that in any average year, out of the millions who play the game as kids, 1,000,000 play in high school, 25,000 play at college level, and ten make it to the big leagues, some for not very long. Even fewer manage to stay up for more than four years.

The odds of making it are probably even longer now. There are millions who want to play this game, all over North and South America and everywhere in between. Yet every year there are only about 640 of us who play in the major leagues. We're specialists. No, we don't always perform as well as we should. But we work at a hard, physical job seven months of the year, with only about three days off each month. And those days are usually given to packing, travelling, always on the move, living out of a suitcase somewhere. There's no way every player is going to be up for every one of the 162 games we play. But most of us try to do our best. We're professionals, and we don't deserve insults any more than any other professional does.

265

I don't want anything to put distance between Toronto Blue Jays fans and the team. I know a lot of distance is created when players don't show respect for the fans by not taking pride in their work, but a lot of distance is also created when fans don't show respect for the players.

To me, you've got to accept the highs and lows of things that come your way in life. Not everything is going to be easy. I believe an individual has to do that to grow as a person, and I believe that fans have to take the bad times with the good times, too, and not give up or turn negative when things don't go the way they should. Faith from the players and the fans can do wonders for a team. Anybody who doesn't believe that should look at the Dodgers' performance in the '88 World Series.

I watched the series more this year than I did in 1987. Then, it hurt too much to watch because we should have been playing in it. We should have been playing in it this year, too, but it wasn't as disappointing. This year, we didn't play good baseball. Last year, we did. Still, I think we would have made a better showing against Oakland than Boston did. And I think we could have beat the Dodgers if we could've got past Oakland. We had just as good pitching, better defence, and better hitters than the Dodgers.

Good pitching always stops good hitting, and Oakland came up against some well-pitched games. Orel Hershiser is an extremely good pitcher. I've never faced him, but just watching him you can see he hits his spots extremely well. He had a good breaking ball, and he never really missed with location. Belcher threw well for the Dodgers, too. Winning is a matter of executing, and the Dodgers executed and got the big guys out. Shut down the Cansecos, McGwires, and Hendersons and you're going to win.

I guess what will stand out about the series, besides Hershiser's pitching, was Kirk Gibson limping up to the plate with two outs in the ninth and hitting a two-run homer to win the game. Why a guy has a knack for dramatics like that, I don't know. He did the same thing to beat the Padres in the '84 World Series when he was with Detroit, hitting a three-run home run off Goose Gossage to put the Tigers ahead. He did it to us in the last game in Toronto against the Tigers in '87. He hadn't hit the ball hard all day. Two outs in the ninth, and he hits it. He's an impact-type player. I don't know why. Maybe he just gets pumped up for those situations. He's able to stay within himself and not let the pressure get to him. Maybe he feels there's more pressure on the pitcher than there is on him, and when that happens a player will often be successful.

A lot of times I'll catch myself coming up with the bases loaded, and I'll swing at the first pitch even if it's a foot off the plate or in the dirt. That's when I have to step back and think, "Wait a minute. The pressure's not on me. The pressure's on him. He's the guy who's got the bases loaded." You try and talk to yourself and relax in situations like that. It's easier for a hitter to do that than for a pitcher because the pitcher has to throw the ball over a 17-inch plate, knowing that if he doesn't throw it for a strike,

266

a run might come in. Relax, see the ball, make sure it's a good pitch that you can handle and hit it. Gibson's a specialist at that.

I questioned the pitch selection of Hassey and Eckersley. The only pitch Gibson could hit was a breaking ball and Eckersley had thrown nothing but fastballs that whole inning. Gibson was fighting the fastball off. He couldn't put any body into it, and you foul a lot of fastballs off using only your hands. Gibson wasn't handling the outside ball at all, and to throw him the first breaking ball of the inning on a 3-2 pitch was questionable. A guy who can't extend or really use his legs can only use his hands, and with a breaking ball your hands are all you're supposed to use. You might commit your body, but you have to keep your hands back. That's the only way you're going to hit it. With your hands back, you'll have more time to get the bat head through the hitting zone. Oakland did him a favour by throwing a breaking ball.

267

I'm sure a lot of people said, "Well, Eckersley hung the breaking ball. If he'd gotten it in a better location, he might have gotten him out." He had him fooled on it. But that's the fun of second guessing the pitcher and catcher. Gibson could have just as easily popped that pitch up, then Hassey and Eckersley would have been geniuses.

Sitting home watching the series on TV instead of playing in it bothered me some, but in a way it also made me feel good. I'm an optimist, and I thought, "That could happen to us next year. We could be there, too." The more I watched, the more excited I got at the thought that with the team we have, there's no reason why we shouldn't be playing in a World Series.

The Blue Jays had 48 hours after the end of the last game of the series to announce whether they were going to exercise their option on my contract. On the Thursday evening before what turned out to be the last game, Pat Gillick phoned to inform me that there would be an announcement at noon Friday that the club was going to exercise its right to pick up my option for the '89 season.

I told him I was happy about that. He asked how Chris and the kids were doing, I asked about Doris and their daughter, Kimberley. We talked a bit about the Dodgers and what I'd been doing lately. I said the addition to the house was keeping me busy with contractors and bids for the job.

He said, "Well, I've got to go. I'm on my way to the game." Maybe to see Paul and talk about my advance.

I was really glad to have the option picked up. Another of my goals the last couple of years has been to hang on and hope to be behind the plate when the Blue Jays take the field in the dome for the first time. It'll be interesting to play both indoors and outdoors at home, depending on the weather. It'll take some getting used to. From what I hear, there are still a few issues to resolve. The ball club thinks of it as an open stadium that's closed in inclement weather. The stadium people talk about it as a closed stadium that can be opened on good days. That's a little difference that could make a big difference. Will the umpires say, "Close the roof"? It'll be interesting, too, to hear what it sounds like indoors when the fans yell, "Ernie, Ern-ie," when I come up to the plate. I'm looking forward to that.

It was good to have the security of a contract, but it didn't last long. The arbitrator looking into the collusion of the owners against free agents in 1986 finally brought down a ruling on October 24th. I was declared a free agent, but it really didn't mean that much to me. At this point in my career, I'm pretty well set in my ways. I hope to be compensated financially for being a victim of the owners' collusion, but free agency wasn't what I was after.

I don't hold any grudges against the Blue Jays. They were just acting in concert with the other owners. They all felt this was the way they could stop free agency and the bidding wars for players. It was a business decision, a bad one, and the Blue Jays knew that with no other team willing to show any interest in me they wouldn't have to give me what the market value should have been. I feel I'll be compensated, even though it might take years to come through.

I wouldn't want to play for any other team. Players like to think that the grass is always greener on the other side, but I don't think that's the case. The Blue Jay organization has always treated me well. When I look at everything they've done for me, there have been too many plusses. There's a sense of loyalty involved, too. The fans have always been supportive of me and I don't want to leave them right now. I guess that's partly because I'm one of the last of the originals, and I don't feel we've finished the job we started back in 1977. I want to see this thing through to when we bring a World Championship to Toronto.

When the ruling came down, I decided I wasn't going to take the phone off the hook. I'd listen to anyone who was interested enough to call. But it would take a blockbuster deal to get me to move at this time. With the business interests I have in Toronto, with all the investments I've made in Ontario, and all the charity work I do, I've just got too much going to leave. My feet are too firmly set for me to move on.

I guess if Detroit offered more money than Toronto, I'd have to consider it. I'd be able to live at home half the year instead of out of a suitcase in some hotel or rented house. I'd be with my family. But I still have goals to achieve. I want to be on a team that can win it all, and I'm not sure that Detroit has the right mix of veterans and young players to do that in the next few years. I know that Toronto has.

Besides, it took two years to get the ruling, and those were two really productive years that I had with the Blue Jays. I feel that I've still got a lot more games left in me, but I'm two years older. Other organizations might think that I'm coming to the end of my career.

Maybe. I could probably stay in the game for years like Pudge Fisk or Bob Boone. Catchers do seem to have long careers these days. It was kind of funny to think back and remember how I felt as a rookie hoping to get the backup job to the established star, Carleton Fisk. That was almost fifteen years ago, and who should knock me out of my '87 position as the top ranked catcher of the American League but Pudge himself. Amazing. I could stay in the game for years, but I don't know that I want to. At this point, I know I'm good through the 1989 season. After that, who knows? My only thought has always been that I'd like to leave the field when it stops being fun going to the ball park every day. If there ever comes a time when I feel I'm not up to making a big contribution, I'll take the gear off and hang it up. I never want to feel that I'm cheating the organization, the fans, or myself. I'd rather go that way than be told that I'm no longer wanted.

What the future holds, I don't know. There are pulls in all different directions. I know I want to spend a lot more time with my family. My kids are all so involved with different activities, and I always hear about the interesting and fun things going on at home. But that's all I do. I hear about it, but I don't get to see it. I miss it a lot. This year, it got so bad that after a Sunday afternoon game in Toronto, I'd drive home to Detroit for dinner, spend a few hours with Chris and the kids, then drive back Monday morning for that night's game.

There's also the pull of my good fortune in being able to do what I enjoy doing and getting well paid for doing it. I know that I can pick and choose whatever I want to do in the future without worrying about the bills coming in. But I love playing baseball. I've been living a dream I had when I was seven years old. I wanted to be the catcher for a big league team. I wanted to be out on the field with the people cheering and the batter waiting to be outsmarted by me and my pitcher looking in. I thought that would be the neatest thing in the world at the time, and that turned out to be the case. I had to endure a lot of uncertainty and disappointments, a lot of punishment, and a lot of setbacks along the way, but I've endured. I worked hard. I believed in myself. I didn't let anyone tell me that I wasn't good enough. I made my dream come

270

true, and I'm sure it won't be an easy thing to say, "All right. The dream is over. It's time to go."

And there's still that strong pull towards going out a winner. I want a World Series ring. I want the satisfaction of knowing that I played with a group of guys recognized as the best baseball team in the world.

The Blue Jays are an incredibly talented team. There's no reason why we shouldn't win our division, win the pennant, and take on the best the National League has to offer and come out on top. No reason in the world. We've got the talent, the organization, the management, and the fans behind us, as long as we work hard on the field. Bringing a world championship to Toronto would be the greatest feeling I can imagine. Sure, we've got some problems to work out. That's life, not just baseball. There are always problems to work out. And we're still in the game's toughest division, with some extremely talented teams to battle for the top spot over a long season.

It'll be a challenge. But I always go to spring training **271** with optimism, thinking we can have a good year.